Praise for *James Dean Died Here*
A BookSense 76 Selection

"*James Dean Died Here* is an addictively irresistible tour through pop culture past and present."
– Chicago Tribune

"The whereabouts of 600-plus places that have helped shape national identity, from the momentous (site of the world's first A-bomb explosion) to the ridiculous (where Zsa Zsa slapped that hunky Beverly Hills cop)."
– USA Today

"Who says Americans don't know much about history? . . . Epting's quirky factoids are most appealing."
– Publishers Weekly

"Chris Epting has written a guidebook to a broad range of historic and often hysterical American landmarks – more than 700 in all. *James Dean Died Here* includes the spot where the young movie icon perished in a car accident, the location of the *Brady Bunch* house, and the hangar where the final scene of *Casablanca* may have been shot."
– National Public Radio's "All Things Considered"

"Chris Epting's omnibus picks up where standard guidebooks leave off, directing couch potatoes to the spots they've always imagined but never seen. . . . 49 states are represented, the 600-plus locations are almost entirely free to visit, and you'll never again lose $40 to take a stupid 'star tour.'"
– Arthur Frommer's Budget Travel

"Just in time for summer road trips comes a cool new book that lists the location of about 650 pilgrimage-worthy pop culture sites across the United States. *James Dean Died Here: The Locations of America's Pop Culture Landmarks* is a guide to sites morbid, trashy and profound. Epting has assembled a treasure trove of pop landmarks!"
–Albuquerque Journal

"Want to know where Zsa Zsa Gabor was arrested? The house that was built on the Indian burial ground in *Poltergeist*? Where Elvis recorded 'Heartbreak Hotel'? It's all in here, Baby!"
– BookSense 76

"This book bulges with facts!"
– Los Angeles Times

"With sweep both noble and tacky, Chris Eptin[...] *Locations of America's Pop Culture Landmarks*, is[...] their American history unadulterated by the usual[...] sticking to that armchair or planning a road trip[...] spirited companion, one that will steer you off the[...] exalted, tragically charged and hopelessly hokey l[...]
– Baltimore Sun

D1004533

Praise for
The Ruby Slippers, Madonna's Bra and Einstein's Brain

The Rock and Roll Landmarks of North America

LED ZEPPELIN CRASHED HERE

NO VACANCY

Chris Epting

SANTA
MONICA
PRESS

S A N T A
M O N I C A
P R E S S

Published by:
Santa Monica Press LLC
P.O. Box 1076
Santa Monica, CA 90406-1076
1-800-784-9553
www.santamonicapress.com
books@santamonicapress.com

Printed in the United States

Santa Monica Press books are available at special quantity discounts when purchased in bulk by corporations, organizations, or groups. Please call our Special Sales department at 1-800-784-9553.

ISBN-10: 1-59580-018-2
ISBN-13: 978-1-59580-018-3

Library of Congress Cataloging-in-Publication Data

Epting, Chris, 1961-
   Led Zeppelin crashed here : the rock and roll landmarks of North America / by Chris Epting.
      p. cm.
   ISBN-13: 978-1-59580-018-3
   ISBN-10: 1-59580-018-2
   1. Rock music—United States—History and criticism. 2. Musical landmarks—United States—Guidebooks. 3. United States—Guidebooks. I. Title.

ML3534.3.E68 2007
781.660973—dc22

2007006246

Cover and interior design and production by Future Studio

781.660973
EPTI

Back cover photos:

Top row (left to right): Jim Morrison's hotel room; Johnny Ramone's monument; The Beach Boys' birthplace; Capitol Records building; Gram Parsons's death site

Bottom row (left to right): The author, pictured in Studio 1 at Sunset Sound, where several songs from his favorite album, *Exile on Main St.*, were recorded; Site of the infamous Altamont concert; Johnny Thunders's death site; The Beatles and the Rolling Stones play New Orleans; The famous RockWalk at Guitar Center

contents

Introduction | 9

It's Only Rock 'n' Roll (But I Like It):
Sex, Drugs, and Rock 'n' Roll Mayhem | 13

Roll Over Beethoven:
The Beatles, Bob Dylan, Elvis Presley, and The Rolling Stones | 77

Kick Out the Jams:
Concert Sites and Live Performance Locations | 117

The Song Remains the Same:
Music, Film, and TV Recording Sites | 159

Sweet Home Chicago:
Blues and Jazz Shrines | 185

Don't Fear the Reaper:
Homicides, Suicides, and a Bad Moon Rising | 203

Knockin' on Heaven's Door:
R.I.P. | 225

Can't Buy Me Love:
Rock 'n' Roll Museums, Restaurants, Hotels,
and Other Places to Spend Your Cash | 269

B-Sides:
Record Stores, Road Trip Music Suggestions, and
Other Rock 'n' Roll Miscellany | 295
100 Classic Road Trip Songs
100 Rockin' Road Trip Albums
My Top Live 25
30 Great North American Music Stores

Appendix: Rock 'n' Roll Landmarks by State | 319

Acknowledgments | 326

Photo Credits | 327

On a drizzly May 1, 1975, the Rolling Stones created a bit of bedlam in Lower Manhattan. To announce the dates of their Tour of the Americas, they had scheduled a press conference at One Fifth Avenue. As reporters gathered inside the hotel to wait for the band, a commotion was noticed outside. A rumbling was heard coming down Fifth Avenue and lo and behold, it was the Rolling Stones on the back of a flatbed truck performing "Brown Sugar." Stunning the lunchtime crowd, they ran through the song before tossing out leaflets to those on the street. On the sheets of paper were the tour dates. The flatbed then drove around the corner; the band jumped into waiting cars and was gone in a flash. The idea for the impromptu concert came from Stones drummer Charlie Watts, who'd read that jazz bands would sometimes promote their evening concerts with truck tours around the city.

I was in 8th grade at the time, 13 years old, and in the previous year or two had become a huge fan of the Rolling Stones. When I got home from school that day, I was glued to the news reports of the event. I knew exactly where that truck had pulled up and could not believe that the Stones, in the flesh, had actually performed within inches of people on the street. That night, my father told me he had gotten tickets through his company for us to see the Stones at Madison Square Garden and I began counting down the days until June 22nd. When I hear people who grew up in the 1960s talk about seeing The Beatles on *Ed Sullivan* and how that changed their lives, well, that's what May 1, 1975 was for me: a lightning bolt. The day I developed a serious emotional attachment to rock 'n' roll.

My two favorite American creations are baseball and rock 'n' roll, and since I'd already written a book about baseball it only seemed natural to pen one on rock 'n' roll. Because it was born here in America, with roots going back to Congo Square in New Orleans, there are many landmarks, shrines, and touchstones throughout North America and that's what led me to approach rock 'n' roll from a geographic angle. From the store where Elvis bought his first guitar to the site of Buddy Holly's plane crash to the location of The Beatles first performance in America, the landscape is laced with hundreds of places relevant not just to rock 'n' roll, but to rock's building blocks as well. Sites related to jazz and the blues are just as important in a book like this to help form a foundational perspective, and so they are included, too.

Obviously, there are many sites in this book that involve a certain level of mayhem and excess. This is rock 'n' roll, after all, and it goes with the territory. That said, something that struck me while writing this book is how different music would be today if the likes of Jim Morrison, Jimi Hendrix, Janis Joplin, and so many other artists taken from the world so early in life were still here. Their early exits parallel those of other icons like Marilyn Monroe and James Dean in that they remain forever young, but it's interesting to think about how music might have been altered had they not died. The thought of Gram Parsons joining the Rolling Stones onstage today, or a joint Hendrix/Joplin tour—so many intriguing possibilities struck down by drugs and/or bad luck. But again, that's rock 'n' roll.

The other day, my son and I were in the car listening to Delta blues legend Robert Johnson. Charlie, who at this writing is 13, snapped to attention when a song called "If I Had Possession over Judgment Day" started playing. "That's 'Rollin' and Tumblin'" he said excitedly, referring to a song off the current Bob Dylan album *Modern Times*. It struck me once again what a powerful force music is in our lives, and how our homegrown American art form gets passed down from generation to generation. The Robert Johnson song had been adapted over the years by Muddy Waters, Cream, and, most recently, Bob Dylan. Now, the musical roots from the Mississippi Delta had found their way to our driveway in Huntington Beach, California, and connected with yet another young rock 'n' roll fan. (This experience also helps explain why I included a chapter on Blues and Jazz in this book. As Muddy Waters wrote and sang, "The blues had a baby and they named it rock and roll.")

I hope you enjoy this collection of places and get a chance to go out and visit a bunch of them. Rock 'n' roll combined with road trips is a timeless combination, after all.

To all of you who remember those pre-MTV days, when albums and radio ruled so much of our lives, I hope this book brings back a few memories. To the younger readers, who knows, maybe reading about all of these legends will inspire you to go start a band. And we can always use a few good new bands.

Chris Epting
Huntington Beach, California

Write the author at chris@chrisepting.com and visit www.chrisepting.com for additional information on this book as well as other titles by Chris Epting.

This book is dedicated to the memory of my friend, Jeffrey Flower.

May the good Lord shine a light on you.
Warm like the evening sun.

"Shine a Light"
Jagger/Richards

IT'S ONLY ROCK 'N' ROLL (BUT I LIKE IT): SEX, DRUGS, AND ROCK 'N' ROLL MAYHEM

Abdul, Paula

Delmonico's
16358 Ventura Boulevard
Encino, California
818-986-0777

At about at 1:30 P.M. on July 18, 1995, singer/host Paula Abdul arrived here at Delmonico's restaurant and became the victim of an afternoon car theft. After briefly leaving her white 300SL Mercedes-Benz running unattended in the front of the restaurant (she had gone to get a valet parking ticket), two men jumped into her car and sped away.

Aerosmith

The Anchorage at Sunapee Harbor
17 Garnet Street
Sunapee, New Hampshire
603-763-3334

Aerosmith was born right here, when New York drummer Steven Tyler met guitarist Joe Perry at this restaurant where Perry worked in 1970. According to legend, Tyler ate the best French fries he had ever had, and he wanted to meet the cook who made them. He walked into the kitchen and met the cook, who happened to be Joe Perry.

They ended up forming a power trio with Tom Hamilton on bass, and before long, they'd added drummer Joey Kramer and guitarist Brad Whitford. Today, 30 years later, Steven Tyler still eats at the Anchorage. Another Aerosmith landmark is Nipmuc Regional High School, located in nearby Upton, at 90 Pleasant Street. It was there on November 6, 1970, that Aerosmith appeared in their first-ever public performance.

Aerosmith

1325 Commonwealth Avenue #2B
Boston, Massachusetts

This building was pictured in the 1991 video for the classic song "Sweet Emotion," and it was here from 1970 to 1972 that the band members of Aerosmith lived, wrote, played, and ate (and maybe even slept a little) until being signed by Columbia Records.

"There were six of us in the group, some of us were living in the kitchen, eating brown rice and Campbell's soup. Those days, you know, when a quart of beer was heaven. It was hard times and it was really good. During lunch we would set up all our equipment outside of BU [Boston University] in the main square and just start wailing. That's basically how we got billed. We never got much publicity in the magazines and newspapers." (Steven Tyler speaking to *Circus Magazine* in June 1975.)

Alice's Restaurant

Housatonic Church-The Guthrie Center
4 Van Deusenville Road
Great Barrington, Massachusetts
413-528-1955

Alice's Restaurant isn't around anymore, but, as the song says, "Alice didn't live in a restaurant. She lived in the church nearby the restaurant. . . ." And the old Trinity Church, where Alice once lived and where the saga began, has become home to The Guthrie Center and The Guthrie Foundation. Arlo Guthrie, working to provide a place to bring together individuals for spiritual service, founded the Guthrie Center, an Interfaith Church, in 1991. So the Trinity Church where the song "The Alice's Restaurant Massacree" began and where the movie *Alice's Restaurant* was filmed, continues to service the local and international community.

Allman Brothers

The Big House
2321 Vineville Avenue
Macon, Georgia

Back in the 1960s and early 1970s, this big, rambling house was where The Allman Brothers lived communally. On the fateful night that guitarist Duane Allman was killed in a traffic accident, this was the last place he stopped.

Ballard-Hudson High School

1070 Anthony Road
Macon, Georgia

Both singing legends Otis Redding and Little Richard attended this high school. In fact, when Redding dropped out in the tenth grade he got a gig as part of Little Richard's then band, the Upsetters.

The Band

8841 Evanview Drive
West Hollywood, California

Sammy Davis, Jr., once lived here, but this is also where The Band cut their brilliant second album, *The Band,* in 1969.

Beach Boys' Hamburger Stand

Foster's Freeze
11969 Hawthorne Boulevard (just north of 120th Street)
Hawthorne, California
310-644-9653

The Beach Boys grew up in Hawthorne, California, and the "hamburger stand" mentioned in their hit song, "Fun, Fun, Fun," was actually this very Foster's Freeze (which they nicknamed "Frostie's"). It seems that Brian Wilson spotted a friend here driving by in her daddy's T-Bird. This Foster's Freeze is still open for business.

Beach Boys' Home

3701 W. 119th Street
Hawthorne, California

The site of the Wilson home, the childhood home of Brian, Dennis, and Carl Wilson (three of the original five Beach Boys), was once located at what would have been this address, which is now near the intersection of West 119th and Kornblum Avenue in Hawthorne. However, it was demolished for the construction of the 105 Freeway in Los Angeles County back in the mid-1980s.

A commemorative landmark plaque and monument was dedicated on May 20, 2005, at the site of the house where the Wilson brothers grew up and The Beach Boys began as a group. Harry Jarnagan, with help from Paula Bondi-Springer, worked with the Hawthorne City Council and the state Historical Resources Commission to install the incredible landmark plaque. The project had the full support of the Wilson family, who were out in full force for the ceremony. (Dennis's eldest son Scott Wilson provided con-

struction services for the monument.) About 1,000 people attended the event, which was hosted by Fred Vail and included speakers and musical performances. Brian Wilson and members of his current touring band sang "In My Room" and "Surfer Girl." Fellow Beach Boys Alan Jardine and David Marks were also there.

Bee Gees

Sunny Isles Bridge
Miami, Florida

Each evening on the way to Criteria Studios, the Bee Gees would drive across the Sunny Isles Bridge, and the tires of their car would make a "chunka-chunka" sound as they crossed some railroad tracks. One night, Barry Gibb's wife, Linda, turned to her husband and said, "Hey, listen to that noise. It's the same every night. It's our drive talking." Barry looked at her and started to sing a song that evolved into their second number one single, "Jive Talkin'."

Ben Frank's

8585 Sunset Boulevard
West Hollywood, California

Today it's a Mel's retro diner, but back in the 1960s it was one of the ultimate rock 'n' roll hangouts: Ben Frank's diner. It was a favorite of Frank Zappa's and many other musicians over the years, including the Rolling Stones and Andy Warhol. What's fortunate is that the building has been preserved in all its "Googie"-style architecture glory that harkens back to the 1950s.

Berry, Chuck

2520 Goode Avenue
St. Louis, Missouri

Rocker Chuck Berry was born in San Jose, California, on October 18, 1926. As an infant, Berry moved with his family to this modest house here in St. Louis where they lived for two years. However, Berry would eventually use the name of the street to christen his most famous character in song, Johnny B. Goode.

Berry, Chuck

Berry Park
Buckner Road
Wentzville (suburb of St. Louis), Missouri

In the 1950s, rock 'n' roll icon Chuck Berry bought this 30-acre parcel of land with the intent of turning it into a full-fledged recreation site. A public pool and fishing spot opened in 1960, but that was about as far as the grand vision got. Berry Park has remained as Berry's homebase and several interesting scenes from the movie of Berry's life, *Hail, Hail Rock and Roll* (with Keith Richards) were shot here. It is no longer open to the public, but can be found by driving south on Interstate 70 to Highway Z (Church Street). After passing Highway N, head west on Buckner Road.

Bingenheimer, Rodney

7561 Sunset Boulevard
Hollywood, California

In the early 1970s, this was the center of glitter and glam rock 'n' roll along Sunset Boulevard. Rodney Bingenheimer's English Disco was where David Bowie, Marc Bolan, Led Zeppelin, Queen, and dozens of others congregated to listen to live music and hang out. Bingenheimer himself was a local legend—a DJ and tastemaker who earned the unofficial title of "Mayor of Sunset Strip." While Bingenheimer is no longer the fashionable tastemaker he was back in the 1970s and early '80s (when he was instrumental in popularizing the punk rock and new wave genres), he's still on the radio in L.A. with a fervent fan base.

Bonaduce, Danny

St. Croix Villas
100 E. Fillmore Street
Phoenix, Arizona

This is where police found former Partridge Family "bassist" Danny Bonaduce hiding naked beneath a pile of clothes in a closet back in 1991. Bonaduce was arrested; he was on the lam for having allegedly beaten up a transvestite prostitute. Since then, Bonaduce has gone on to forge a successful career as a radio personality while also co-hosting a TV talk show for men.

Bowie, David

Flagship Americana Hotel
Rochester, New York

On March 21, 1976, David Bowie and Iggy Pop were arrested at this hotel for drug possession. Bowie was in the midst of his Thin White Duke tour when they were busted on suspicion of possession of 8 oz. of marijuana. Bowie was later given a bail of $2,000, which he posted for both himself and Iggy Pop. They also ended up paying a fine later on.

Brown, James

WIBB Radio
830 Mulberry Street
Macon, Georgia

In 1955, this was the location of WIBB 1280 AM, a local radio station that allowed a young singer named James Brown to cut a demo of what became his first hit single, "Please Please Please." A DJ at the station, Hamp Swain, played the song over and over until it caught fire, thus putting James Brown on the map. Today, the building still exists, but it's an insurance office, not a radio station.

Brown, James

430 Douglas Road
Beach Island, South Carolina

On July 7, 2000, an electric company repairman showed up here at the residence of the Godfather of Soul, James Brown. Brown allegedly swung a steak knife at the man and called him "you son-of-a-bitch white trash." No charges were filed against Brown, who's had a history of run-ins with the law. (In 1988, Brown pleaded no contest to PCP possession and guilty to carrying a gun and resisting arrest. He received a two-year suspended sentence and $1,200 fine. Another time, Brown interrupted an insurance seminar at his headquarters in Georgia by waving a rifle and demanding to know who had used his personal bathroom. The subsequent police chase through two states ended with Brown being sentenced to a six-year jail term.) Sadly, Brown passed away in December 2006.

Carpenters

"Close to You" and "Only Just Begun" Apartments
8356 5th Street
Downey, California

Born in New Haven, Connecticut, Karen Carpenter moved with her family to Downey, California, in 1963. Karen's older brother, Richard Carpenter, decided to put together an instrumental trio with him on the piano, Karen on the drums and their friend Wes Jacobs on the bass and tuba. In a battle of the bands at the Hollywood Bowl in 1966, the group won first place and landed a contract with RCA Records. Stardom would soon follow with the smash hit, "Close to You," which had been written in 1964, first turning up on the debut album of Dionne Warwick. It became a number-one record for the Carpenters in the summer of 1970, and with their royalties they bought an apartment building and named it "Close to You."

Soon after, they bought the building across the street and named it, "Only Just Begun" after their big hit that was written by Paul Williams (and originally appeared in a bank commercial). Today, the buildings remain as they did back in the '70s: monuments to two locals who made good. More Carpenters in Downey: The Downey Library at 11121 Brookshire Avenue houses The Carpenters Collection. Donated by Richard Carpenter, it comprises CDs, books, songbooks, albums, videocassettes, a fan club newsletter series, and publicity materials. Many of the books, CDs, and videos may be checked out. Other materials are housed in a display case located near the circulation desk.

The Carter Family Memorial Music Center

A.P. Carter Highway
Hiltons, Virginia
276-386-9480

The Carter family is the most influential group in country music history. Their emphasis on vocals instead of hillbilly instrumentals greatly influenced, and thereby made many of their songs a part of, the standard country music canon, and made a style of guitar playing, "Carter-picking," the dominant technique for decades. Today, they celebrate their legacy in their own backyard.

Their center serves fans and supporters of old-time country and folk music through the presentation of weekly performances here at the Carter Family Fold. It also honors the memory of the first family of country music, the legendary Carter Family (A.P. Carter, Sara Carter, and Maybelle Carter), whose first recordings (in 1927) are credited with giving birth to the commercial country music industry. Here in this beautiful rural area, within several miles of each other, are several historic landmarks connected to the Carters.

One such site is A.P.'s birthplace, an old log cabin that is now an officially designated National Historic Site, which has been moved from an inaccessible, remote area unavailable to automobiles and visitors. It now is in the final stages of restoration and is permanently positioned right next door to the Carter Fold.

The two houses—A.P. and Sara's house, and Maybelle and Ezra's home—are still owned and occupied by family members so they're not open to the public, but they may be seen from the A.P. Carter Highway. The A.P. Carter Store, a general store owned and operated by A.P. Carter in the later years of his life, is now the Carter Family Museum. Located right next door to the Fold, it is open on Saturdays and during the festival each year. Tours at other times can be pre-arranged by calling 276-386-9480.

Cleveland Rocks

Some gone but not forgotten rock 'n' roll sites in Cleveland, Ohio.

La Cave de Café

10615 Euclid Avenue

At one time it was a favorite place for The Velvet Underground to play, but alas, the folk-rock paradise still wound up becoming a parking lot. Open from 1962-1969, Le Cave also hosted Phil Ochs, the Jeff Beck Group, and many other artists.

Pirate's Cove

1059 Old River Road

Today it's where the dance club Heaven & Earth is located but back in the 1970s this was the punk heaven known as Pirate's Cove, where famous local underground acts such as Pere Ubu, Devo, and the Dead Boys all cut their teeth.

Record Rendezvous

300 Prospect Avenue

Was this the birthplace of the term "rock 'n' roll"? At one time a top record store owned by a man named Leo Mintz stood here, and he was the guy who sponsored the very first Moondog Coronation Ball. Many claim that it was Mintz, not DJ Alan Freed, who coined the term "rock 'n' roll" at his store. Mintz also revolutionized how records were marketed because it was here that he saw an increasing number of white teenagers buying rhythm and blues records. Based on this, Mintz convinced Freed to start playing these records on his radio show. On July 11, 1951, calling himself "Moondog," Freed went on the air and became among the first to program rhythm and blues for a white teenage audience. Other small stations followed, eventually forcing the larger stations to join in.

Swingo's

1800 Euclid Avenue

At one time, Swingo's may have been the country's ultimate rock 'n' roll hotel. In the '50s Elvis used to crash here and the Rolling Stones were regulars in the '60s (with dozens of other name bands), but Zeppelin made a real mark on the place in the early 1970s by tossing trays full of food out of their room and then calling the front desk to blame the chaos on another guest in the hotel—Elton John. Today, Swingo's still stands, but it has become a Comfort Inn.

Costello, Elvis

Holiday Inn City Center
175 East Town Street
Columbus, Ohio
614-221-3281

Elvis Costello found himself in hot water in 1979 after making racist comments about Ray Charles and James Brown. While on tour promoting his new *Armed Forces* album, Costello was at this Holiday Inn bar discussing British and American music with Stephen Stills and Bonnie Bramlett, when the remarks were made. Bramlett responded by punching Costello in the face, thereby ending the discussion. After much publicity about the incident, Costello held a press conference and apologized.

Crosby, David

Medallion Plaza
6400 East Northwest Highway
Dallas, Texas

On April 12, 1982, back when it was a Cardi's nightclub, this was where singer/songwriter David Crosby was caught freebasing cocaine backstage. (The cops arresting Crosby also found he was in possession of a loaded .45 pistol.) He was arrested and eventually did time at a rehab center in New Jersey before skipping out and winding up in the Texas State Penitentiary.

Dead Man's Curve

Sunset Boulevard near Whittier Drive
Beverly Hills, California

The story of "Dead Man's Curve," made famous in the Jan & Dean song, ironically came true near this site on April 12, 1966, when singer Jan Berry had a near-fatal car accident in his Corvette Stingray 427 that left him permanently disabled. The infamous curve originally mentioned in their hit song referred to a curve slightly west on Sunset Boulevard, near Groverton Place, just north of UCLA.

Disco Demolition Night

Comiskey Park
333 West 35th Street
Chicago, Illinois

Chicago DJ Steve Dahl is credited by many with single-handedly ending the disco era. On July 12, 1979, after several smaller anti-disco events, Dahl's "Disco Demolition" between games of a twi-night double-header at old Comiskey Park ended up with the field completely trashed, and the White Sox forced to forfeit the second game.

The Doors

Alta Cienega Motel

1005 N. La Cienega Avenue
West Hollywood, California
310-652-5797

Jim Morrison kept a room here from 1968-1970, as the sign on room 32 attests. Inside the tiny space, fans from all over the world have scrawled messages upon the wall. Inside the motel office, an interview with Morrison that was conducted within that very room hangs on the wall.

Cinematique 16

8818 Sunset Boulevard
West Hollywood, California

Today it's the wonderful store Book Soup, but back in he 1960s it was a small movie theater called Cinematique 16, and it was here where Jim Morrison read his poetry during a Norman Mailer Benefit on May 30-31, 1969. He was accompanied by former Doors member Robby Krieger on guitar, and the song "Far Arden Blues" was recorded during this stint and later appeared on the album called *An American Prayer*.

The Doors

Coconut Grove Exhibition Center

2700 South Bayshore Drive (at Pan American Way)
Coconut Grove, Florida
305-579-3310

On March 1, 1969, at Miami's Dinner Key Auditorium, Jim Morrison of The Doors was arrested for allegedly exposing his penis during the show. Morrison was officially charged with lewd and lascivious behavior, indecent behavior, open profanity, and public drunkenness. Found guilty in October 1970 of indecent exposure and profanity, his sentence totaled eight months hard labor and a $500 fine. The case was still on appeal when Morrison died in Paris in 1971. The auditorium still stands, but has been enveloped by the Coconut Grove Exhibition Center.

The Cock 'n' Bull

9170 Sunset Boulevard
Hollywood, California

This was at one time a prime rock 'n' roll hangout in L.A. and also a place where you could often find Jim Morrison eating. Infamously, back in 1970, he supposedly left here drunk and began acting like a matador out on Sunset Boulevard in front of the restaurant, waving his jacket at passing cars.

Courson, Pamela

108 N. Sycamore Avenue
Hollywood, California

It was in this house that Jim Morrison's longtime girlfriend Pamela Courson died of a heroin overdose on April 25, 1974. She is laid to rest at:
Fairhaven Cemetery
16572 E. Fairhaven Avenue
Santa Ana, California

The Doors' Office

8512 Santa Monica Boulevard
West Hollywood, California

This building, now the Benvenuto Café, once housed The Doors' office (up on the second floor), and the classic album *L.A. Woman* was recorded in the space they used downstairs.

The Doors

The Extension

8500 Santa Monica Boulevard
West Hollywood, California

Today it's an Al and Ed's Autosound, but back in the 1960s it was called The Extension and it was a regular hangout for Jim Morrison. This is where he'd often meet with journalists to give interviews and, in fact, the now famous *Rolling Stone* magazine interview with Jerry Hopkins was conducted at this site.

George Washington High School

1005 Mount Vernon Avenue
Alexandria, Virginia

From 1958 until he graduated two-and-a-half years later, this is where Jim Morrison spent some formative high school years. His dad had been transferred to work at the Pentagon and that's what brought the Morrison family out from Alameda, California. (Morrison skipped the graduation ceremonies.)

Gil Turner's Liquor Store

9101 Sunset Boulevard
West Hollywood, California
310-652-1000

This is sometimes called the "liquor store to the stars" and The Doors would often walk over here from the nearby Whisky in between sets to buy booze (the Whisky did not yet have a liquor license).

Kaleidoscope

8433 Sunset Boulevard
West Hollywood, California

Today it's the world famous Comedy Store, but back in the 1960s, after first starting out as Ciro's restaurant and nightclub, it was known as The Kaleidoscope. Many bands played here during that time, including The Doors, who appeared here April 21–23, 1967.

The Doors

New Haven Arena

State and Grove Streets
New Haven, Connecticut

There's a parking lot here where the arena used to be, where on December 9, 1967, Doors lead singer Jim Morrison had one of his more memorable run-ins with the law. Morrison had been found entertaining a woman in a shower stall before the show by a cop who, not recognizing the singer, maced him. Later, onstage, Morrison recounted the episode for the crowd during the song "Back Door Man" and was then arrested and charged with "indecent and immoral exhibition."

Monaco Liquor

8513 Santa Monica Boulevard
West Hollywood, California
310-652-5091

This liquor store is where The Doors would often buy booze in between rehearsal breaks. Its close proximity to the band's studio, offices, and other haunts made it the perfect spot to stock up and it remains virtually unchanged today.

Morrison Hotel

1246 South Hope Street
Los Angeles, California

The squalid hotel depicted on the cover of The Doors' album Morrison Hotel is located in downtown L.A., just two blocks east of the Los Angeles Convention Center. The hotel's owner supposedly chased The Doors away when they came by to shoot the cover for the 1970 LP, but they snuck back and grabbed the shot anyway (the picture was taken by famed photographer, Henry Diltz).

Morrison's Last Residence

8216 ½ Norton Avenue
West Hollywood, California

This was Jim Morrison's last residence. He lived here in 1970 with Pamela Courson (who was never legally married to the singer). It was here where Chuck Berry came to visit Morrison, who, according to his friends, was surprised and thrilled to be visited by the rock 'n' roll legend.

The Doors

Mural

1811 Speedway
Venice, California

This is a landmark for Doors fans, a huge painting of Jim Morrison located right near several other key Doors spots in Venice. Well-known painter Rip Cronk created the mural.

Olivia's (former site)

2615 Main Street
Santa Monica, California

At one time there was a restaurant called Olivia's here and it's the place that inspired Jim Morrison to write the song "Soul Kitchen."

The Palms

8572 Santa Monica Boulevard
West Hollywood, California

During band rehearsals, Jim Morrison would frequent this bar to drink beer and whiskey during the breaks in the action. It is now a lesbian nightspot.

The Doors

Themis

947 La Cienega Boulevard
West Hollywood, California

This antique store also plays a part in the history of Jim Morrison. It's the former site of Themis, the boutique run by Morrison's girlfriend Pamela Courson. It was basically financed by Morrison and was in business for about three years starting in the late 1960s. Back then, it would not be uncommon to find the singer hanging out here.

TTG Studios

1441 N. McCadden Place
Hollywood, California

Today this place is called Shooting Star International, but it used to be TTG Studios and it's where The Doors recorded their third album called *Waiting for the Sun*.

Turkey Joint West

116 Santa Monica Boulevard
Santa Monica, California

Rick and the Ravens (Ray Manzarek's band) played at this club as the house band in the mid-1960s and it was here on June 5, 1965, that Jim Morrison made his first public appearance as a singer. Today, it's a popular English pub called Ye Olde King's Head.

Topanga Corral

2034 Topanga Canyon Boulevard
Topanga Canyon, California

There used to be a restaurant here that served as the inspiration for the Doors song "Roadhouse Blues." A fire destroyed it back in the 1960s, and there was a cabin behind the restaurant that Jim Morrison bought for his girlfriend Pamela Courson (in the song he referred to the cabin as a "bungalow").

Emerson, Greg

Shilo Inn
206 SW Temple Street
Salt Lake City, Utah

Back in the early 1970s, Greg Lake of the monster progressive band Emerson, Lake and Palmer was busted here for swimming nude in the pool.

Eminem

8427 Timken Street
Warren, Michigan

This is the house that rapper Eminem grew up in a three-bedroom, two-bath house that has been in his family for over 50 years (until his uncle sold it to two businessmen who put it up for auction on eBay—the high bid: $11 million).

Fender Guitars

Corner of Santa Fe and Pomona Streets
Fullerton, California

Guitar design-whiz Leo Fender once operated his factory on this site, where he mass-produced his breakthrough creations such as the Fender Broadcaster, the Telecaster, and the Fender Precision Bass from 1945-1952. Though he never played guitar himself, Fender was inducted into the Rock and Roll Hall of Fame a few months after his death in 1991.

Franklin, Aretha

New Bethel Baptist Church
8450 C.L. Franklin Boulevard
Detroit, Michigan

In the 1950s, the Reverend C.L. Franklin preached and sang here (he was also a recording artist on Chess Records in Chicago). His three daughters performed here as well, one of whom was Aretha Franklin.

The Grateful Dead

The Château

838 Santa Cruz Avenue
Menlo Park, California

Back in the early 1960s, a rambling old house stood here, sort of a hostel for various musicians, artists, and beatniks. Banjo player Jerry Garcia resided here with lyricist Robert Hunter. So, for many fans, this is the group's spiritual birthplace. Once they started up as The Warlocks (they would change their name soon after), they played a local pizza place, Magoo's Pizza Parlor, which had been located at 639 Santa Cruz Avenue in Menlo Park. Today, the site is a furniture store.

Grateful Dead House

710 Ashbury
San Francisco, California

This house was home to Jerry Garcia, Pigpen, manager Rock Scully, and other Dead associates. It was a popular community center until 1967, when the police arrested everyone for a very small amount of marijuana that was found on the premises (Garcia and his girlfriend were out shopping at the time). In March of 1968, the band performed a farewell concert from the back of a flatbed truck with power lines attached to the Straight Theatre. The band then moved to Marin County.

The Grateful Dead

Lesh, Phil

1012 High Street
Palo Alto, California

The Warlocks met here at band member Phil Lesh's house in 1965 and decided a name change was in order. Thumbing through an encyclopedia, they came upon a reference to "the grateful dead" and settled on that as the new group name. Their first gig under that name took place in December 1965.

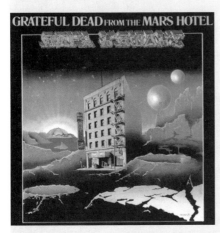

Mars Hotel

192 Fourth Street
San Francisco, California

This rundown, skid row flophouse was immortalized by the band on their 1974 album *From the Mars Hotel*.

The Onion

9550 Haskell Avenue
Sepulveda, California
818-894-9251

The odd-shaped, onion-dome church can be rented today for many different kinds of events. But, in February 1966, the Grateful Dead played here as part of the infamous Acid Test Series, organized by the LSD-touting group the Merry Pranksters.

Royal Sonesta Hotel

300 Bourbon Street
New Orleans, Louisiana
504-586-0300

In the legendary Grateful Dead song, "Truckin'," the band sings of being "Busted, down on Bourbon Street." The lyric was based on a real incident that took place in room 2134 of this Big Easy hotel in January 1970. Though marijuana and hashish were recovered in the room by undercover cops, charges against several band members were eventually dropped.

Green, Al

Full Gospel Tabernacle
787 Hale Road
Whitehaven, Tennessee

Just a few miles south of Graceland is a place where you can hear one of soul's sweetest voices at work. This is where the Reverend Al Green preaches (when he's not on the road). When he's there, he packs them in just as he did at concert halls in the 1970s. Green found faith in the '70s after a girlfriend threw a hot pan of grits in his face.

Green Day

924 Gilman Street Project
924 Gilman Street
Berkeley, California
510-525-9926

This Berkeley club has seen it all since it opened in the 1980s, from punk legends the Dead Kennedys to current punk-pop megastars (and owners of two Grammy Awards) Green Day, who first honed their chops here in the late 1980s.

Guns N' Roses

1114 North Clark Street
Hollywood, California

In the early 1980s, this apartment complex was where the band Guns N' Roses lived with their then-manager, Vicky Hamilton. The pad is located right near the famous Whisky nightclub, where the band would often hang out.

Haight Ashbury Free Medical Clinic

558 Clayton Street
San Francisco, California
415-487-5632

This clinic has long aided the locals when they become ill, and when the band Nirvana came here in 1989 for treatment of the flu, they noticed a public service poster that was used to encourage drug users to "bleach their works." The band members got the idea from the poster to name their next release "*Bleach.*"

Haley, Bill

Corner of Crosby and Fifth Streets
Chester, Pennsylvania

Located about 14 miles southwest of Philadelphia, a star embedded in the sidewalk here marks the former home (it burned down many years ago) of rocker Bill Haley of "Rock Around the Clock" fame.

Hall and Oates

Adelphia Ballroom
1400 North 52nd Street
Philadelphia, Pennsylvania

This is where Daryl Hall first met John Oates. It happened in 1967 when both young singers were part of competing doo-wop groups. A gang fight broke out and they made their acquaintance while hiding out in the freight elevator of the theater. (They didn't go on to record together until 1972.)

Hard Rock Cafe

300 East 5th Street
Los Angeles, California

This was where photographer Henry Diltz shot the back of The Doors' 1969 album, *Morrison Hotel*. (The front cover had been shot a few blocks away at a place called the Morrison Hotel.) The flophouse bar is long gone in this tough L.A. neighborhood.

Says Diltz: "I guess though sometime the next year after the album came out with that picture on the back, they got a call from England and this guy says, 'Hello. Would you mind if we use that name on the back of your album? We're starting a cafe over here in London and we would like to use that name." And they said no, go ahead, and that was the beginning of it. Now every time I go into a Hard Rock Cafe, whatever city I'm in, I always feel like I should get a free hamburger."

Jimi Hendrix

Ashbury Tobacco Center

1524 Haight Street, near Ashbury
San Francisco, California

The Hendrix song "Red House" was supposedly written about this old Victorian mansion, which at the time in the 1960s was painted red. Though he never lived here full-time, Hendrix did spend many nights here as he kept two girlfriends living on the second and third floors.

Café Wha?

115 Macdougal Street
Greenwich Village, New York
212-254-3630

An early Bob Dylan hangout, this is where Animals bassist Chas Chandler first saw the unknown Jimi Hendrix play in 1966. Under Chandler's guidance, Hendrix soon moved to England, where his career began to crystallize.

Jimi Hendrix

Drake Swissotel

440 Park Avenue
New York, New York

In April of 1968, Jimi Hendrix stayed here after being tossed out of the nearby Warwick Hotel. In his room (which cannot be identified at this time–anyone know?) he recorded a batch of songs including "Cherokee" and "Angel Mist." This is also the hotel where Led Zeppelin's gate receipts from their Madison Square Garden concerts were supposedly stolen in 1973, worth upwards of $200,000.

Electric Lady Studios

52 West 8th Street
New York, New York
212-677-4700

In 1968, Jimi Hendrix was looking to buy a recording studio when he found the Generation Club on West 8th Street in the heart of Greenwich Village. After shelling out the $50,000 asking price, Hendrix turned it into a recording facility, becoming the first major artist to own and operate his own studio. Sadly, Jimi died within a month after the studio opened.

In June 1997, the original, distinctive, curved brick facade entrance to Electric Lady Studios was demolished (the New York Landmark Society unsuccessfully attempted to halt the renovation of the building, which would have been eligible for landmark status in just three years).

Freedman's Loans

1208 1st Avenue
Seattle, Washington
206-622-3086

Jimi Hendrix's father, Al, had once bought himself a saxophone from this pawnshop. Thirty years later, he bought his son, Jimi, his first guitar here. It's still in business after all these years.

Jimi Hendrix

Greenwood Memorial Park

4th Street and Monroe Avenue
Renton, Washington

This is the grave of Jimi Hendrix, who overdosed in London on September 18, 1970. Today, it's become a shrine for Hendrix fans all over the world. The graveyard is located in Renton, a suburb of Seattle, which was Jimi's birthplace. Another interesting Hendrix landmark is Garfield High School (400 23rd Avenue) in Seattle, from which Hendrix was booted (though he later returned to play a concert in the gym).

Hilton Hotel

720 South Michigan Avenue
Chicago, Illinois

The Plaster Casters were a bunch of 1960s groupies whose claim to fame was immortalizing their rock 'n' roll conquests in the form of plastic molds. That's right—they'd actually make molds of the rock star's private parts. Jimi Hendrix became immortalized in February 1968, in room 1628 of the Chicago Hilton. (And no, the hotel does not acknowledge what took place here.)

Hotel Theresa

2090 Adam Clayton Powell Boulevard
New York, New York

The office building you'll find here today was once one of Harlem's finest hotels. Many musicians and celebrities stayed here; it's even where Cuban president Fidel Castro stayed in 1960. When Jimi Hendrix first came to the Big Apple in January 1964, he stayed here as well. In fact, during that stay Hendrix won the Apollo Theater's weekly amateur contest. In May of 1965, Hendrix returned to the hotel, staying in room 416 while playing in Little Richard's band during an Apollo stand (under the name Maurice James).

Buddy Holly

Childhood Home

1911 6th Street
Lubbock, Texas

This is the house where the Holley family lived at the time their fourth child, Charles Hardin Holley, was born on September 7, 1936. He would one day become "Buddy," and would also drop the "e" from his last name. A vacant lot sits where the house used to stand.

Fair Park Coliseum

Avenue A and 10th Street
Lubbock, Texas

Back in the mid-1950s, Buddy Holly and The Crickets played as an opening act for both Elvis Presley and Bill Haley and the Comets here at this local arena (which still stands today).

Hutchinson Junior High

3102 Canton Avenue
Lubbock, Texas

Buddy formed a duet here with his friend Bob Montgomery. Calling themselves "The Bob and Buddy Show," they'd regularly entertain at school functions.

Buddy Holly

KDAV Radio (now KRFE AM 580)

**6602 Martin Luther King Boulevard
Lubbock, Texas
806-745-1197**

Today it's an easy listening station, but back in 1953 Buddy Holly did a weekly radio show here with his partner Bob Montgomery. It's believed by many that KDAV was the first full-time country music station in the United States.

Buddy Holly and Montgomery were initially given a chance to perform on the air during *The Sunday Party*. This later evolved into a regular slot at 2:30 P.M. every Sunday for what by then had become a trio (Holly, Montgomery, and bassist Larry Welborn). The segment was called *The Buddy and Bob Show* and featured a unique blend of country and western and rhythm and blues. Tours are offered today, so you can get a chance to see the actual studio where Buddy Holly cut his very first records.

Riverside Ballroom

**115 Newhall Street
Green Bay, Wisconsin**

On February 1, 1959, what would be Buddy Holly's final tour, The Winter Dance Party, became stranded en route to Appleton, Wisconsin. The bus had broken down with temperatures at 30 degrees below zero and no source of heat. Still, the tour somehow rolled on and Buddy and his crew (including Ritchie Valens) performed that night at the Riverside Ballroom here in Green Bay, Wisconsin (built in 1929).

It was their second to last performance (the last show was performed the next night in Clear Lake Iowa at the Surf Ballroom, all details of which appear in *James Dean Died Here*). However, outside the club is a touching memorial to the three fallen singers, commemorating their appearance here in Wisconsin.

Buddy Holly

Statue

8th Street and Avenue Q
Lubbock, Texas

Lubbock pays tribute to its famous son with an eight-foot bronze statue of Buddy Holly at the entrance to the city's civic center. Nearby is a walk of fame honoring other Texas favorites including Waylon Jennings and Roy Orbison.

Idol, Billy

Corner of Gordon and Fountain
Hollywood, California

On February 6, 1990, rocker Billy Idol crashed his motorcycle here at about 8 A.M. He had just finished his *Charmed Life* album, and wound up breaking both an arm and a leg. The accident forced the cancellation of his original role in *The Doors*, but director Oliver Stone found another part for Idol, and the character of Cat is actually portrayed on crutches. Five leg operations later, Idol rebounded from the accident with an extensive world tour, which began in August of 1990.

Jackson Five

2300 Jackson Street
Gary, Indiana

This two-bedroom clapboard house is where Joe and Katherine Jackson lived with their nine children before striking it rich with the Jackson Five and moving to Southern California. Note: the street is not named for the family—it had already been named for President Jackson.

Jackson, Janet

Reliant Stadium
Houston, Texas

Reliant Stadium, the first NFL stadium with a retractable roof, hosted the 2004 Super Bowl XXXVIII between the New England Patriots and the Carolina Panthers. (The Patriots won 32-29 on Adam Vinatieri's 41-yard field goal with four seconds remaining.) The event also featured history's most controversial halftime show, the now infamous "Wardrobe Malfunction" that saw Janet Jackson bare her breast during a song and dance routine with Justin Timberlake. The CBS network was heavily fined for the incident and though all parties involved claim the incident was unintentional, broad skepticism remained, many feeling that it was a calculated stunt designed to produce a shock effect (which it did).

Michael Jackson

Garnett Elementary School

2131 Jackson Street
Gary, Indiana

One of Michael Jackson's first big performing moments happened here at the school that all of the Jackson Five attended. In 1963, the five-year-old singer brought the house down with his version of "Climb Every Mountain" from *The Sound of Music*. Michael's first professional debut happened a year later at a club called Mr. Lucky's Lounge, which is still located at 1100 Grant Street in Gary.

Jackson Family Home

641 Hayvenhurst Avenue
Encino, California

In November of 1993, police searched singer Michael Jackson's famous family compound here in the San Fernando Valley, looking for evidence that might support charges of child molestation against Jackson. (The criminal case was eventually dropped for lack of evidence.) Michael Jackson later settled the civil lawsuit out of court with the boy (for a reported $20 million), while insisting that he was innocent of any and all charges. Michael's sister, LaToya Jackson, had earlier alleged that she had been abused as a child by her father at this same Jackson family home, though the rest of the family heatedly denied all of her explosive charges.

Pasadena Civic Auditorium

300 East Green Street
Pasadena, California
626-449-7360

On March 25, 1983, Michael Jackson, in front of his Motown brethren, slid across the stage and introduced "moonwalking" to the strains of a pre-recorded "Billie Jean" during the Motown 25th anniversary television show. Both the live and television audiences went wild at the sight of Jackson seemingly floating above the floor.

Michael Jackson

Neverland Ranch

Figueroa Mountain Road
Los Olivos, California
Directions: Neverland is located on Figueroa Mountain Road, six miles north
of Los Olivos, California. Los Olivos is in the Santa Ynez Valley, 25 miles
north of Santa Barbara.

You can't get beyond the guard at the gate, but within this sprawling complex is where Michael Jackson houses his zoo, amusement park, and theater. It's from here that he broadcast his 1993 speech declaring his innocence when charges of child molestation arose.

Santa Maria Courthouse

312 East Cook Street
Building E
Santa Maria, California

Singer Michael Jackson was arraigned here in Santa Maria on January 16, 2004, at the court of Santa Maria. He was admonished by the judge for turning up 20 minutes late and entered a plea of "Not Guilty." Hundreds of fans and an international media circus surrounded the event, which became notable for Jackson's bizarre, post-plea circus whereby he jumped on a van front of the courthouse and began dancing for the throngs of people who showed up (as well as for the ever-present videographer Jackson had hired for the day).

Jefferson Airplane

2400 Fulton Street at Willard Street North (facing the northern side of Golden
Gate Park)
San Francisco, California

This is where the Jefferson Airplane parked it during their heyday in the late '60s and early '70s. Many of rock's royalty paid a visit to this stately manor for what are considered some of the most legendary parties in rock 'n' roll history.

Joel, Billy

Route 114
Sag Harbor, New York

In January of 2003, singer/songwriter Billy Joel, then 53, was driving his blue 2002 Mercedes-Benz south on Route 114 near Walker Avenue in Sag Harbor at about 10:30 P.M. on a Saturday night when he apparently lost control of his vehicle, veered off the road, and struck a tree. Paramedics rushed him by ambulance to East Hampton Airport, where he was airlifted to Stony Brook University Hospital. He was not given a Breathalyzer test and faced no charges in the incident.

Joplin, Janis

380 West Baltimore Avenue
Larkspur, California

This rustic, redwood-paneled home was Janis Joplin's last official residence. Situated up in the then-bohemian Marin County, one of her neighbors was Jerry Garcia. Joplin moved in here in December 1969, and spent a reasonably peaceful last year of her life here before dying of a heroin overdose in Hollywood.

Joplin, Janis

Eleventh Door
Red River and 11th Street
Austin, Texas

It's now called Symphony Square, but when it was a small club back in the 1960s it was the first place Janis Joplin sang professionally before trucking herself off to fame in San Francisco.

Journey Headquarters

1111 Columbus Avenue
San Francisco, California

By 1981, Journey had become one of the most popular and financially successful bands on the planet. Adding to the "corporate rock" aspect surrounding the band was this building, which became the headquarters for everything Journey. The planning, finances, design—it all was based here in this impressive redwood building, a palace that testified to the success of the band. Today, in a post-Journey world, the consulate of Indonesia owns the building.

KISS

**10 East 23rd Street
New York, New York**

Back in the pre-makeup days of 1972, this is where the band KISS (Gene Simmons, Paul Stanley, Ace Frehley, and Peter Criss) got together to start rehearsing, up in a loft on the fourth floor. Today it is the site of Cosmic Comics.

Laurel Canyon Country Store

**2108 Laurel Canyon Boulevard
Los Angeles, California
323-654-8091**

Built in 1919, this casual market has served as a location for several films and is also a hangout for many Laurel Canyon artists, musicians, and actors. It feels like a small-town store—a cozy place where you just might run into Liam Neeson, Sophia Loren, or Mick Jagger. Back in the early 1970s, members of the Eagles, The Byrds, The Doors, and other local rock 'n' roll residents could always be found here. (A stone's throw from the market is a wood house where Jim Morrison used to live.)

Led Zeppelin

Absinthe Bar
400 Bourbon Street
New Orleans, Louisiana
504-525-8108

This famous bar, the walls of which are covered with thousands of yellowed business cards and dollar bills, was re-created in a London studio for the cover of the band's last album, 1979's *In Through the Out Door.* The actual bar had long been a Zeppelin hangout; Jimmie Page even met his wife there, and so the band wanted to pay tribute.

Led Zeppelin

Edgewater Inn
Pier 67
2411 Alaskan Way
Seattle, Washington
1-800-624-0670

Located on the edge of beautiful Puget Sound, this hotel (now called simply The Edgewater) is the site of the infamous 1969 Led Zeppelin "Shark Incident." On July 25th, Zeppelin checked into this hotel, which back then was a favorite with musicians because guests could fish from their rooms. (Zeppelin was in town to play at the Seattle Pops Festival scheduled for July 25-27, at Woodenville, Washington.) The band caught some red snapper, and then, though versions vary, partook in some unseemly behavior with a seventeen-year-old redhead named Jackie in room 242. (Members of the band Vanilla Fudge were also present.)

Lewis, Jerry Lee

1595 Malone Road
Nesbit, Mississippi
662-429-1290

Incredibly, you can take a personal tour at the home and ranch of the "Killer" himself, Jerry Lee Lewis. You can see the gold records, the pianos, the piano-shaped swimming pool as well as tons of personal effects (plus the "Killer Kar Kollection," as Jerry Lee calls it). You may even see Jerry Lee himself if he's home. There are few (if any) other chances to witness a living legend in his own surroundings, and note, you have to call to book a tour reservation—don't just show up. Also, if you want more Jerry Lee, visit the Jerry Lee Lewis Family Museum in Ferriday, Louisiana. Jerry's sister, Frankie Jean Lewis, will personally guide you through the museum, which is located at 712 Louisiana Avenue in Ferriday. Call 318-757-2460 for tours. The museum (located in Jerry Lee's childhood home) is filled with pictures and "Killer" memorabilia.

Lewis, Jerry Lee

4908 East Shore Drive
Memphis, Tennessee

When Jerry Lee Lewis married his young cousin Myra in 1957, they shocked the world. After all, she was just 12 when they met the year before and he was already married! This is the house where Myra lived and where Jerry Lee first met her in 1956. The couple stayed married until 1970, though the bad publicity from the unconventional union is thought to have marred the rest of Lewis's career.

Limp Bizkit

Peacock's Tattoo Studio
11233 Beach Boulevard
Jacksonville, Florida
904-642-0037

This is where Fred Durst famously tattooed the band Korn while they were in town for a gig. He slipped them his Limp Bizkit demo tape while giving them their tattoos, thus launching the band's career.

Love, Courtney

Plaid
76 East 13th Street
New York, New York

Singer Courtney Love, while in the midst of a series of arrests (and bizarre public behavior), gave a surprise performance at Plaid, a lower Manhattan nightclub, for about 400 patrons on March 17, 2004. While on stage with her band, Love hurled a microphone stand into the audience and struck a 24-year-old man in the head. The man was taken to Cabrini Hospital (he fully recovered) while Love was booked at the 9th Precinct in the East Village and charged with reckless endangerment. Love had gone to the club after a controversial appearance earlier in the evening on *The David Letterman Show*.

Lynyrd Skynyrd

Robert E. Lee High School
1200 South McDuff Avenue
Jacksonville, Florida

This was where the unpopular gym teacher Leonard Skinner taught—the hardass eventually made famous when some students changed the name of their band from "My Backyard" to "Lynyrd Skynyrd" in honor of him.

MacArthur Park

Wilshire Boulevard (near Alvarado Street)
Los Angeles, California

MacArthur Park is most famous for the song named after it: a smash hit written by Jimmy Webb and performed by Richard Harris in 1968. In 1978, a disco version by Donna

Summer again hit the top of the charts. Running more than seven minutes, it is apparently about a lost love and a rendezvous in the park. It has been covered more than 50 times, including versions by Waylon Jennings, Glenn Campbell, and Liza Minelli.

MacArthur Park was originally named "Westlake Park," and built in the 1880s. It was renamed shortly after the end of World War II for General Douglas MacArthur.

Madonna

234 East 4th Street
New York, New York

When she first set out to conquer the music world, this is where Madonna lived. Trained as a dancer at the University of Michigan before moving to New York City, her albums *Madonna* (1983) and *Like a Virgin* (1984) secured her position as a universal pop icon.

Mayfield, Curtis

Wingate Field
Wintrop Street and Brooklyn Avenue
East Flatbush
Brooklyn, New York

On August 14, 1990, at an outdoor concert at Wingate Field in the East Flatbush section of Brooklyn, legendary soul artist Curtis Mayfield was struck and paralyzed from the neck down by a lighting scaffold that fell during a windstorm. He released a new album in 1996, *New World Order,* on which he only sang given that he could no longer play guitar. Sadly, he died on December 26, 1999. Mayfield is remembered for such hits as "It's All Right," "People Get Ready," and "Freddie's Dead," to name a few.

Metallica

3140 Carlson Boulevard
El Cerrito, California

This Bay-Area house is where the band Metallica lived together from 1983 to 1986. During this time they wrote and rehearsed the albums *Ride the Lightning* and *Master of Puppets* in the garage before recording both sets. Perhaps the ultimate heavy metal landmark.

Metallica

Tommy's Joynt
1101 Geary at Van Ness
San Francisco, California
415-775-4216

In September of 1986, Metallica bassist Cliff Burton was killed in a bus crash while the band was on tour in Sweden. After auditioning a slew of other bassists as potential candidates to replace Burton, they brought Jason Newsted here to this legendary San Francisco eatery (famous for its beef stew) to offer him the job.

Michael, George

Will Rogers Memorial Park
9650 Sunset Boulevard (just across from the Beverly Hills Hotel)
Beverly Hills, California

On April 8, 1998, pop star George Michael decided to enter the men's room at this well-mannered park and engage in what police described as a "lewd act." (The park was under fairly regular surveillance after cops realized that it had become a "hot zone.") Michael was alone in the restroom at the time—which is located near the northwest corner of the park. Michael was arrested, found guilty of the charge, and eventually sentenced to perform community service.

Milli Vanilli

Le Mondrian Hotel
8440 Sunset Boulevard
West Hollywood, California
323-650-8999

This is where one of the lead "singers" for the pop duo Milli Vanilli tried to kill himself in 1991. The dreadlocked pair had won the Grammy Award for Best New Artist of 1989, but the statue was taken away from them after it was discovered that the two singers hadn't sung at all on their debut item: they had only lip-synched the songs.

One member of the duo, Rob Pilatus (from Germany), took an overdose of pills, slashed his wrists, and tried to jump out of the ninth-floor window of this hotel before the police finally stopped him. Five years later, on North Van Ness Street in Hollywood, Pilatus was arrested on charges of attempted burglary and making terrorist threats, after he first tried to steal a car and then tried to break into a man's home. His attempt failed when the victim hit Pilatus over the head with a baseball bat. On April 3, 1998, Pilatus was found dead of an apparent overdose in a Frankfurt, Germany, hotel room.

Mitchell, Joni

Garden of Allah
Southwest corner of Sunset and Crescent Heights
Hollywood, California

"They paved paradise, and put up a parking lot," sang Joni Mitchell wistfully about the end of the Garden of Allah, Hollywood's famed apartment-hotel that welcomed transient show business guests from 1935–1955. It was actually a collection of private bungalows, frequented by stars such as Errol Flynn, Clark Gable, Greta Garbo, W.C. Fields, Humphrey Bogart, F. Scott Fitzgerald, the Marx Brothers, and Orson Welles. Legend has it that

Tallulah Bankhead swam naked in the pool here, and Marilyn Monroe was discovered sipping a Coke next to that same swimming pool. Today, the site contains a modern strip mall. Until recently, the bank at the mall had a model of the hotel complex in a glass case, but the bank changed names and the model is now gone.

The Miyako Hotel

1625 Post Street
San Francisco, California

After the famous *The Last Waltz* concert in 1976 featuring the final shows of The Band (with many musical guests) the cast and crew came here to the Garden Bar at the Miyako to listen to Dr. John and Bob Dylan play together along with many of the other musicians in one of the most famous post-concert parties ever.

Neil, Vince

**The Esplanade at Sapphire Street
Redondo Beach, California**

Mötley Crüe frontman Vince Neil had been living it up at his Redondo Beach home for three days when he decided to make a run to a local liquor store for more booze. Nicholas "Razzle" Dingley (a member of the Finnish punk band Hanoi Rocks), went along for the ride. Coming home from the booze run, Neil, driving with a personal blood alcohol level almost twice the legal limit, swerved sharply to avoid a parked fire truck. His red 1972 Ford Pantera then smashed into a white Volkswagen, killing "Razzle" Dingley. Neil escaped with minor injuries, but the man in the Volkswagen was left with brain damage and paralysis. Though Neil was arrested for vehicular manslaughter, amazingly, he got off with just a 30-day jail sentence.

New York Dolls

**Gem Spa
131 Second Avenue
New York, New York
212-995-1866**

Open 24 hours every day of the year, the Gem Spa newsstand has been in business for nearly 70 years. In addition to making what many New Yorkers consider to be the world's best egg cream, this is also where the legendary New York Dolls posed for the back cover of their first album in 1973 (the record was produced by Todd Rundgren). David Johansen, Johnny Thunders, and the rest of the Dolls returned for a follow-up shoot in 1977, after the original group had dissolved.

Nirvana

Maria's Hair Design

107 S. M Street
Aberdeen, Washington

Maria's Hair Design is the shop owned by Nirvana bassist Krist Novoselic's mom, and it's where Krist and Kurt Cobain practiced many a night during the early days of Nirvana.

Morrison Riverfront Park

Sargent Boulevard
Aberdeen, Washington

Riverfront Park is the site of the much publicized fan vigil the night of Kurt Cobain's death.

Seafirst Bank Building

Market Street and Broadway
Aberdeen, Washington

On July 23rd, 1985, Kurt Cobain was arrested for vandalism when he was caught writing "Ain'T goT no how waTchamacalliT" on the alley wall behind this bank (though today it's a Bank of America).

No Doubt

1173 Beacon Avenue
Anaheim, California

The members of the Southern California band No Doubt moved into this house, the former home of Eric and Gwen Stefani's grandparents. They built a recording studio in the garage, which is where they cut their initial demos (not to mention a few of the songs that would wind up on their breakout 1996 album *Tragic Kingdom*).

Ozzy Osbourne

Epic Records

Century Park East and Little Santa Monica Boulevard
Los Angeles, California

In May of 1981, a drunk Ozzy Osbourne bit the head off of a live dove during a promotional visit to the Epic Records building. He was promptly banned from ever re-entering the building and proceeded to release an album under the Epic label, *The Blizzard of Oz,* that would become a triple platinum hit.

Veterans Memorial Auditorium

833 5th Avenue
Des Moines, Iowa
515-242-2946

During the 1981–82 "Blizzard of Oz" tour, rocker Ozzy Osbourne would bite the heads off of rubber bats as part of his show. Fans got into the act, and throughout the course of the tour would throw their own offerings onstage. On January 20, 1982, someone tossed a very real, very stunned bat on to the stage. Oz, thinking it was a rubber prop, chomped the head off it and thus sealed his own legend as a satanic, ritualistic animal killer. He was taken to the hospital right after the show and checked for rabies.

The Alamo

300 Alamo Plaza
San Antonio, Texas
210-225-1391

We know of Ozzy's exploits of biting the head off of bats and pigeons, but this hallowed American landmark is the scene of another classic Ozzy moment back in the early

1980s. It was here where, after donning one of his wife's dresses, he wandered out in a drunken state and relieved himself in public. (Contrary to myth, not on the actual Alamo wall, but on a monument called the Cenotaph in Alamo Plaza, across the street from the landmark.) Ozzy was arrested and banned from appearing in the city.

Paul, Les

1514 Curson Avenue
Hollywood, California

This is the former site of where guitar genius and innovator Les Paul lived in the 1940s and 1950s with his wife, singer Mary Ford. In the garage that used to be located here, Paul developed his famous multi-track recording technique and the guitar that today bears his name.

Perkins, Carl

Route 13 (between Dover and Woodside, about one mile north of Woodside)
Dover, Delaware

Carl Perkins was traveling on March 2, 1956, from Memphis to appear on Perry Como's TV show in New York when, at about 6:40 A.M. after an all-night drive, the car he and his band were driving struck the rear of a truck heading in the same direction. Perkins was riding the huge success of "Blue Suede Shoes" at the time—it would make it to #2 on the charts.

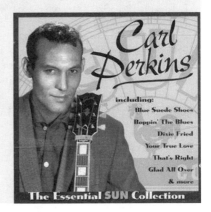

The driver of the truck was killed in the wreck and Perkins's brother Jay died later. His career never recovered from the six months he had to spend in the hospital recuperating, and his legend remains one who might have been.

Prince

Paisley Park Studios
7801 Audubon Road
Chanhassen, Minnesota

Though not open to the public, this is the nerve center and recording/production studio of the artist once again known as Prince. He's recorded most of his music here since 1987 (along with some other bands) and although the Purple One doesn't allow visitors, you can get a postcard view of the place from downtown Minneapolis.

Ramone, Joey

**11 East 9th Street
New York, New York**

This apartment building was the longtime home of the Ramones' lead singer Joey Ramone, who passed away in 2001 from cancer at just 49 years old. Joey (real name Jeffrey Hyman) co-founded the Ramones, a pioneering punk band whose influence stretched all the way from the Sex Pistols and The Clash to U2 and Nirvana. The band recorded 21 albums and its hits included the punchy, three-chord classics "Blitzkrieg Bop," "Teenage Lobotomy," and "Rock 'n' Roll High School."

R.E.M.

The small city of Athens, located about 70 miles northeast of Atlanta, is home to the 30,000-plus students of the University of Georgia. It is also famous for being the fertile, creative launching pad of R.E.M. (and also the B-52s). Here are a few R.E.M. landmarks:

The Church

**394 Oconee Street
Athens, Georgia**

Back in the late 1970s, this church had been converted into inexpensive student apartments. And it was here that guitarist Peter Buck and singer Michael Stipe lived and eventually formed the band R.E.M. In fact, it was here that a yet-to-be-named R.E.M. made its debut at a friend's birthday party on April 5, 1980.

A person in attendance who managed the local club called Tyrone's offered them a gig that May (paying $100) and the rest is history. Today, only the steeple of the church remains, and nearby is the railway trestle bridge that was pictured on the back of the album *Murmur*.

R.E.M.

Weaver D's Delicious Fine Foods

1016 East Broad Street
Athens, Georgia
706-353-7797

The slogan on the outside of this down-home cafe reads, Delicious Fine Foods—
Automatic for the People. The slogan inspired the name of the 1992 smash album by
R.E.M., and soon Weaver D's (home of delicious southern fried chicken and vegetables
served on molded styrofoam plates) became a national phenomenon.

Wuxtry Records

197 East Clayton Street
Athens, Georgia
706-369-9428

It was at this legendary new and used
record store that then-store assistant
Peter Buck met Michael Stipe and the
two decided to try and form a band.
Years later, Buck tried again to work
here, but his success got in the way
because too many fans asked him to
sign records. The store (and its sister
shop in Atlanta) remains a vital
resource for music lovers (and they
also have an upstairs area with tons of
comics and other pop culture
ephemera).

Replacements

2215 Bryant Avenue South
Minneapolis, Minnesota

Bob Stinson and his brother Tommy (guitar and bass players, respectively) lived here,
and it was in the basement of the house where their band the Replacements was formed
and cultivated. Their first public show took place in 1979 at an alcoholic's halfway house.

"Riot" House

Hyatt on Sunset
8401 Sunset Boulevard
West Hollywood, California
323-656-1234

When British bands first invaded this hotel in the 1960s, it was simply known as the Continental Hyatt House. It didn't take long before the place picked up a more appropriate nickname: the "Riot House." Led Zeppelin supposedly had the most fun at the hotel, riding Harleys down the hallways, parading groupies in and out, and tossing TVs out of windows. Room 1015 bares the distinction of being where Rolling Stone Keith Richards mooned the world, and in 1986, Guns N' Roses frontman Axl Rose tossed sizzling steaks to fans below after the fire department showed up to halt his balcony barbecue. Recently renovated, the hotel still has a sense of what makes it famous, as evidenced by the poster of a long-haired musician posted at the front desk. It says: "Be kind to this customer. He may just have sold a million records."

Rolling Stone Magazine

746 Brannan Street
San Francisco, California

It was in the loft here on November 9, 1967, that editor Jann Wenner (and staff) rolled out the very first issue of *Rolling Stone* magazine. Several years later, in 1975, Wenner moved his now hot publication to nicer offices in New York City.

Roth, David Lee

Washington Square Park
Greenwich Village, New York

On April 18, 1993, former Van Halen singer David Lee Roth was arrested here for purchasing marijuana for $10. Roth kept his record clean for the next year and so charges were dropped.

Rundgren, Todd

147 West 24th Street
New York, New York

In the early 1970s, Todd Rundgren built a recording studio here in the top story loft of keyboardist Moogy Klingman. Dubbing it "The Secret Sound," the visionary musician and sought-after producer Rundgren recorded and produced several notable albums here including the Hall and Oates album *War Babies*. For himself, he recorded *A Wizard, A True Star*, and *Todd*, among others. In the late 1970s, Rundgren left the city and headed north to Woodstock, New York, where he would live and record for several years. Today, a candy company occupies the loft space where Rundgren worked.

Rubin, Rick

Weinstein Residence Hall
5-11 University Place
New York, New York

It was in this dorm building, room 203 to be exact, that Rick Rubin started his influential Def Jam Records with Russell Simmons while a student at New York University. His work with L.L. Cool J, the Beastie Boys, and Jazzy Jay attracted the attention of Columbia Records, who, just one year later, paid Rubin more than half a million dollars for a distribution deal.

Sex Pistols

Great Southeast Music Hall and Emporium
3871 Peachtree Road, NE
Brookhaven, Georgia

It's no longer there, but this one-time punk club near Atlanta is where the Sex Pistols played their first American show of their first (and only) American tour on January 5, 1978. It's now the site of the Lindbergh Plaza Shopping Center. The band stayed at the nearby Squire Inn, now called the La Quinta Inn at 2115 Piedmont.

Simon and Garfunkel

P.S. 164
77th Avenue and 137th Street
Forest Hills, New York

When they were both about nine, Paul Simon and Art Garfunkel met at this public school when they appeared together in a production of *Alice in Wonderland* (Paul was the White Rabbit; Art the Cheshire Cat). In their early teens, they were in a doo-wop group called the Sparks, and they soon became a duo (originally calling themselves "Tom and Jerry"). You know what happened after that.

Sixx, Nikki

Aladdin Theatre for the Performing Arts
3667 Las Vegas Boulevard
Las Vegas, Nevada

On August 11, 1997, during a concert by the band Mötley Crüe, bassist Nikki Sixx incited the crowd at the Aladdin Theatre to riot—and riot they did. Sixx was charged with provoking a breach of the peace, though the charge was later dropped.

Soundgarden

7600 Sand Point Way
Seattle, Washington

The Seattle-based band Soundgarden formed in the mid-1980s, naming themselves after a statue called "The Sound Garden" that stands at the Lake Washington shore in Seattle. The statue makes odd, howling tones when the wind blows through its tuned pipes.

Spears, Britney

Aquarium and Pet Center
826 Wilshire Boulevard
Santa Monica, California

In the spring of 2004, Britney Spears, her sister Jamie Lynn, and her mom visited this pet store to purchase a pair of puppies. As always, the paparazzi swarmed and according to one photographer, while Britney's mom was backing out of the parking lot, she hit him with her Toyota Scion. Video shot at the event shows only the aftermath with the cameraman on the pavement. The footage also captured a very upset Britney Spears, who implored to her mother, "Mama, get in the car, get in the damn car." Cops called to the scene prevented the Spears family from fleeing and when an ambulance arrived, the photographer, identified as Colin Reavley, was taken to the hospital where he was given x-rays (revealing no broken bones).

Spencer, Jeremy

Hollywood Hawaiian Hotel
Corner of Yucca Street and Grace Avenue
Hollywood, California

In 1971, a pre-Stevie Nicks/Lindsay Buckingham version of Fleetwood Mac rolled into Hollywood, two weeks into their American tour. While staying at the Hawaiian Hotel, guitarist Jeremy Spencer went for a stroll to buy some newspapers at a bookstore on Hollywood Boulevard. He was approached by a member of a religious group called the Children of God and almost instantly fell under their spell. When the guitarist failed to show up for that evening's gig, the police were contacted, and after five worry-filled days Spencer was traced to the Children of God headquarters at a warehouse in downtown L.A.

In order to get in to see Spencer, Fleetwood Mac manager Clifford Davis had to make up a story about Jeremy's wife, Fiona, being seriously ill. According to a Fleetwood Mac roadie who was at the scene, Spencer "was walking around in a daze like a zombie . . . he'd been brainwashed. It nearly killed me to see him." His head had been shaved and he now answered to the biblical name "Jonathan."

In the course of a three-hour talk, (during which members of the cult rubbed Jeremy's arms and chanted "Jesus loves you"), Spencer explained that he had tired of the hedonistic rock 'n' roll lifestyle and that he was through with the group. With six weeks left on the tour, Fleetwood Mac persuaded eccentric former guitarist Peter Green to fly in and finish the tour. Today, it is believed that Jeremy Spencer is still involved with the Children of God, and he is still playing and composing music. As for the Hawaiian Hotel, the building still exists, only now it's the Princess Grace Apartments.

Bruce Springsteen

Civic Center

**143 West 4th Street
St. Paul, Minnesota
612-224-7403**

Bruce Springsteen kicked off his massive "Born in the U.S.A." tour here at this 18,000-seat arena in June of 1984. However, he returned a month later to shoot his "Dancing in the Dark" video, where he pulled a then-unknown Courteney Cox out of the crowd to dance with him.

"E" Street

Belmar, New Jersey (just south of Asbury Park, along the Jersey Shore)

This is the road that gave Springsteen his band's name. A one-way street running for just a few blocks east of Highway 71 (the main route in and out of town), it's where David Sancious's (an early keyboard player in the E Street Band) mom lived.

First New Jersey Home

**87 Randolph Street
Freehold, New Jersey**

Today the site is a driveway for the St. Rose of Lima church, but until 1957 it was where Springsteen lived with his grandparents, mom, and dad. In a 1987 song called "Walk Like a Man," Springsteen references the home with the line, "By Our Lady of the Roses, we lived in the shadow of the elms."

Bruce Springsteen

Freehold High School

Broadway at Robertsville Road
Freehold, New Jersey

It was while attending high school here in 1965 that Bruce Springsteen formed his first band, The Castilles. He graduated from the school two years later, but missed the graduation ceremony after teachers told him his hair was too long.

The Castilles played their first performance in 1965 at the Woodhaven Swim Club in Woodhaven, New Jersey, earning $35. The group closed the show with Springsteen's arrangement of Glenn Miller's "In the Mood." Today, the swim club has become the local YMCA and it's located at 470 East Freehold Road in Freehold.

Second New Jersey Home

39½ Institute Street
Freehold, New Jersey

This was the Boss's household from 1958-1961. Interestingly, the Boss himself turned up here in the early 1980s and had his photo snapped leaning against the sycamore tree in the front yard—that shot became the underlay image of the *Born in the U.S.A.* album lyric sheet.

The Student Prince

911 Kingsley Street
Asbury Park, New Jersey

It was at this club in the summer of 1971 that Bruce Springsteen first met the man who become one of the foundations of the E Street Band, and the ultimate onstage foil for Springsteen—sax player Clarence Clemons.

Third New Jersey Home

68 South Street
Freehold, New Jersey

Bruce Springsteen and his family moved here in 1961, and it was on the roof of this home where he'd teach himself to play the guitar on summer nights.

Stern, Howard

WRNW-FM
55 Woodside Avenue
Briarcliff Manor, New York

After graduating from Boston College in 1976, legendary radio personality Howard Stern started working as a DJ for the progressive FM station WRNW in Briarcliff, New York (located in Westchester County). This was his first real on-air job, and while here he eventually took over several other duties, including both program and production direction. Stern lasted about two years at WRNW before moving to Hartford, Connecticut, to work for WCCC. In Stern's autobiographical movie, *Private Parts* (based on his wildly successful book), you can actually see the building where WRNW used to exist, as Stern used the exterior in the movie. (Today, it houses other businesses.)

Stevens, Rick

Edenvale Elementary School
285 Azucar Street
San Jose, California

The band Tower of Power has released 18 albums over the years, the latest being 2003's return to form *Oakland Zone*. In addition, the horn section has become well-known as a backing unit for other artists. The TOP horn section has appeared on many artist's recordings, including Little Feat, The Monkees, Santana, Elton John, Linda Lewis, John Lee Hooker, Rod Stewart, Jefferson Starship, Heart, Huey Lewis and the News, Lyle Lovett, Poison, Phish, and Aerosmith. But there is a dark spot in the band's career. In February of 1976, the lead singer for Tower of Power, Rick Stevens, surrendered to police here on the playgrounds at this school and was arrested for a double murder (for which he was sentenced to life).

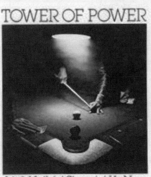

The Sunset Grill

7439 Sunset Boulevard
Hollywood, California
323-851-5557

This hamburger stand is the subject of Don Henley's "Sunset Grill" from his *Building the Perfect Beast* album. When the tune came out, the Sunset Grill's owner, Joe Frolich, had no idea he and his establishment had been immortalized. After customers started telling him that he and his restaurant were being sung about by the ex-Eagle, Joe's wife, Eva, finally recognized Henley at the Grill one day. By that time, tourists had already started gawking and pulling up to take snapshots. Henley was quoted back then as saying the song was an indictment not of Southern California, but of urban sprawl in general and the changing nature of American cityscapes.

The Supremes

Brewster Douglas Housing Project
Just north of downtown, and west of the Chrysler Freeway
Detroit, Michigan

This former public housing project (the original buildings have been torn down) is where The Supremes singing group first came together. Florence Ballard had recruited a couple of neighbors, Diana Ross and Mary Wilson, for her group called the Primettes and together they visited the soon-to-be famous Hitsville studios, where they went in to sing backup and provide handclaps to records being recorded there. Soon, they became The Supremes; one of Motown's most successful acts.

"Take It Easy"

The Northwest corner of Kinsley Avenue and Second Street
Winslow, Arizona

Mention the name "Winslow, Arizona" and it's sure to trigger the song lyric, "Well I was standing on a corner in Winslow, Arizona," right? The lyrics from the popular Eagles song "Take It Easy," written by Jackson Browne and Glenn Frey, inspired the city to turn this very corner into a park right on historic Route 66. A bronze sculpture of a young man wearing blue jeans with a guitar in hand sums up the hopes and musical dreams of a generation. It's called "Standin' on the Corner Park." The park features the artwork of muralist John Pugh and sculptor Ron Adamson.

The Talking Heads

Rhode Island School of Design
2 College Street
Providence, Rhode Island
401-454-6100

Though it was at New York's famed underground club CBGB's that The Talking Heads first were noticed, it was here where three of the band's members first met. In the early 1970s, Chris Frantz, David Byrne, and Tina Weymouth were all design students here when they met on campus. Frantz and Byrne formed a band called The Artistics, which played for a while on campus and soon after moving to New York the trio formed The Talking Heads.

The Tropicana Motel

8585 Santa Monica Boulevard
West Hollywood, California

Today it's a Ramada Inn, but back in the 1960s and 1970s, Jim Morrison of the Doors lived here, as did Tom Waits. The Tropicana was a den of rock and roll excess for years, catering to not just bands on the way up but also some of the biggest acts on the planet. Frequent rock 'n' roll guests included Janis Joplin, Alice Cooper, Van Morrison, Bruce Springsteen, Eddie Cochran, the Beach Boys, The Byrds, Led Zeppelin and Frank Zappa, whose "freak-out" parties here were legendary. The Tropicana was torn down in the 1980s.

Turner, Ike and Tina

4263 Olympiad Drive
Baldwin Hills, California

In this L.A. suburb, the Turners lived throughout their heyday years in the 1960s and '70s. It was the center of much of the torment Tina Turner allegedly suffered at the hands of her husband, and, in fact, was also used in the film about her life, *What's Love Got to Do with It,* starring actress Angela Bassett.

"Valley Girl"

Sherman Oaks Galleria
Ventura and Sepulveda Boulevards (northwest corner)
Sherman Oaks, California

Though it's hard to peg who came up with the actual term "Valley girl," for sure the phrase gained widespread recognition in 1982 with the release of the Frank Zappa novelty hit, "Valley Girl." The minor rap mocked the speech and attitudes of rich teenage girls in Southern California, particularly the San Fernando Valley (where Zappa's daughter Moon Unit used to observe the obnoxious brats). In fact, that's Moon Unit herself

dueting with her father on the song. Of course, the Galleria (now an office/shopping complex) was prominently featured in the tune.

Van Halen

Body Shop
8520 Sunset Boulevard
Hollywood, California

This strip club on the legendary "Strip" was the site of a famous rock 'n' roll presentation: in 1977 Warner Bros. executives gave Van Halen their first gold record here. The ceremony was hosted by the late comedy legend Milton Berle, who was the uncle of their then-manager.

Velvet Underground

Café Bizarre

106 West 3rd Street
New York, New York

This is the famed club where Andy Warhol discovered The Velvet Underground. He took them under his wing and made them "his" group. The Velvets had become a kind of house group until the famed artist plucked them from the obscure layers of the New York underground. Today, the site is occupied by a college dorm.

Electric Circus

23 St. Mark's Place
New York, New York

The brainchild of William Morris agent Jerry Brandt, this former club played host to many crazy shows from 1967-1970, including those featuring The Exploding Plastic Inevitable, an explosive, shocking light/costume/sound revue featuring The Velvet Underground. Today, it's a rehabilitation center.

Velvet Underground

Reed-Morrison Loft

450 Grand Street
New York, New York

Lou Reed and Velvet Underground band mate, the late Sterling Morrison, lived in a fifth-floor loft here in 1965. One wintry day that same year, the Velvets were hanging out here when legendary journalist Al Aronowitz popped in to check up on a claim Reed had made about being the fastest guitar player in the world.

Waiting out in Aronowitz's limo was Rolling Stone Brian Jones. Velvet guitarist John Cale rushed out to meet Jones, who was a hero of his. But too late—Jones supposedly had gone off to score acid in this rundown part of Little Italy. (Cale's apartment back then was at 56 Ludlow Street in New York.)

Summit High School

125 Kent Place Boulevard
Summit, New Jersey

On December 11, 1965, The Velvet Underground made their performing debut in this high school auditorium, playing a school dance. It was a triple bill with The Myddle Class as headliners and The Forty Fingers as co-support. This gig was arranged by journalist Al Aronowitz, who was also The Myddle Class' manager.

The Who

Moon, Keith

Days Inn
2207 West Bristol Road
Flint, Michigan
810-239-4681

Talk about a memorable birthday. On August 23, 1968, The Who drummer Keith Moon turned 21 and this hotel (then a Holiday Inn) may never be the same as a result. The party started early in the morning but as the day rolled on, Moon wanted to commemorate it in a special way so he hijacked a brand new Lincoln Continental and drove it into

the swimming pool, waiting until it nearly hit bottom before climbing out. In all, paint for six cars, a piano, a pool, and several rooms were trashed, all to the tune of $40,000, which the band paid.

Moon, Keith

Stage 43
CBS Television City
7800 Beverly Boulevard
Los Angeles, California
323-575-2458

On September 15, 1967, Keith Moon affixed explosives in his drums for The Who's appearance on *The Smothers Brothers Comedy Hour*. At the end of their second song (lip-synching to a live version of "My Generation"), Moon ignited his drums, causing a ferocious explosion, which is what originally impaired guitarist Pete Townshend's hearing. Game shows use the stage today.

The Who

The Who

Cow Palace
2600 Geneva Boulevard
Daly City (San Francisco), California
415-404-4111

During a November 20, 1973, concert here, Who drummer Keith Moon collapsed onstage during the song "Won't Get Fooled Again." The roadies carried him backstage into the dressing room, where he was placed in a cold shower and brought to. After a 30-minute delay, Moon was unable to continue playing, and, in fact, was taken to a local hospital.

Who guitarist Pete Townshend took the microphone and said, "Hey, can anybody out there play drums? I mean good. Any takers come up here onstage." Scott Halpin, a 19-year-old, made his way to the stage and took over. Townshend introduced him, called for the song "Naked Eye," and they were off. The Who ran through two other songs, "Magic Bus" and "My Generation" before finishing the set with the substitute drummer.

The Who

Riverfront Coliseum
100 Broadway
Cincinnati, Ohio

Eleven people tragically died here at a 1979 Who concert during the band's first tour after Keith Moon's death some three months earlier. The fans were trampled in a stampede that developed when they were trying to reach unreserved "festival" seating. An episode of the TV show *WKRP in Cincinnati* later made the incident a focal point of one of its shows.

Williams, Hank

Municipal Auditorium
Louis Armstrong Park, off North Rampart and St. Peter Streets
New Orleans, Louisiana

Country legend Hank Williams actually got married twice here on the same day in October 1952, to Billie Jean Eshlimar. They sold tickets to the event ($1.50 per ticket) and the couple banked more than $25,000 that day.

Wilson, Brian

10452 Bellagio Road
Beverly Hills, California

The musical genius Brian Wilson once painted this mansion purple, much to the ire of his neighbors. It also contained the home studio where he recorded much of the albums *Smile, Wild Honey, Friends, 20/20, Sunflower,* and *Surf's Up.*

ROLL OVER BEETHOVEN:
The Beatles, Bob Dylan, Elvis Presley, and The Rolling Stones

The Beatles

Astor Towers Hotel

1340 North Astor Street
Chicago, Illinois

The Beatles' last U.S. tour in 1966 had a different feel than the first tour two years earlier. Much of the mania had died down and on August 11th John Lennon created a PR nightmare during a televised press conference in this hotel. Grilled about an interview he had given a few months earlier on religion (where he had stated that The Beatles were "more popular than Jesus now"), Lennon on this day apologized for his remarks as a means of trying to quell the numerous Beatle record burnings that were taking place throughout the Bible Belt. The hotel has since been converted into an apartment building.

Blue Jay Way

North of Sunset Strip
Hollywood, California
Directions: Turn north on Sunset Plaza Drive off Sunset Boulevard. Head north to Rising Glen when Sunset Plaza goes east. Go left on Thrasher, follow it around west, then turn north on Blue Jay Way.

On August 1, 1967, George Harrison was staying at a rented house on this street. He wrote the song "Blue Jay Way" while awaiting the arrival of former Beatles publicity man Derek Taylor, who had gotten lost in the fog. Shortly thereafter, the piece was recorded by The Beatles for the *Magical Mystery Tour* film and soundtrack record. You may have a hard time determining if you are actually on Blue Jay Way, because folks keep stealing the sign.

Candlestick Park

602 Jamestown Avenue
San Francisco, California
408-562-4949

On August 31, 1966, The Beatles gave their final American concert at Candlestick Park in San Francisco. The official song list that cold and windy night included: "Rock and Roll Music," "She's a Woman," "If I Needed Someone," "Day Tripper," "Baby's in Black," "I Feel Fine," "Yesterday," "I Wanna Be Your Man," "Nowhere Man," "Paperback Writer," and "Long Tall Sally."

Davlen Studio

4162 Lankershim Boulevard
Universal City, California

In early 2003, an American Internet auction house claimed to have proof that The Beatles reunited in secret in the mid-1970s to record a final album. The website said the recordings had been made at a session in 1976 that ended in an argument between the members of the group. This created a huge controversy, utterly disputed by the remaining band members and management.

The tape label listed the songs "Happy Feeling," "Back Home, Rockin' Once Again," "People of the Third World," and "Little Girl." But the tape itself was said to be "bulk erased" by The Beatles because the session ended in a disagreement. Larrabee Studios North currently occupies the building where this supposedly mysterious recording happened.

Deauville Hotel

6701 Collins Avenue
Miami Beach, Florida
305-865-8511

On February 16, 1964, The Beatles made their second TV appearance on *The Ed Sullivan Show*. However, this time the performance was broadcast from the Napoleon Room of this popular resort hotel, not the Sullivan Theater in New York. The nightclub still exists and is located just off the hotel's main lobby. During their stay, The Beatles visited Muhammad Ali (then Cassius Clay), who was there training for his upcoming championship fight with Sonny Liston.

Delmonico Hotel

502 Park Avenue
New York, New York
212-355-2500

This midtown hotel actually hosted two significant Beatle events. The first was in late 1963 when their manager Brian Epstein visited Ed Sullivan (who lived in the hotel) to square away details for The Beatles' first U.S. TV appearance on Sullivan's show in a few months. The next year, on August 28th, Bob Dylan paid a visit to the group's hotel room while they were in the middle of their first U.S. tour and introduced them to pot, thus getting them high for the very first time.

The Ed Sullivan Theater

1697 Broadway Avenue
New York, New York

This is where The Beatles made their United States television debut on February 9, 1964, during a musical segment of *The Ed Sullivan Show*. The CBS Television office had more than 50,000 requests for tickets to a studio that held 700. It is estimated that 73,700,000 viewers watched The Beatles' historic debut. Their thirteen-and-a-half minute performance included the songs "All My Loving," "Till There Was You," "She Loves You," "I Saw Her Standing There," and "I Want to Hold Your Hand." Today, of course, this theater is famous as the place where David Letterman does his show.

John Lennon

Fairmont The Queen Elizabeth

900 Rene Levesque Boulevard West
Montreal, Canada
514-861-3511

On May 26, 1969, newlyweds John Lennon and Yoko Ono took the corner suite rooms (1738-40-42) at the elegant Queen Elizabeth Hotel to stage their week-long "bed-in for peace." A couple of weeks before that, the couple had bedded down in the Amsterdam Hilton for their first bed-in for peace, as documented in the song, "The Ballad of John and Yoko." On June 1st, the lovebirds ordered up some recording equipment, and with comedian Tommy Smothers playing guitar, the song "Give Peace a Chance" was recorded. Joining them in the suite to sing were Dr. Timothy Leary, Montreal rabbi Abraham Feinberg, musicians Derek Taylor and Petula Clark, and members of the Canadian Radha Krishna Temple. The single was released a month later. Today, couples can make their own peace in the same bed as John and Yoko in that very suite. The weekend package includes a souvenir photo of the 1969 event, breakfast for two, a bottle of wine, and a welcome gift.

John Lennon

First New York Apartment

105 Bank Street
New York, New York

John and Yoko first moved to New York City in 1971 and lived in this small West Village apartment. Lennon loved the fact that he could live in relative quiet and anonymity among the busy New Yorkers and soon, he and Yoko relocated to a more grand residence at the Dakota Building, a famous landmark at 72nd Street and Central Park West. Tragically, it was at the Dakota where Lennon was shot to death on December 8, 1980.

Doug Weston's Troubadour

9081 Santa Monica Boulevard
West Hollywood, California
310-276-1158

This legendary club has seen its share of history. The Troubador is where Elton John performed his first show in the United States on August 25, 1970 (he was introduced by Neil Diamond). Randy Newman started out here. Cheech & Chong were discovered on its stage. And on and on.

But it was also here on March 12, 1974, that a drunken, despondent, Yoko-less John Lennon made infamous headlines when, after he and (also drunk) Harry Nilsson were about to get tossed for heckling the Smothers Brothers, he taped a Kotex to his forehead. When a waitress refused to give him what he thought was proper respect, he snapped, "Don't you know who I am?" "Yeah, you're some asshole with a Kotex on his head," was her response.

John Lennon

Strawberry Fields

Central Park West
New York, New York

Strawberry Fields memorial is the name given to a landscaped section in New York's Central Park that is dedicated to the memory of musician John Lennon, and named after one of his songs, "Strawberry Fields Forever." It was designed by landscape architect Bruce Kelly, one of the principal members of the Central Park Conservancy's management at the time and the chief landscape architect for the Conservancy's restoration planning team. Yoko Ono, who had underwritten the project, inaugurated it on John Lennon's birthday, October 9, 1985.

The entrance to the memorial is located on Central Park West at 72nd Street, directly across from the Dakota Apartments, where Lennon lived for the latter part of his life. It is not uncommon for the memorial to be covered with flowers, candles in glasses and other belongings left behind by fans of Lennon and The Beatles. On Lennon's birthday and on the anniversary of his death (December 8th), people gather to sing songs and pay tribute, staying late into what is often a cold night.

Paul McCartney

WKNR

15001 Michigan Avenue
Detroit, Michigan

Remember the infamous "Paul is dead" rumor that hinted that Beatle Paul McCartney had secretly died and was replaced by a look-alike? This is where it started. On October 12, 1969, WKNR-FM's popular DJ Russ Gibb opened the phone lines for his usual Sunday afternoon "rap" with his listeners. Then came the call that changed history.

Eastern Michigan University student Tom Zarski called with questions about the supposed death of Paul, thus beginning the tale that would immortalize both Russ and station WKNR-FM in Beatle lore. DJs, television news reporters, newspapers, and magazines picked up on the story (which had been rumored for a year or two after a supposed car accident McCartney had) and began to look for clues.

The rumor eventually became a full-fledged conspiracy theory as members of the media and Beatles fans searched album artwork and song lyrics for clues to the cover-up and McCartney's supposed death.

Believers had many theories, several of which revolved around the cover of the famed *Abbey Road* album. The cover photo was thought to be a funeral procession, with John Lennon leading the way while wearing white (symbolizing clergy) and Ringo Starr, dressed in black (playing the undertaker). Paul, the corpse, is out of step with the other Beatles, pictured barefoot and with his eyes closed. George Harrison is wearing work clothes, supposedly as the gravedigger.

Behind the band on the left side of the street is a Volkswagen Beetle with a license plate reading "28IF," suggesting that Paul would have been 28 years old if he were still alive. (Paul would actually have been just 27 when *Abbey Road* was released.) There's more: Believers eventually decided that McCartney had died in a car accident that happened at 5:00 A.M. on a Wednesday morning (the time and day mentioned in the song "She's Leaving Home"), and that "he hadn't noticed that the lights had changed" ("A Day in the Life") because he was busy watching the pretty girl on the sidewalk ("Lovely Rita").

According to the rumor, McCartney had been replaced with the winner of a McCartney look-alike contest. The name of this look-alike has been recorded as either William Campbell or William Shears. Though all four members have denied it numerous times, many fans are convinced that the rumor was a hoax perpetrated deliberately by The Beatles as a joke. Today the building that once housed WKNR is empty.

Paul McCartney

The Truckee Hotel

10007 Bridge Street
Truckee, California
530-587-4444

In early 2003, regulars enjoying the Truckee Hotel's usual Thursday night jazz duo got a shock when Paul McCartney took to the small stage for an impromptu song he called "Truckee Blues." McCartney sang at about 10:30 P.M. Thursday after he and wife

Heather Mills dined incognito at Moody's Bistro and Lounge in the Sierra ski town's historic hotel about 15 miles from Lake Tahoe.

Delicia's

6106 Paseo Delicias
Rancho Santa Fe, CA

In February 2004, a wealthy individual in the exclusive California community of Rancho Santa Fe hired Paul McCartney and his band for a reported one million dollars to play a private party at this tony restaurant held in honor of his wife's 50th birthday.

Washington Coliseum

3rd and M Streets, NE
Washington, D.C.

On February 11, 1964, just two days after their debut on Ed Sullivan, The Beatles gave their first concert in the United States at the Washington Coliseum. Today, the building is used as a parking and storage facility for garbage trucks.

Bob Dylan

Birthplace

519 North 3rd Avenue East
Duluth, Minnesota

Dylan was born Robert Allen Zimmerman on May 24, 1941, in Duluth, and spent his first six years in this port city at the end of Lake Superior. The Zimmermans lived on the top floor of this house, which incidentally was auctioned off on eBay in 2001 for $94,600. When Dylan was in kindergarten, his family moved to his mother's hometown of Hibbing, a mining town about 75 miles north of Duluth.

The Bitter End

147 Bleecker Street at La Guardia Place
New York, New York
212-673-7030

When Dylan started hanging out again in Greenwich in the summer of 1975, he made several appearances here with the likes of Patti Smith, Ramblin' Jack Elliot, Bobby Neuwirth, and others before hitting the road with the Rolling Thunder Revue tour. The club is now called The Other End.

Cedar Street Tavern

82 University Place
New York, New York
212-741-9754

An old-fashioned tavern that was once a popular watering hole of artists such as Jackson Pollock, Willem de Kooning, and Mark Rothko in the 1950s, by the '60s it had become a favorite Dylan hangout.

Childhood Home

2425 7th Avenue East
Hibbing, Minnesota

For most of Dylan's life in Hibbing, he lived here. He graduated from Hibbing High School in 1959 (the 1959 yearbook is locked in a cabinet at Hibbing Public Library) and moved to Minneapolis to attend the University of Minnesota. In 1960, he dropped out of the university and moved to New York City. His first album, *Bob Dylan,* was released in 1962. That year, he legally changed his name from Robert Allen Zimmerman to Bob Dylan. A collection relating to Dylan's life and accomplishments is located at the Hibbing Public Library at 2020 East 5th Avenue.

The Commons

130 West 3rd Street
New York, New York
212-533-4790

Dylan played here at The Commons, a sprawling basement club, within a week of his arrival in New York City. It was also here, in 1962, that Dylan started writing a song. After finishing it, he took it over to Folk City and played it for Gil Turner, who thought it was incredible. Gil got up on the stage and played it for the audience, while Bob stood in the shadows at the bar—which is how the world first heard the Dylan classic, "Blowin' in the Wind."

Denver Home

1736 East 17th Avenue
Denver, Colorado

Bob Dylan lived at this address for a short period in the early 1960s—around the time he was playing regularly at the legendary Satire Lounge located at 1920 East Colfax Avenue. Incidentally, the Satire Lounge was also the starting point for Tommy and Dick Smothers, better known as the Smothers Brothers (they lived in the only apartment above the Satire). Judy Collins also played here many times—she attended East High School just a few blocks away.

Duluth National Guard Armory

Armory Arts & Music Center
2416 London Road #779
Duluth, Minnesota

At the 1998 Grammy Awards, Bob Dylan spoke about a pivotal moment in his life. "When I was about 16 or 17 years old, I went to see Buddy Holly play at Duluth National Guard Armory," said Bob, "and I was three seats away from him, and he looked at me, and I don't know how or why, but I know he was with us all the time we were making this record in some kind of way." Dylan witnessed this performance on January 31, 1959. Buddy Holly would die in a plane crash just a few days later. Today the armory remains standing and is in the process of being restored.

Forrest Hills Tennis Stadium

1 Tennis Place
Forest Hills, New York

The U.S. Open Tennis Tournament used to be held in this classic, ivy-covered, open-air stadium. They've held big concerts here, too, including The Beatles, Jimi Hendrix, Talking Heads, Hall and Oates, and others. None were bigger, though, than the show held by Bob Dylan in the summer of 1965. It was just a month after Dylan's controversial "electric" set at the Newport Folk Festival and Dylan wasn't ready to stop pushing the envelope. The first set was acoustic, as the folkies liked. But he tore into the second set with an electric band headed by Robbie Robertson and Levon Helm. Much of the crowd booed and pelted the stage with garbage and it remains another defining night in Bob Dylan's illustrious career.

The Freewheelin' Bob Dylan

161 West Fourth Street
New York, New York

Dylan and his girlfriend, Suze Rotolo, first lived here in an apartment between Jones Street and Sixth Avenue. They moved here in December 1961, just after Dylan had fin-

ished recording his debut album for Columbia. Outside the apartment, in the middle of West Fourth Street, Dylan and Suze were photographed together in February 1963 for the cover of *The Freewheelin' Bob Dylan* album by Columbia staff photographer Don Hunstein (even though they had been separated for seven months at that point). The shot features Dylan and Suze walking toward West 4th with the camera facing Bleecker Street.

Gaslight Cafe/Kettle of Fish Bar

116 MacDougal Street
New York, New York

One of young Dylan's favorite haunts, the Gaslight was originally a "basket house," where performers were paid the proceeds of a passed-around basket. Opened in 1958 by John Mitchell—legendary pioneer of Greenwich Village coffeehouses—the Gaslight had already become a showcase for beat poets Allen Ginsberg and Gregory Corso. However, it was transformed into a folk club when Sam Hood took it over. It was here that Dylan premiered "Masters of War" and many other of his songs. The Kettle of Fish Bar, located upstairs above the Gaslight, was also a regular drinking hangout for Dylan and other bohemian artists of the day.

Gerde's Folk City

11 West 4th Street
New York, New York

This former folk music landmark is where Bob Dylan played his first professional gig on April 11, 1961, supporting blues legend John Lee Hooker. He played here again on September 26th of that same year, a show that was reviewed by Robert Shelton in the *New York Times*. The rave review helped set the Dylan legend in full motion. The site is today occupied by the Hebrew Union College.

Greenwich Village Townhouse

94 MacDougal Street
New York, New York

When the Dylan family left Woodstock in 1970, they moved into this tasteful Greenwich Village townhouse. It was here that Dylan found himself constantly (and infamously) harangued by the seemingly obsessed Dylan expert, A.J. Weberman. It was outside this very house that Weberman made off with the Dylan family's garbage for further study of the legend.

Greystone Park Psychiatric Hospital

West Hanover Avenue
Morris Plains, New Jersey
973-292-4096

 When Bob Dylan first came east in February 1961, he headed straight here to visit his hero, the long-ailing Woody Guthrie, famous singer, ballad-maker, and poet. This marked the beginning of a deep friendship between the two singers. Although separated by 30 years and two generations, they were united on many personal and artistic levels. Woody Guthrie was eventually transferred to Brooklyn State Hospital, where he spent the rest of his life. The Greystone Hospital still houses some patients, but many of the buildings are vacant and in need of repair.

Hard Rock Cafe

279 Yonge Street
Toronto, Canada
416-362-3636

The first plaque marking a rock 'n' roll historic site in Toronto was installed at the Hard Rock Cafe in January 2002. It commemorates the spot where Bob Dylan first rehearsed with Levon and the Hawks. The plaque inscription reads: "An event that *Time* magazine once called 'the most decisive moment in rock history' took place a few steps from where you are now standing. Here in the early morning of Thursday, September 16, 1965, Bob Dylan first heard Levon and the Hawks, a hard-edged Toronto rock group, later to become famous as The Band. After the show, Dylan began rehearsing with The Hawks for what turned out to be his stunning eight-month debut tour on electric instruments."

At the time, this building was famous as the Friar's Tavern. It was one of Toronto's most popular nightclubs and Levon and the Hawks were the city's top band. One of their biggest fans was Mary Martin, a Toronto woman who in 1965 was working in New York City for Albert Grossman, Bob Dylan's manager. Mary watched as Dylan grew fed up playing folk guitar alone in front of silent, reverential crowds. She also witnessed his electric first performance at the Newport Folk Festival.

So Mary Martin decided to play matchmaker. She knew that Dylan needed a fiery band like The Hawks to help him launch his new direction, and that the Hawks needed a star like Dylan to take them beyond the Friar's. On September 15, 1965, Dylan arrived in Toronto. For the next two nights, after hours, he rehearsed with The Hawks on a stage along the north wall—now the window side of the restaurant. One week later, their tour opened in Austin, Texas, unleashing a whole new sound.

Hibbing High School

801 East 21st Street
Hibbing, Minnesota
218-263-3675

A grand staircase leads to the medieval castle-like framework of the historic school, built in the early 1920s for almost $4 million. Unique hand-molded ceilings in the foyer welcome visitors and accent the breathtaking auditorium designed after the Capitol Theatre in New York City. Cut-glass chandeliers of crystal, imported from Belgium, light the 1,800-velvet-seat grand auditorium. The cost of each chandelier in 1920 was $15,000 and today they are insured for $250,000 each. The auditorium boasts a magnificent Barton pipe organ, one of only two that still exist in the United States. Containing over 1,900 pipes, the organ can play any orchestra instrument except the violin. Bob Dylan attended this school and played some legendary performances here in 1958 and 1959.

Hotel Earle

163 Waverly Place
New York, New York
212-777-9515

In the early 1960s, Dylan lived at this onetime rundown hotel (today, as the Washington Square Hotel, it's much nicer) in room 305. Dylan pal and fellow musician Ramblin' Jack Elliott lived in room 312 and Red Indian folksinger Peter LaFarge lived in room 306—LaFarge wrote "The Ballad of Ira Hayes," eventually recorded by both Johnny Cash and Dylan.

"Like a Rolling Stone"

Columbia Studios
799 Seventh Avenue
New York City, New York

Bob Dylan's classic "Like a Rolling Stone" was recorded on June 15, 1965, in Studio A at what was then the New York headquarters of Columbia Records. The studio has since been relocated.

Motorcycle Accident

Zena Road, south of Highway 212
Woodstock, New York

On July 29, 1966, the back wheels of Dylan's Triumph 500 locked and threw him over the handlebars, disabling him for 18 months. This near-fatal motorcycle accident, which broke his neck, caused him to retreat to his home in Woodstock to mend and spend time with his new family.

A few months later, The Band joined him at the rented home (called the "Big Pink") and they began recording. Many of the tapes made there were finally released eight years later as *The Basement Tapes* after being bootlegged by Dylan's fans. The supposed exact site is one mile south of Highway 212, where Zena Road sharply turns, near a rustic barn called the Old Zena Mill.

Newport Folk Festival

Festival Field
Intersection of Girard Avenue and Admiral Kalbfus Road
Newport, Rhode Island

On July 25, 1965, Bob Dylan (and band) upset the folk music generation by plugging in at the Newport Folk Festival and cranking out "Maggie's Farm," "Like a Rolling Stone," and a few other choice selections. While Dylan's seminal show allegedly generated way more disgust than glee amongst the crowd, it became a turning point in his career (and the course of popular music). In one shining moment, he had fused rock 'n' roll with protest songs. The field where the festival was held in 1965 is now the sight of the Festival Field Apartments.

Rotolos' Apartment

One Sheridan Square
New York, New York

Formerly the location of the legendary club called Cafe Society Downtown, it was above this little theater that the Rotolos lived (mother Mary, a widow, and her two daughters, Carla and Suze). Seventeen-year-old Suze Rotolo had fallen for Dylan after seeing him play at a folk music day at the Riverside Church on July 29, 1961. Dylan crashed at a friend's place here on the fourth floor and soon, he and Suze were lovers. It's believed that after Suze left Dylan in May 1962, the heartache inspired him to compose such classic love songs as "Tomorrow Is a Long Time," and "Don't Think Twice, It's All Right."

Sound 80

2709 East 25th Street
Minneapolis, Minnesota

At this one-time recording studio called Sound 80, Bob Dylan recorded his classic mid-1970s album, *Blood on the Tracks,* which featured both "Tangled Up In Blue" and "Idiot Wind," among others. The popular studio had also been used by Leo Kottke and Cat Stevens; the 1980 dance hit "Funkytown" was also cut here. Today, the building where so much musical history was made is used by Orfield Laboratories for testing products' acoustical properties.

The Ten O'Clock Scholar

416 14th Avenue SE
Minneapolis, Minnesota

Robert Zimmerman entered the arts school of the University of Minnesota, located in Minneapolis, in the fall of 1959. While a student at the university, he performed his first solo shows here at the Ten O'Clock Scholar, a local coffeehouse. In October 1959, Robert Zimmerman went into the coffeehouse to see if he could play there. When asked his name by owner David Lee, he responded "Bob Dylan." He maintained a regular job playing at the Scholar until May 1960. Today, the site is a video store parking lot.

Tinker Street Café

59 Tinker Street
Woodstock, New York

Today it's the Center for Photography at Woodstock, but until recently this was the Tinker Street Café, a popular cafe/hangout in the famously bohemian town. Hendrix, Joplin, Van Morrison, and many others ate and played here over the years, but the building had a famous tenant, too. In a room above the cafe, Bob Dylan wrote songs for *Another Side of Bob Dylan* and *Bringing It All Back Home* while living here in 1964.

Village Gate

158 Bleecker Street
New York, New York

In 1962, in the basement apartment of the renowned Village Gate theater, Dylan wrote the song "A Hard Rain's A-Gonna Fall." (The small apartment was then occupied by Chip Monck, later to become one of the most sought-after lighting directors in rock music.) Today, the Village Gate still presents music and theater; it's now called The Village Theater.

White Horse Tavern

567 Hudson Street (at 11th Street)
New York, New York
212-243-9260

This 18th-century bar was a popular Dylan haunt back in 1961, where he would come to hear the Clancy Brothers play. It's also famous as the place where the Welsh poet Dylan Thomas ate his last meal before drinking himself to death. His last words were supposedly, "I've had 19 straight whiskies. I believe that's the record." He died later that night. Founded in 1880, the White House Tavern is the second oldest bar in New York City.

Elvis Presley

Arcade Restaurant

540 South Main Street
Memphis, Tennessee
901-526-5757

Here at the Arcade, you can sit in a booth (on the very same cushions no less) that a young Elvis sat on while sipping malts during his breaks as a driver for Crown Electric. After he became famous in the late 1950s, he still came, but he'd sit by the side door to avoid being recognized right away. There's even a small silver plaque that reads, "Elvis Presley's Booth Since 1953." The Arcade is the oldest restaurant in Memphis; it opened in 1919.

ARCADE RESTAURANT
MEMPHIS' OLDEST CAFE
HAS BEEN PLACED ON THE
NATIONAL REGISTER
OF HISTORIC PLACES
BY THE UNITED STATES
DEPARTMENT OF THE INTERIOR
Est. 1919

Baptist Memorial Hospital

899 Madison Avenue
Memphis, Tennessee

Elvis had checked in and out of here for various ailments over the years, but he was pronounced dead here in August 1977. (Lisa Marie Presley was born here in February of 1968.) The hospital was recently torn down.

Bloch Arena

Building 161 Bloch Arena
Pearl Harbor
Oahu, Hawaii
808-422-0139

On March 25, 1961, Elvis Presley made his first post-Army appearance for the Navy. The King performed in a charity fund-raiser here at Bloch Arena to revitalize the flagging U.S.S. *Arizona* Memorial building fund. It is an event largely unremembered, even though Elvis essentially saved the day.

More than a thousand U.S. sailors were entombed in the battleship in Pearl Harbor when a bomb ripped apart the bow, splitting the hull. It sank in minutes and the bodies were never recovered. Dozens of plans were proposed to memorialize the crew of the *Arizona*, the U.S. Navy's single greatest loss of life, but for nearly 20 years military efforts at raising funds were fumbling and disorganized. There was also no agreement on the size and shape of the memorial.

Enter Elvis, who performed for charity to help pay for the memorial. (Minnie Pearl, a comedy "hillbilly" singer and star of the *Grand Ole Opry* radio and TV show received "special guest" billing.) Elvis brought his complete road show and touring band. They included most of the original musicians and singers on Elvis's first records: D.J. Fontana on drums, Scotty Moore on guitar, and the Jordanaires as backup singers. This was Elvis's last concert for almost a decade.

Civic Arena

66 Mario Lemieux Place
Pittsburgh, Pennsylvania

When it first opened in 1961, the Mellon Arena was known as the Civic Arena. (In December of 1999, the resident Pittsburgh Penguins signed an $18-million, 10-year agreement to rename the Civic Arena the Mellon Arena, after the Pittsburgh-based bank.) Over the years The Beatles played here and part of The Doors' *Absolutely Live* was recorded here, but it's also where Elvis played his very last New Year's Eve show in 1976. His dad Vernon and daughter Lisa Marie were watching that night, and it's thought to be one of Presley's most memorable shows in the last year or so of his life.

De Neve Park

Beverly Glen Boulevard (one block north of Sunset Boulevard)
Los Angeles, California

Elvis Presley's Southern California life in the early to mid-1960s was a hectic tangle of recording, movies, and television. To help unwind on the weekends, Elvis and his entourage would organize spirited touch football games in De Neve Park, not far from where he lived in Bel Air. Their favorite opponent was pop singer and television star Ricky Nelson and his band, although other celebrities—including Pat Boone and Max Baer, Jr.—also took part in the games.

Elvis and Priscilla Honeymoon

1350 Ladera Circle
Palm Springs, California
760-322-1192

On September 16, 1966, Elvis leased this estate in Palm Springs, California, for one year for $21,000. The futuristic house is famous today as being the place where, on May 1, 1967, Elvis and Priscilla Presley spent their wedding night. Recently restored, the estate is open for tours, not to mention weddings, corporate meetings, and, wouldn't you know, honeymoons.

Fool's Gold Loaf

4490 East Virginia Avenue
Glendale, Colorado

On the night of February 1, 1976, Elvis Presley was at Graceland hosting Captain Jerry Kennedy, a member of the Denver police force, and Ron Pietrafeso, who was in charge of Colorado's Strike Force Against Crime. Talking with the guys, Elvis began to crave a Denver-area specialty he had indulged in before: the Fool's Gold Loaf.

He'd had it just once, when he'd visited a restaurant called the Colorado Gold Mine Company Steakhouse in Glendale, a suburb of Denver. It was named this for its exorbitant price—$49.95—and Elvis wanted one that night. They hopped into the King's stretch Mercedes along with a couple of Elvis's buddies, drove to the Memphis airport and hopped aboard Elvis's jet, the *Lisa Marie* (named after his daughter). Next stop, Denver's Stapleton Airport!

The Colorado Gold Mine Company Steakhouse frantically prepared their specialty of the house (22 orders of it, in fact) and had it waiting on the tarmac when the *Lisa Marie* landed a couple of hours later. (A case of Perrier and a case of champagne went with the sandwiches, as ordered.) Elvis and crew landed at 1:40 A.M. at Stapleton Airport and taxied to a private hangar. The owner of the restaurant served them personally and for two hours the entourage and Elvis feasted on the Fool's Gold.

And just what exactly is Fool's Gold Loaf? An entire loaf of bread is warmed and then hollowed out. The loaf is then stuffed with peanut butter and jelly. Lastly, a pound of lean bacon fills the belly of the loaf. Served hot, supposedly the serving size was one loaf per person! Today, the restaurant at this site that prepared the Fool's Gold Loaf is gone, replaced by a construction company, but the memory lingers on.

Forest Hill Cemetery

1661 Elvis Presley Boulevard
Memphis, Tennessee

In August 1977, Elvis was originally laid to rest here, right next to his mother, Gladys. But several months later, both Elvis and his mom were moved to Graceland after attempts were made to steal Elvis's body.

Fountainbleau Hotel

4441 Collins Avenue
Miami Beach, Florida
305-538-2000

Though more of a Rat Pack haunt than a rock 'n' roll hangout, it was from this hotel's Grand Ballroom that Elvis dueted with Frank Sinatra (on one of Frank's many TV spe-

cials) in a very famous TV appearance in 1960 immediately after returning from the army. They sang "Witchcraft" and "Love Me Tender" and part of the performance can be seen in the movie *This is Elvis.*

The Frontier Hotel

3120 Las Vegas Boulevard South
Las Vegas, Nevada
1-800-634-6966

In 1956, Elvis made his first appearance in Vegas at this hotel, opening for comedian Shecky Green in the Venus Room. He would go over much bigger when he came back 13 years later. (This is also where The Supremes performed their last show with Diana Ross on January 14, 1970.)

Hampton Coliseum

1000 Coliseum Drive
Hampton, Virginia
757-838-5650

This famous arena has hosted everyone from the Rolling Stones to Metallica to Elvis Presley. But only Elvis has a special door. Not many know about the "Elvis Door," but it really exists. It was specially cut out of the Coliseum during one of the King's 1970s appearances so Elvis could go directly from his dressing room to his limo. Elvis's third and final visit to the Coliseum occurred on July 31 and August 1, 1976. Also, the documentary *Elvis on Tour* was filmed in the building during his 1972 appearances. Today, Elvis's shows here are commemorated on a bronze plaque located on the south concourse level of the Coliseum.

Elvis's Homes

These are some homes Elvis owned or rented during the years he lived at Graceland:

906 Oak Hill Drive
Killeen, Texas
A home Elvis rented in 1958 during basic training at Ft. Hood, Texas.

10539 Bellagio Road
Bel Air, California
Elvis rented this home from November 1961 to January 1963.

1174 Hillcrest Avenue
Beverly Hills, California
Elvis and Priscilla bought this home in November 1967 for $400,000.

845 Chino Canyon Road
Palm Springs, California
Elvis and Priscilla bought this home in April 1970 paying $13,187.83 down and signing a mortgage for $85,000.

Humes High School

659 North Manassas Street
Memphis, Tennessee

Elvis graduated from this high school in 1953. Today, there is a mini-Elvis museum, and the school auditorium is now dedicated to him.

Kaiser Arena

10 Tenth Street
Oakland, California
510-238-7765

Elvis Presley's first western swings included a big show in Oakland on June 3, 1956. It took place at the Auditorium Arena (now called the Henry J. Kaiser Arena). Tickets cost just $2.50. When he returned to the arena on October 27, 1957, prices had gone up a bit ($2.75–$3.75). Elvis's last East Bay performance took place at the Oakland (now McAfee) Coliseum on November 11, 1972, where he performed a memorable greatest-hits set for more than 14,000 fans.

Lansky Brothers Clothing Store

126 Beale Street
Memphis, Tennessee

This shop (which closed in 1990) billed itself as "Outfitter to the King" for years, as it was where Elvis bought many on- and offstage outfits. On the building's west wall is a mural dedicated to Memphis history, in which Elvis figures prominently.

Libertyland

940 Early Maxwell Boulevard
Memphis, Tennessee

After he became famous, Elvis would sometimes rent out this entire amusement park so he could throw parties and ride the Zippin' Pippin roller coaster. (Back then it was called the Fairgrounds Amusement Park.)

Market Square Arena

300 East Market Street
Indianapolis, Indiana

Elvis Presley gave his last concert at Market Square Arena on June 26, 1977. Twenty-five years later, a commemorative plaque was placed here (the marker is in a gravel parking lot where the arena stood before being demolished). A time capsule encased within holds Presley memorabilia, including a scarf of Presley's and a bootlegged recording of one of his last shows. A bronze plaque reading "Ladies and Gentlemen, Elvis has left the building" sits atop a stone column, just as Elvis's show announcer Al Dvorin would say at the end of each of Presley's shows.

Elvis Presley Memorabilia

Cars

Automobile Museum at Graceland
3734 Elvis Presley Boulevard
Memphis, Tennessee
901-332-3322

When people visit the famed Graceland, they're not always aware that in addition to touring the home of Elvis, there are other tours available through Graceland that give you an additional glimpse into the life of Elvis Presley. Case in point, the Elvis Automobile Museum.

Located at the south end of the plaza, a green Cadillac convertible marks the entrance to this classic Elvis shrine. Guests walk down a landscaped, curbed, tree-lined "highway" past colorful exhibits of vehicles owned and enjoyed by Elvis. Highlights include his famous 1955 pink Cadillac, 1956 purple Cadillac convertible, 1973 Stutz Blackhawk, the red MG Elvis drove in the movie *Blue Hawaii*, his Harley Davidson motorcycles, and his three-wheeled supercycles.

Also on display are personal items such as his leather motorcycle jackets, his gasoline credit cards, and his driver's license. A modern-day tribute to Elvis's passion for cars features two official 1998 race cars with Elvis-themed designs: the Elvis N.A.S.C.A.R. that was driven by racing star Rusty Wallace and the Elvis N.H.R.A. "funny car" that was driven by John Force. The tour is self-guided and may be visited anytime during business hours. Then, if you're up for it (and who wouldn't be?), there are the planes of Elvis, also part of Graceland Tours.

Elvis Presley Memorabilia

Cars

Tupelo Automobile Museum
Located 1/2 block off Highway 45, Main Street Exit
Adjacent to Bancorp South Center on Otis Boulevard
Tupelo, Mississippi
662-842-4242

This great museum features 120,000 square feet of automobile displays and open-viewing restoration bays. There are over 100 antique, classic, and collectible automobiles, chronologically displayed, illustrating the progress of over 100 years of automobile design and engineering. And there's an Elvis connection. The Tupelo Automobile Museum has a 1976 Lincoln Mark IV that was given to them as a gift by Elvis Presley himself.

Elvis often played shows in Denver, Colorado, where he formed a close relationship with Jerry Kennedy, captain of the Denver Police Vice and Drug Control Bureau. Captain Kennedy was in charge of security for Elvis when he appeared in Denver. On January 14, 1976, Elvis visited the Kumpf Lincoln Mercury Dealership at 9th Avenue and Broadway in Denver. There he purchased a 1976 Lincoln Mark IV for $13,386.69. The check to the dealership, made out in Elvis's own handwriting, can be seen in the museum. Elvis gave the brand-new car to Captain Jerry Kennedy as a gift.

The Tupelo Automobile Museum also owns a 1939 Plymouth, the same model driven by Elvis's family when they moved from Tupelo to Memphis. This car is on permanent display in the Elvis Presley Birthplace and Museum in Tupelo. Beyond Elvis, your self-guided tour through the museum will cover an 1886 Benz, representing the birth of the automobile, and a never-driven 1994 Dodge Viper. The collection, valued at over $6 million, also includes a rare Tucker, movie and celebrity vehicles, Hispano Suizas, a Duesenberg, and many more rare brands and American favorites.

Cars

Sierra Sid's Truck Stop Casino
200 North McCarran Boulevard
Sparks, Nevada
775-359-0550

Sierra Sid's is home to Elvis's guns as well as other Elvis memorabilia—all purchased from the estate of Elvis's father, Vernon Presley, in 1981. In one of the many display cases next to the nickel slot machines, you'll find jewelry (including a tiger-eye ring, a watch, and diamonds) that Elvis gave to his father. You'll also find four .45 handguns (one of which Elvis reportedly used to shoot a TV set) and two complete sets of Elvis's 52 gold albums.

Elvis Presley Memorabilia

Jets

Graceland
3734 Elvis Presley Boulevard
Memphis, Tennessee
901-332-3322

Located at the north end of the plaza, this tour begins in a re-created airport terminal setting with an entertaining video on the history of the planes. Guests step outside to take a quick peek at the small *Hound Dog II* Lockheed JetStar plane, and then walk aboard the much larger customized *Lisa Marie* jet, which Elvis named after his daughter and often referred to as his "flying Graceland." Highlights include the luxuriously appointed living room, conference room, sitting room, and private bedroom on the jet.

Limo and Speedboat

Elvis-a-Rama Museum
3401 Industrial Road
Las Vegas, Nevada
702-309-7200

It started as a hobby for Chris Davidson, but now it's the real deal.The Elvis-a-Rama Museum is perhaps the most amazing Elvis museum on the planet. Davidson has amassed an incredible amount of Elvis stuff, from his cars—the world famous '55 Concert Tour Limo—and stage-worn jumpsuits to more than $500,000 in Elvis's personal jewelry, Hollywood movie clothing, personal documents, and hand-written letters . . . even the King's personal speedboat.

Elvis-a-Rama also boasts a theater for Elvis-style live shows. Daily performances in the Rock 'n' Roll Theater are free with museum admission. A museum gift shop stocks souvenirs, and as new material is added to exhibits, a larger collection of investment quality, documented Presley memorabilia goes on sale.

Elvis Presley Memorabilia

Report Card

Graceland Too
200 East Gholson Avenue
Holly Springs, Mississippi
662-252-2515

Graceland Too attracts music fans seven days a week, 24 hours a day. Paul McLeod and his son, Elvis Presley McLeod, love to show off the tribute to the King of Rock and Roll they have created at their home, just off of the town square. Visitors from around the world have toured Graceland Too, many calling it the greatest tribute to Elvis they've ever seen. For a small admission, you can tour Paul's home and see such items as Elvis's report card from 1951, a gold lamé suit supposedly worn by Elvis during a 1957 concert, and a casket that plays "Return to Sender," which McLeod plans to be buried in.

Mississippi–Alabama Fairground

Mulberry Alley off West Mains Street
Tupelo, Mississippi

This now rundown fairground is where Elvis Presley made his first public performance on October 3, 1945, after being entered in a talent contest by one of his teachers (the 10-year-old Elvis sang a tune called "Old Shep" and won five dollars). Eleven years later, he played the same spot, only by this time he'd become an international star and was promoting his first film, *The Reno Brothers* (later renamed *Love Me Tender*.)

Overton Shell

1928 Poplar Avenue
Memphis, Tennessee

On July 30, 1954, Elvis gave his first paid professional performance on this stage, opening for Slim Whitman and Billy Walker. Since 1936, the Overton Shell has been an important Memphis landmark, and in 1982 it was named the Raoul Wallenberg Shell after the Swedish diplomat responsible for saving thousands of Jews from Nazi death camps.

RCA Nashville

1525 McGavock Street
Nashville, Tennessee

When Elvis Presley signed with RCA in 1955, this was their main Nashville studio (though many more would soon be opened). On January 10, 1956, Elvis came in for his first RCA sessions and recorded some of his most formative singles, including: "Heartbreak Hotel," "I Got a Woman," and "Money Honey." Today, it's a production studio for The Nashville Network.

RCA Studios

55 East 24th Street
New York, New York

It now houses classrooms, but in 1956 you could find RCA's Studio "A" in this building, and it was here that Elvis Presley cut three of his most timeless singles: "Hound Dog," "Don't Be Cruel," and "Blue Suede Shoes."

Schwab Dry Goods

163 Beale Street
Memphis, Tennessee
901-523-9782

It's been in business since 1876, with the motto "If you can't find it at A. Schwab's, you're better off without it!" Elvis used to shop here, and today the store has lots of Elvis souvenirs.

Sun Studio

706 Union Avenue
Memphis, Tennessee
800-441-6249

Opened in 1950 by a local radio station engineer named Sam
Phillips, some of the most legendary moments in rock 'n' roll history were captured at this tiny Memphis studio, and many artifacts from over the years remain here today in this living music
museum—including Elvis Presley's microphone and Johnny
Cash's dollar-strung guitar.

Phillips started Sun Records in 1952; two years later, a nervous
local teenager came in to lay down a few vocal tracks. The date
was July 5, 1954. "It was just an audition," remembers Scotty
Moore, the country guitarist brought in to back up a green Elvis
Presley for his Sun Records tryout. Near the end of the day, Presley broke into an
obscure blues tune, "That's All Right," and history was made.

Eventually, Phillips sold his discovery's contract to R.C.A. for $40,000, a huge sum at
the time. A few years before Elvis, a local DJ named Ike Turner produced a session at
Sun with teenager Jackie Brenston. Their 1951 version of "Rocket 88" is considered by
many to be the first genuine rock 'n' roll record. And don't forget that Jerry Lee Lewis
recorded "Great Balls of Fire" and "Whole Lotta Shakin' Goin' On" at Sun.

The studio was restored with Sam Phillips's help, and in 1987 opened its doors as both a
tourist attraction and a working recording studio. Ringo Starr, Def Leppard, John
Fogerty, Tom Petty, Paul Simon, Bonnie Raitt, U2, and Matchbox 20 are only some of the
recent music greats who have come to record at Sun Studio since it reopened. In the studio's own words: "Today, Sun Studio carries on the Rock N' Roll Revolution begun here
in 1950, by providing a place where a kid with a guitar case full of dreams can stand in
the footsteps of giants and carve out a legend." Tours are given on a daily basis.

Rolling Stones

Black and Blue

Sanibel Island Beach
Sanibel Island, Florida

In February 1976, the Rolling Stones flew here to be photographed by famed fashion photographer Hiro for their album *Black and Blue*. It was the first release that new member Ron Wood played on officially.

Brown Palace Hotel

321 17th Street
Denver, Colorado
800-321-2599

In 1972, the Rolling Stones hired famed photographer/filmmaker Robert Frank to document their legendary tour of America. The movie was never released, in part because it included a few too many moments of unchecked debauchery, including a famous incident that Frank caught on film at this hotel. This is where guitarist Keith Richards and sax player Bobby Keys are shown dropping a television out of their window, guffawing as it smashes on the ground below.

Fordyce, Arkansas

(Near 100 S. Main Street)

Fordyce (population about 5,000) is located at the intersection of two U.S. Highways, 79 and 167, and State Highway 8. On July 5, 1975, police pulled over a rented Chevy after the car swerved on the roadway. Among the car's occupants were guitarists Keith Richards and Ron Wood of the Rolling Stones. Richards was later charged with reckless driving and possession of a knife and his bodyguard Fred Sessler was charged with possession of a controlled substance. (Richards was released on $160 bail and later paid a fine.) Earlier that day the group had dined at the 4-Dice Restaurant in Fordyce.

Fort Harrison Hotel

210 South Fort Harrison Avenue
Clearwater, Florida

The Rolling Stones played to 3,000 teenagers at Jack Russell Stadium in May, 1965, performing only four songs before the crowd turned rowdy and the police stepped in,

ending the show. That night, Keith Richards awoke in his room at the Jack Tar Harrison Hotel (today it's the Fort Harrison) with the opening guitar riff of "Satisfaction" in his head. He grabbed his guitar, got the notes on tape, and went back to sleep. The next day, he woke and worked with Mick Jagger on the rest of the song by the hotel pool. Today, the building is owned by the Church of Scientology.

Gosman's Dock

500 West Lake Drive
Montauk, New York
631-668-5330

Gosman's Dock was founded in 1943 and has since become a legend out on the eastern tip of Long Island, a true seafood lover's paradise. It's no wonder Mick Jagger came

here to eat back in the summer of 1975 while the Rolling Stones rehearsed for their upcoming "Tour of the Americas" at Andy Warhol's nearby Montauk compound. But Jagger got a little more than he bargained for. On May 17, 1975, upon leaving the restaurant, the head Stone inadvertently put his hand through the plate-glass door, opening a huge gash on his wrist. The wound required 20 stitches but, thankfully, did not end up delaying the June 1st start of the tour.

Harbour Castle Westin

1 Harbour Square
Toronto, Canada
416-869-1600

On February 27, 1977, Royal Canadian Mounted Police crashed into suite 2223 in this hotel and found five grams of cocaine, 22 grams of heroin, and Keith Richards, who was promptly arrested. After a six-month court battle, stunningly, Richards got off with a slap on the wrist (the Stones were made to play a charity show in Toronto to benefit the blind). The arrest followed club gigs at the El Mocambo, where the Stones had recorded portions of their 1977 concert album *Love You Live.* The El Mocambo Club is located at 494 Spadina Avenue (416-968-2001).

"Have You Seen Your Mother Baby"

24th Street between Park Avenue South and Lexington Avenue
New York, New York

In 1966 the Rolling Stones released the hit single, "Have You Seen Your Mother Baby (Standing in the Shadow)." To promote it they created an outrageous photo featuring the band in full drag. It was shot by renowned photographer Jerry Schatzberg at this location, and the preparation for the photo took place at Schatzberg's studio, located at 333 Park Avenue South.

Long View Farm

Stoddard Road
North Brookfield, Massachusetts
508-867-7662

This rustic, isolated recording studio was home to the Rolling Stones from August through September 1981, as they rehearsed and prepared for their upcoming world tour. (Mick Jagger even invited several local high school kids up here to interview him for their school paper, creating a press opportunity that no national media got to enjoy.) Long View Farm was a former dairy farm that had been converted to a recording studio, and Stevie Wonder, J Geils, Mötley Crüe, and James Taylor are just a few of the artists who have recorded here in the beautiful Massachusetts countryside.

"Memory Motel"

692 Montauk Highway
Montauk (Long Island), New York
631-668-2702

The Memory Motel is a small, 13-room motel and bar immortalized by the Rolling Stones in the pretty ballad of the same name (which appeared on the band's 1976 album *Black and Blue*). During the mid-1970s, the Rolling Stones—and in particular Mick Jagger—were regulars out on the remote reaches of Montauk, hanging out with artist Andy Warhol at his nearby compound, among other places.

Jagger supposedly spent time at the motel because it had a pool table and a decent jukebox, and one night while here he reputedly was inspired to write the beautiful song about "Hannah, a honey of a girl," and where they spent "a lonely night at the Memory Motel." (Rumor has it he actually wrote part of the tune at the bar.)

Muscle Shoals Recording Studios

3614 Jackson Highway
Shefield, Alabama

In the 1970 film *Gimme Shelter*, the Rolling Stones are seen recording "Brown Sugar" and "Wild Horses" in this recording studio. The building was then used to sell used refrigerators and stoves but today, thankfully, it's become a museum dedicated to the great music created within the building.

Press Conference

One Fifth Avenue
New York, New York

On May 1, 1975, there was a press conference scheduled at the restaurant called Feathers of Fifth Avenue to announce the Stones' "Tour of the Americas." Professor Irwin Corey, the famous American comedian was the M.C. Instead, a flatbed truck with the band on top playing "Brown Sugar" came down Fifth Avenue, stopping in front of the hotel. It was so exciting that everybody ran out into the street to watch. The Stones then carried on down the road, tossing out leaflets with tour dates. When they finished the song, they pulled away in their truck, turned the corner, jumped into limos, and were gone.

RCA Records

6363 Sunset Boulevard
Hollywood, California

From the early 1960s through the early 1990s, some of the most famous records of all time were recorded in this building. Elvis was here in the '70s, The Monkees recorded here, the Jefferson Airplane, etc. But the band that perhaps did the most damage was the Rolling Stones, who recorded (among other songs) "Satisfaction," "Paint it Black," "19th Nervous Breakdown," and "Let's Spend the Night Together" at this location. Today, the building houses the Los Angeles Film School.

Sir Morgan's Cove

89 Green Street
Worcester, Massachusetts
508-363-1888

On September 14, 1981, the Rolling Stones played a surprise concert here at this small club on the heels of launching their massive 1981 tour of the United States. The Stones were nearing the end of a six-week stay at Long View Farm, where they were rehearsing for their upcoming tour that would showcase the album *Tattoo You.*

Local radio station WAAF announced the show and handled the 350 tickets for the lucky fans, who got to witness the first live Stones show in three years, a nearly two-hour set that opened with "Under My Thumb" and included such classics as "Satisfaction," "Honky Tonk Woman," and "Tumblin' Dice." The next Stones show would be a little more than a week later in front of 90,000 people at Philadelphia's J.F.K. stadium. Today, the club has been renamed the Lucky Dog Music Hall.

Swing Auditorium

G Street (just south of Rialto, next to the railroad tracks)
San Bernardino, California

The Rolling Stones gave their debut American concert on July 5, 1964, at the Swing Auditorium in San Bernardino, California. They played a total of 11 songs to 4,400 fans. Over the years, everyone from Jimi Hendrix to the Grateful Dead to Led Zeppelin played at the Swing. On September 11, 1981, an airplane crashed into the Swing Auditorium, killing the pilot and his passenger. The building was so badly damaged that remaining parts of the structure had to be demolished.

Theodore Francis Green State Airport

2000 Post Road
Warwick, Rhode Island
401-737-4000

On July 19, 1972, Mick Jagger, Keith Richards, and three members of the Rolling Stones entourage were arrested in Warwick, Rhode Island, on charges of assault and obstructing police. The five were involved in a scuffle with a photographer as they made their way through the small airport. They pleaded guilty and were released, but the incident caused a four-hour delay of their concert in Boston that night (which, by many accounts, was one of the greatest shows they've ever played).

"Waiting on a Friend"

132 1st Avenue
New York, New York

At one time this bar was called the St. Marks Bar & Grill, and in the 1981 video for their hit, "Waiting on a Friend," Mick Jagger and Keith Richards met the rest of the Rolling Stones here (after Mick waited for Keith on the stoop of the building seen on the cover of Led Zeppelin's *Physical Graffiti* album). The band was filmed performing in this tiny space for the rest of the day, and for years the bar sold T-shirts commemorating the event.

Kick Out the Jams: Concert Sites and Live Performance Locations

Altamont Concert

Altamont Raceway
17001 Midway Road
Tracy, California
925-606-0274

It was billed as a West Coast Woodstock—a huge free concert in a windswept racetrack headlined by the Rolling Stones. Instead, the gathering became one of the most violent days in the history of rock 'n' roll. For the final show of their 1969 American tour, the Rolling Stones "hosted" a one-day concert at the Altamont Speedway in Livermore, California. The show took place on December 6, 1969, and was intended as a thank-you gesture to Stones fans. In addition to the Rolling Stones, the show's lineup included Santana; the Jefferson Airplane; The Flying Burrito Brothers; and Crosby, Stills, Nash and Young. The Grateful Dead never got to play, though they were scheduled to perform.

The haphazardly organized festival was "policed" by the Oakland chapter of the Hell's Angels motorcycle gang, a move that haunts the Stones to this day. The calamitous festival reached its climax during the Stones' set, when 18-year-old Meredith Hunter rushed the stage with a gun and was stabbed to death before the band's eyes. The moment is the ugly centerpiece of the Maysles Brothers' classic 1970 documentary *Gimme Shelter.*

Apollo Theater

253 Martin Luther King Boulevard
Harlem, New York
212-479-5838

The Apollo Theater is one of the most famous clubs for popular music in the United States, and certainly the most famous club associated almost exclusively with African-American performers. The Apollo grew to prominence during the Harlem Renaissance of the pre-World War II years. In 1934, it introduced its regular Amateur Night shows. Billing itself as a place "where stars are born and legends are made," the Apollo became famous for launching the careers of artists like Ella Fitzgerald, James Brown, Gladys Knight, Michael Jackson and The Jackson 5, Lauryn Hill, and Sarah Vaughan. The Apollo also featured the performances of old-time vaudeville favorites like Tim Moore, Stepin Fetchit, Dewey "Pigmeat" Markham, Jackie "Moms" Mabley, Marshall "Garbage" Rogers, and Johnny Lee.

The club fell into decline in the 1960s and 1970s, but was revived in 1983, when it obtained federal, state, and city landmark status. It fully reopened in 1985, and was bought by the State of New York in 1991. It is now run by a nonprofit organization, the Apollo Theater Foundation Inc., and draws an estimated 1.3 million visitors annually. In 2005, Ben Harper and The Blind Boys of Alabama released an album, *Live at the Apollo*, in honor of the Harlem music scene.

Atlanta Pop Festival

Atlanta Motor Speedway
1500 Highway 41
Byron, Georgia

 From July 3-5, 1970, here in the tiny central Georgia town of Byron (10 miles south of Macon), smack in the middle of a pecan grove (and on what was then known as the Middle Georgia Raceway) somewhere between 350,000 to 500,000 people witnessed the second annual Atlanta International Pop Festival. Exactly like Woodstock the previous summer (but with more people), the event was promoted as "three days of peace, love and music." On the bill were Jimi Hendrix, The Allman Brothers, Jethro Tull, B.B. King, Ravi Shankar, 10 Years After, Johnny Winter, John Sebastian, and others. (Tickets for the music festival were $14).

Atlantic City Pop Festival

Atlantic City Racetrack
4501 Black Horse Pike
Mays Landing, New Jersey
609-641-2190

From August 1-3, 1969, 110,000 people attended this festival at the Atlantic City Racetrack—a sort of tune-up for Woodstock. Thirty or so bands played, many of whom then headed up to play Woodstock the next week. The show featured (among others) Joan Baez; Arlo Guthrie; Tim Harden; Richie Havens; Ravi Shankar; Sweetwater; Canned Heat; Creedence Clearwater Revival; the Grateful Dead; the Jefferson Airplane; Mountain; The Who; The Band; Blood, Sweat & Tears; Joe Cocker; Crosby, Stills & Nash; Santana; Jimi Hendrix; Ten Years After; Johnny Winter; and Sha Na Na.

Avalon Ballroom

Regency II Theater
1268 Sutter Street (at Van Ness)
San Francisco, California
415-776-8054

In the 1960s, this is where Janis Joplin debuted with Big Brother and the Holding Company. A legendary concert venue through the 1960s, the Avalon's trademark was the swirly, psychedelic lights that were projected on the backdrop behind the stage. The area that served as the ballroom is on the second floor of this theater and access is not allowed to the public.

Band Shell

Golden Gate Park
San Francisco, California

This quaint band shell located near the Steinhart Aquarium has been the site of many legendary performances including shows by the Jerry Garcia Band and Todd Rundgren, who actually recorded live audience vocals here for his song "Sons of 1984" in 1973.

Boarding House

960 Bush Street
San Francisco, California

At one time the Boarding House was the premier rock 'n' roll nightclub venue in the Bay Area. Among the many landmark events that took place at this legendary venue (founded by David Allen) include the recording of Steve Martin's classic comedy album *Let's Get Small*, plus the Bay-Area debuts of Albert Brooks, Martin Mull, Robin Williams, and George Carlin. Neil Young tested out all of 1978's *Rust Never Sleeps* here, among many other memorable concerts that took place at this site. The Boarding House is no longer in existence; condos now occupy the location.

Boston Arena

St. Botolph Street
Boston, Massachusetts

Located on the campus of Northeastern University, Boston Arena (now called Matthews Arena) was built in 1910 and is currently home to both the men's and women's hockey teams at the school. But it was once home to two famous musical events: The Big Beat Show and the Motown Revue.

The first took place on May 3, 1958, when a concert staged by legendary disc jockey Alan Freed resulted in a riot. Freed would soon be in trouble for all of the infamous "payola" scandals and many believe this concert riot was the beginning of his end. "The Big Beat Show" featured Buddy Holly & the Crickets, Chuck Berry, Jo-Anne Campbell, and Jerry Lee Lewis. Secondly, in 1962, the first ever Motown Revue was held here. The famous traveling show featured many acts including Mary Wells, Marvin Gaye, and The Supremes.

Boston Tea Party

53 Berkeley Street
Boston, Massachusetts

This former synagogue once held a place as one of the country's prime rock palaces. Opened in 1967 as the Boston Tea Party, this was where everyone from Led Zeppelin to The Velvet Underground played back in the late 1960s. In fact, it was here that band member John Cale played his last gig with the influential group, to be replaced by Boston local Doug Yule (who had chatted with the members backstage). In 1969, the Boston Tea Party moved to a location adjacent to Fenway Park, where it remains today as The Avalon.

The Bottom Line

15 West 4th Street
New York, New York

The Bottom Line was an intimate music venue in New York City's Greenwich Village, at West Fourth Street between Broadway and Washington Square Park. During the 1970s, it played a major role in maintaining Greenwich Village's status as a cultural mecca. It opened in 1974 and enjoyed a multi-year string of successes at pulling in major musical acts and premiering new talent. Bruce Springsteen played legendary showcase gigs, Lou Reed recorded the album *Live: Take No Prisoners* at the club and Todd Rundgren recorded part of his live album *Back to the Bars* here. Its cachet faded with

time, and by 2003, it was deeply in debt and garnering very little attendance. Even with its landlord, New York University, artificially keeping its rent at half of prevailing values, it was unable to stay open, and closed its doors at the end of 2003 rather than accept a takeover bid by Sirius Satellite Radio. Its former owners claim to be seeking another venue that will carry the same name.

Bowie, David

Capitol Theatre
149 Westchester Avenue
Port Chester, New York
914-934-9362

The classic old Capitol is one of the most beautiful movie-vaudeville palaces ever built in Westchester County, New York. Opened in 1926, it was closed in 1966 after many successful years as a movie house and was re-opened as a rock palace shortly after. Until

1971, many legendary acts from Yes to Black Sabbath to Humble Pie played here, but the noise and hassles shook the local community to such a degree that shows were stopped. However, David Bowie came here secretly in 1974 to rehearse his new Diamond Dogs stage show, an elaborate, futuristic spectacle that toured the world for two years. Today the theater is available for private events.

Bowie, David

Cleveland Public Hall Convention Center
500 Lakeside Avenue
Cleveland, Ohio

David Bowie made his American concert debut here in Cleveland on September 22, 1972, when he premiered his outrageously revolutionary Ziggy Stardust show with the Spiders from Mars at the Cleveland Music Hall. The orange-haired Bowie, who sailed over to America due to a fear of flying, almost saw the show cancelled by his manager, Tony DeFries, over the size of the piano that was provided in the 3,500-seat hall. However, a new piano was borrowed from the Cleveland Symphony Orchestra and the show went on. (The band Fumbal opened the show.) A post-concert party was held that night at the Hollenden House Hotel, which was located in Cleveland at 610 Superior Avenue. (Bowie would return to play this venue in 1974 during his elaborate *Diamond Dogs* tour.)

Cal Jam

Ontario Motor Speedway
Ontario Mills Shopping Center (at the intersection of Interstate 10 and Interstate 15, approximately 40 minutes east of Los Angeles)
One Mills Circle
Ontario, California
909-484-8300

ONTARIO MOTOR SPEEDWAY
ONTARIO, CALIF.

A.B.C. ENTERTAINMENT INC.
BRINGS YOU

033887

"CALIFORNIA JAM"

APR.

SATURDAY 10 A.M. TO 10 P.M.
GATES OPEN AT 8:00 A.M.

6

GENERAL ADMISSION

$10.00 ADVANCE
(INCLUDES PARKING)

1974

COORDINATED BY PACIFIC PRESENTATIONS
NO REFUND — NO EXCHANGE

The "Cal Jam" concerts heralded in a new era of rock festival: organized, detailed, and packaged. Technically, they were slick, and the stage and lighting designs were the prototypes for today's tightly-run festivals. They were also filmed for television's *In Concert* series, giving them an even more polished edge.

Cal Jam I took place on April 6, 1974, and featured the Eagles, Deep Purple, Rare Earth, Emerson, Lake & Palmer, and Black Sabbath. Two hundred thousand fans paid $10 each, so the show grossed $2 million, at that time one of the largest gates in the history of rock 'n' roll.

Aerosmith co-headlined California Jam II on March 18, 1978, in front of 350,000 people. The other performers at that show were Bob Welch, Dave Mason, Santana, Heart, Ted Nugent, Foreigner, Frank Marino & Mahogany Rush, and Rubicon. Aerosmith included a couple of cuts from this show on their *Live Bootleg* LP.

CBGB-OMFUG

315 Bowery at Bleeker Street
New York, New York
212-982-4052

It may stand for "Country, Bluegrass, Blues and Other Music for Uplifting Gourmandisers," but it was ground zero for some of the most influential rock 'n' roll ever spawned. From the mid-'70s on, this hole-in-the-wall club was home to such bands as Television, Blondie, The Dead Boys, the Ramones, The Talking Heads, and many other punk legends. Considered the home to NYC's underground rock scene, it's still a vital place to experience music. Many nights in the '70s, it would not be uncommon to find Debbie Harry, Patti Smith, Joey Ramone, Iggy Pop, David Johansen, or any other number of local legends holding court at the bar. Sadly, the club closed in 2006 and there is a plan afoot to open a new location in Las Vegas.

true life presents
TELEVISION

at C.B.G.B.'s
315 Bowery at Bleeker 982-4052
for four weekends

Devonshire Downs Racetrack

Devonshire Street just west of Zelzah Avenue
Northridge, California

This site, a former racetrack, is probably best known for hosting the famed Newport '69 music festival from June 20-22. Despite the name "Newport," the show (which drew about 150,000 fans) actually took place out in the San Fernando Valley. On the bill were Jethro Tull, Jimi Hendrix, The Animals, Led Zeppelin, Creedence Clearwater Revival, The Chambers Brothers, Johnny Winters, the Young Rascals, Booker T. & MG's, Three Dog Night, The Byrds, The Grassroots, Marvin Gaye, and Mother Earth. The site is now a shopping center.

The Doors

Aquarius Theater

6230 Sunset Boulevard
Hollywood, California

The Aquarius Theater opened in 1938 as the shimmering landmark, the Earl Carroll Theater, a nightclub/theater that was home to the "Most beautiful girls in the world." By 1968, it had become the Aquarius Theater, home of the production of *Hair*. It was also here that Elektra Records staged the comeback of one of their once biggest bands, The Doors. The shows were recorded for the album, *Live at the Aquarius Theater.*

Elektra Sound Recorders

962 La Cienega Boulevard
West Hollywood, California

Here you'll find a postproduction facility today, but at one time it was the Elektra Sound Recorders Studio, where The Doors recorded the albums *The Soft Parade* and *Morrison Hotel.* You can still see the dark brown wooden door off to the side of the building that once served as the studio's main entry.

The Doors

The Warehouse

1820 Tchoupitoulas Street
New Orleans, Louisiana

From 1969 to 1982, a former coffee storage warehouse hosted many memorable rock concerts, including shows from Bowie to Bob Dylan. It was here on December 12, 1970, that The Doors played their final public performance—a supposed disaster that found front man Jim Morrison smashing a hole in the middle of the stage with the mike stand. The building has since been razed.

The Eagles

Disneyland
Anaheim, California
714-781-4565

In June of 1971, then-country singer Linda Ronstadt was performing for about a week on the small stage near the Tomorrowland stage at Disneyland. For the engagement she needed a group of backup musicians and enlisted the help of four California-based players: Don Henley, Bernie Leadon, Randy Meisner, and Glen Frey. This marked the first time they all played together and is now considered to be the birth of the Eagles, because after this engagement they decided to create their own band.

The Experience

7601 Sunset Boulevard
Hollywood, California

In the late 1960s, this famous building featured a huge painting of Jimi Hendrix's head on the front door—so to enter you had to walk through his mouth. Hendrix jammed here many times, as did Led Zeppelin and many others. Today, the building still stands but it's an auction house.

Festival for Peace

Shea Stadium
123-01 Roosevelt Avenue
Flushing, New York
718-507-METS

The Summer Festival for Peace was held here on August 5, 1970, and the scorching hot weather may have played a part in why the festival drew an under-sized crowd. However, those in attendance were treated to performances by Jimi Hendrix, Janis Joplin, Poco, Steppenwolf, James Gang, Janis Joplin, The Rascals, Johnny Winter, Ten Wheel Drive, Tom Paxton, Dionne Warwick, Paul Simon, and several others. An underpublicized, underdocumented event, it was one of the more diverse lineups featured during the spate of music festivals held in the wake of Woodstock.

Fillmore East

105 Second Avenue
New York, New York

The Fillmore East, another of promoter Bill Graham's psychedelic concert venues, hosted hundreds of memorable rock 'n' roll events. Jimi Hendrix's Band of Gypsys played here on New Year's Eve, 1969. John Lennon showed up one time to jam with Frank Zappa. The Jeff Beck Group (featuring Rod Stewart) made their American debut here in 1968, on a bill with the Grateful Dead.

But the most famous aural document from this theater may be the shows taped by The Allman Brothers on March 11-13, 1971. These legendary sets (one of which ended at 7:05 A.M.) became part of a landmark live album, the back cover of which was shot against the theater's back exterior wall. The wall is still there today, though the Fillmore is long gone.

Fillmore West

San Francisco Honda
10 South Van Ness Avenue at Market Street
San Francisco, California
415-441-2000

From 1968 to 1971, the theater at this site (originally called the Carousel Ballroom) hosted everyone from The Who to the Jefferson Airplane to Cream. Famed promoter Bill Graham took it over in 1968, renamed it the Fillmore West, and thus created one of rock 'n' roll's most legendary venues. Today, it's the second floor of a Honda dealership. Supposedly, there's some graffiti in the rear stairwell that's an actual artifact from the theater.

Fox Venice

620 Lincoln Avenue
Venice, California

In the mid-1970s, this theater was one of the most active creative hotspots in the greater Los Angeles area. Movies were screened here, and there were Love-Ins and lots of noted concerts, featuring musical acts such as Little Feat, Big Joe Turner, and Bonnie Raitt. In fact, John Lee Hooker recorded a live album here with Canned Heat (*Live at the Fox Venice*). Today, it still stands, but it's an indoor swap meet.

Frampton, Peter

Marin Civic Center
3501 Civic Center Drive
San Rafael, California
415-479-4920

This pretty Frank Lloyd Wright-designed center has a distinctive round blue roof and sits on the north side of the civic center lake in San Rafael. On June 13, 1975, Peter Frampton and his band recorded a live concert here, much of which was used on *Frampton Comes Alive*, one of the largest selling albums of that decade. The Grateful Dead rented the facility for months in the '80s, using the 2,000-seat concert hall as a recording studio as they laid down the basic tracks for their 1989 release, *Built to Last*.

Gazzarri's

**9039 Sunset Boulevard
West Hollywood, California**

Gazzari's, opened by Sunset Strip legend Bill Gazzarri in 1963, hosted many different musical eras in Southern California. In the 1960s, The Byrds, Buffalo Springfield, and many others found their first fame here. In the '70s and '80s, it was Van Halen, Guns N' Roses, and Metallica among others. After Gazzarri died, the club was torn down in the 1990s, and has since been replaced the The Key Club.

Grand Ole Opry

**Ryman Auditorium
116 Fifth Avenue North
Nashville, Tennessee
615-889-3060**

Opened in 1892, the famous Ryman Auditorium gained its true fame with the coming of the *Grand Ole Opry* show in 1943. After garnering a reputation as the "Mother Church of Country Music," the Opry moved in 1974 to its current home by the Gaylord Opryland Resort and Convention Center, which left the original venerable theater empty. Twenty years later, the Ryman was restored to its original grandeur and is once again a national showplace for country music. Over the years, musicians ranging from Elvis Presley to James Brown to Patsy Cline to Sheryl Crow have performed on the Ryman stage. In 2006, director Jonathan Demme filmed Neil Young's post-brain surgery comeback concert here, which resulted in the touching and powerful *Neil Young: Heart of Gold*.

Grateful Dead

**Soldier Field
425 East McFetridge Drive
Chicago, Illinois**

The Grateful Dead played their last shows here in Chicago on July 8-9, 1995. Guitarist Jerry Garcia died later that year from drug complications, thus ending the band's tenure.

Great Lawn

**Mid-Central Park from 79th to 85th Streets
New York, New York**

The Great Lawn is a 13-acre oval lawn with a carpet of lush Kentucky bluegrass and eight ball fields. This green area is famous for being a beautiful place for reading and contemplation, as well as for playing Frisbee and having a picnic among friends. It has also become a favorite for free concerts by the New York Philharmonic and the Metropolitan Opera. In addition, it has hosted famous concerts by Simon and Garfunkel (their reunion) and Diana Ross (in the rain), among others.

The Greek Theater

The Greek Theater
2700 N. Vermont Avenue
Los Angeles, California
323-660-8400

 The Greek Theater is a beautiful, woodsy, outdoor setting located in Griffith Park. Built in 1929, many bands have played here over the years, including Jefferson Airplane, Supertramp, Jethro Tull, Joe Cocker, Joni Mitchell, The Moody Blues and The Band. Back in 1972, Neil Diamond played ten sold out concerts here and on Thursday, August the 24th, the show was recorded and released as the smash live double album *Hot August Night.* The amphitheater's stage is modeled after a Greek temple, hence the name.

Hendrix, Jimi

Berkeley Community Theater
Milivia Street and Allston Way
Berkeley, California
510-644-8593

In 1944–back when he was named Johnny Allen Hendrix–the two-year-old Jimi lived with a family friend in a housing facility for military families at the corner of Martin Luther King Way and Derby Street in Berkeley as he waited for his father to return from the Army. Jimi returned to Berkeley for two shows here on Memorial Day 1970, as seen in the classic film *Jimi Plays Berkeley.* This is also where a 16-year-old guitarist named Neil Schon sat in with Derek and The Dominoes and impressed bandleader Eric Clapton so much he invited the teen to join the band. Schon declined, opting to take a job with Santana instead (he later played with Journey).

Hendrix, Jimi

Haleakala Crater
Near Kula
Maui, Hawaii

Haleakala is an active, but not currently erupting, volcano on the island of Maui that last released its fury in 1790. And it was here on July 30, 1970, that Jimi Hendrix erupted, performing his last ever American show. This concert was supposed to be part of the film *Rainbow Bridge*, but little of the concert footage was used in the film and *none* of the audio was used on the soundtrack album (this is a widely bootlegged show among Hendrix fans). After this concert, Hendrix went on to play a handful of dates in Europe and died later that year in his sleep, on September 18th, at the Samarkand Hotel in London. He was just 27 years old.

The Hollywood Bowl

The Hollywood Bowl
2301 North Highland Ave
Hollywood, California
323-850-2000

It may be the home of the L. A. Philharmonic, but the renowned Hollywood Bowl has hosted many legendary rock shows, including The Beatles, Elton John, Hendrix, The Doors, Bob Dylan, The Who, Rick Wakeman, Pink Floyd, the Rolling Stones and many

others. Its outstanding acoustics, serene outdoor setting and comfortable box seating makes it an excellent place to see any performance (even though the parking can be a bit tricky due to lack of space). The Bowl opened officially in 1922 on the site of a natural amphitheatre formerly known as the Daisy Dell.

The Hollywood Palladium

**6215 Sunset Boulevard
Hollywood, California**

The classic Palladium opened in 1940 with a show by Frank Sinatra and the Tommy Dorsey Orchestra. But since then, rock 'n' roll has also made its name here. Starting in the 1960s, it became an ideal mid-sized venue for bands that could not yet sell out bigger halls, like the Grateful Dead. Then it became a more intimate venue for bands that wanted a break from arenas, like The Rolling Stones and The Who. In the 1980s, such vital artists as The Clash and The Talking Heads performed here. The Blues Brothers movie concert sequences were filmed here (as were some Partridge Family TV performance segments) and this was also the broadcast home to Lawrence Welk throughout the 1960s and '70s.

I-Beam

**1748 Haight Street
San Francisco, California**

The I-Beam nightclub operated here from October 1978 to July 1992. It was founded and owned by Sanford Kelleman, a former astronomer. The building it was located in was the former Park Masonic Hall, and while it started out as a popular gay disco, it soon became a music venue that hosted the likes of the Ramones, REM, The Buzzcocks, The Replacements, and many other up-and-coming punk/new wave bands of the 1980s and '90s.

KISS

Cobo Hall
600 Civic Center Drive
Detroit, Michigan

Several live albums were recorded here over the years, including *Bob Seger's Live Bullet,* but it was *KISS Alive* that's remembered as one of the true icons of the 1970s, in a city where they were adored, on a night when they truly kicked it out. As the announcer revved up the crowd before they started said, "You wanted the best and you got it—the hottest band in the land . . . KISS!"

KISS

The Coventry
47-03 Queens Boulevard
Queens, New York

Back in the early 1970s, there was a tiny club here, the Coventry, that became one of the primary glitter-rock places in New York. The New York Dolls first started playing here in 1972 but it was KISS that really took the place by storm. In January 1973, with fewer than 10 people in the house, they played one of their first shows ever. Throughout the year, they honed their chops and developed their stage act before unleashing their makeup and fury upon the rest of the world the next year.

KMPX Studios

50 Green Street
San Francisco, California

KMPX was one of the most influential radio stations in rock 'n' roll history and this was the home of the famed station (frequency 106.9) from 1962 to 1978. KMPX is considered by many to be the birthplace of underground FM radio. When they started to include rock 'n' roll music in between foreign-language broadcasts, the ratings soared. And so on August 6, 1967, the 24-hour-a-day music format was heard for the first time ever, changing the history of radio from that point forward.

Joplin, Janis

Harvard Stadium
North Harvard Street
Cambridge, Massachusetts

Janis Joplin performed the last concert of her life here with her Full Tilt Boogie Band on August 12, 1970, in front of 40,000 people. She was to die less than two months later on October 4th, in Los Angeles at the Landmark Hotel.

Led Zeppelin

Auditorium Arena
1245 Champa Street
Denver, Colorado
303-893-4000

On December 26, 1968, Led Zeppelin played its first-ever American show at Denver's Auditorium Arena. The set list included "Train Kept A Rollin'," "Dazed and Confused," "You Shook Me," "Babe I'm Gonna Leave You," and "Communication Breakdown." The tour lasted into February and took the band from Denver to Cleveland to New York to Toronto. Now part of the Denver Center for the Performing Arts, the Auditorium Arena has hosted everything from the Democratic National Convention to auto shows to countless other concerts.

Live Aid

JFK Stadium
Broad Street (near Patterson Avenue)
Philadelphia, Pennsylvania

This is where the American portion of the legendary "Live Aid" benefit concerts was held on July 13, 1985 (the London portion took place at Wembley Arena). That day saw the likes of Bob Dylan, Led Zeppelin, Mick Jagger, Neil Young, and many more come together to help raise funds to feed the world's hungry. J.F.K. Stadium, the longtime home of the Army/Navy football game, was torn down in the 1990s.

Madison Square Garden

4 Pennsylvania Plaza
New York, New York
212-465-MSG1

Aptly nicknamed "The World's Most Famous Arena," the Garden has over five million fans a year passing through its doors. Though the notable musical performances are too numerous to mention here, a few of the more legendary events that have graced

the Garden's stage include: George Harrison's Concert for Bangladesh, the MUSE Concerts, Sly Stone's wedding, Led Zeppelin's *Song Remains the Same* concert sequences, and many of the Rolling Stones' *Gimme Shelter* concert sequences.

Marley, Bob

Paul's Mall
733 Boylston Street
Boston, Massachusetts

Bob Marley and the Wailers made their U.S. live debut at the funky old jazz club called Paul's Mall. The set included the songs, "Lively Up Yourself," "Stir It Up," "Concrete Jungle," and "Get Up Stand Up." The club closed a long time ago but in its day featured the best jazz, blues, and rock 'n' roll artists of the time, including Muddy Waters, B.B. King, and Bruce Springsteen.

Marley's last performance of his life was in Pittsburgh at the Stanley Theater, now called the Benedum Center, located at 719 Liberty Avenue in Pittsburgh, Pennsylvania. The show took place on September 23, 1980, and Marley had already become gravely ill with cancer. He died on May 11, 1981, at the Cedars of Lebanon Hospital in Miami, Florida. Bob Marley was just 36 years old.

The Masque

1655 North Cherokee Avenue
Hollywood, California

The Masque was a seminal punk rock club located in central Hollywood. It was open sporadically from 1977 to 1979 and in that short span served as a spawning ground for many of American punk's most influential bands. X, The Germs, The Mau-Mau's, The Weirdos, The Avengers, The Dils, The Skulls and others played here regularly. An up-and-coming Go-Gos would often rent practice space here. The building was recently renovated and even though the basement where The Masque was located is currently used as storage (and many of the walls have been removed), most of the classic original graffiti created back in the club's heyday still exists along the remaining walls.

Maverick's Flat

4225 Crenshaw
Los Angeles, California

There were some amazing black musical groups that played here at what would become known as the West Coast's answer to New York's Apollo Theater. Such legendary greats as the Ike and Tina Turner Revue, Earth, Wind and Fire, the Commodores, and Parliament-Funkadelic as well as the Temptations, the Four Tops, and The Supremes all played here and the club is still open for business today.

Max's Kansas City

213 Park Avenue South (between 17th and 18th off Union Square)
New York, New York

"Max's Kansas City was the exact spot where Pop Art and Pop Life came together in the 1960s." So said Andy Warhol, and he should know, because he held court here for many years. From the mid-'60s through the end of the '70s, this is where much of New York City's music and artistic culture developed. The house band for a time was The Velvet Underground, followed by the New York Dolls. Aerosmith was discovered here. Bruce Springsteen opened for Bob Marley here.

"Upstairs" at Max's was the place to be in the glitter-packed early '70s, hanging out with Alice Cooper, Todd Rundgren, Mick Jagger, Iggy Pop, David Bowie, and the rest of the then-avant-garde establishment. Today, sadly, it's a gourmet market.

McCartney, Linda

Memorial Stadium
Gayley Road
UC Berkeley Campus
Berkeley, California

An infamous tape in the early 1990s surfaced, purported to be the warblings of Linda McCartney singing background for her husband during an appearance here in 1990. The painfully off-key vocals during the Beatle classic "Hey Jude" became widely circulated and remains a bit of a comedy classic.

Michigan Theater

238 Bagley Street
Detroit, Michigan

The Michigan Theater was at one time a movie theater in Detroit. It was built in August 1926 by the architectural firm of Rapp & Rapp for Detroit philanthropist and movie theater owner John H. Kunsky. With a seating capacity of 4,000, the concert hall/movie house was one of the largest in Michigan. Throughout the 1950s and 1960s, the theater changed ownership several times. It was subsequently used for various events: in the 1960s a closed-circuit television provided views of Red Wings ice hockey games for those who could not attend the actual event in nearby Olympia Stadium, and in the 1970s the theater was a nightclub and concert venue for rock bands (called The Palace). The Stooges recorded the raw live classic *Metallic KO* here in October 1973, but the most lasting image from the Michigan Theater is probably the cover of *KISS Alive*, which was shot here (along with the first two promo films for the band featuring *Rock and Roll All Night* and *C'mon and Love Me*).

The Michigan Theater was permanently closed and partially demolished in 1976. Due to problems with the structural integrity of an adjoining office building, the main hall and lobby were gutted and converted into a parking structure. Cars, Detroit's primary industrial product, now fill the once-bustling theater, and the derelict remains have, for many historians, become a symbol of the decline of Detroit. Ironically, the Michigan Theater is built on the site of the small garage where Henry Ford built his first automobile (the garage was transported brick-by-brick to The Henry Ford Museum in nearby Dearborn).

Monterey Pop Festival

Monterey County Fairgrounds
2004 Fairgrounds Road (off Fremont Street, near Highway 1)
Monterey, California
831-372-5863

Held in Monterey, California, on June 16-18, 1967, the Monterey Pop Festival was the first commercial American rock festival. Dunhill Records executive Lou Adler and John Phillips of The Mamas and the Papas organized the festival around the concept of the successful Monterey Jazz Festival and staged it at that festival's site.

Featuring the first major American appearances of Jimi Hendrix and The Who, it also introduced Janis Joplin to a large audience and featured performances by the Jefferson Airplane, the Grateful Dead, The Byrds, Canned Heat, Buffalo Springfield, Otis Redding, Ravi Shankar, and many others.

Arguably the most famous moment of the festival (and one of the most memorable in rock 'n' roll history), was when Hendrix lit his guitar on fire before smashing it at the climax of "Wild Thing." The stage where the show took place has hardly changed at all since then. At the exact spot where Hendrix knelt and "sacrificed" his guitar, "Jimi Hendrix 1967" has been scrawled into the wood floor.

Interestingly, it was here that Mickey Dolenz of The Monkees (a huge commercial act at the time) decided to take the generally unknown Hendrix on the road as The Monkees' opening act. Several shows into the tour, however, everyone soon realized that Hendrix was not a good fit for the teenybopper audience and he left the tour.

Mount Pocono Festival

Pocono International Speedway
Long Pond Road
Long Pond, Pennsylvania
570-646-2300

Held July 8-9, 1972, over 200,000 fans attended this muddy two-day festival, which featured (among others) Emerson, Lake and Palmer; Humble Pie; Three Dog Night; Rod Stewart & The Faces; Mother Night; Cactus; Edgar Winter; The J. Geils Band; and Black Sabbath. The festival was marred on Saturday by a three-hour rain delay.

Newport Pop Festival

Orange County Fairgrounds
88 Fair Avenue
Costa Mesa, California

On August 4-5, 1968, over 140,000 pre-Woodstock fans gathered here to watch (among others) Tiny Tim, the Jefferson Airplane, Country Joe and the Fish, the Grateful Dead, The Chambers Brothers, Charles Lloyd, James Cotton Blues Band, Quicksilver Messenger Service, The Byrds, Alice Cooper, Steppenwolf, Sonny and Cher, Canned Heat, Electric Flag, Butterfield Blues Band, Eric Burdon and the Animals, Blue Cheer, Iron Butterfly, Illinois Speed Press, and Things To Come. Admission was just $5.50 per day and the festival was produced by "Humble" Harvey Miller, a top Los Angeles disc jockey. The site still hosts the popular Orange County Fair each year.

Pandora's Box

Sunset Boulevard and Crescent Heights
Hollywood, California

It was the tearing down of this club in 1966 that helped fuel the Sunset Strip riots. During late 1966, Pandora's Box was a center of controversy. One of the few underage clubs of its day, it became a flashpoint of the era as defiant teenagers got into fights with cops who began handing out curfew violations. These riots are what inspired the Buffalo Springfield song "For What It's Worth." The exact location of the club is the island in the middle of Sunset at Crescent Heights.

The Panhandle

Golden Gate Park, between Oak and Fell Streets
San Francisco, California

Just past this famous park's entranceway is an island of grass (just a few blocks north of the Haight) called The Panhandle. Back in the 1960s, some legendary concerts took place here including one in 1966 when the Grateful Dead played in honor of LSD being made illegal and also a 1967 show when the Jimi Hendrix Experience played here.

Paramount Theater

385 Flatbush Avenue Extension
Brooklyn, New York

The Brooklyn Paramount movie theater was built in 1928 and closed in 1962. Disc Jockeys staged many famous rock 'n' roll shows here between 1955-1958 including performances by Chuck Berry, Buddy Holly and Little Richard. Today, the theater serves as a gymnasium for Long Island University, and although the classic old Paramount has lost some of its original look, the building still contains the original Wurlitzer organ, which, incredibly, is still maintained and used for the college's basketball games. Many argue that the gymnasium's organ is the finest in the country, if not the world.

Peppermint Lounge

128 West 45th (in the Knickerbocker Hotel)
New York, New York

This became a hotspot in 1961 after the house band Joey Dee and the Starliters released the record, *The Peppermint Twist*. The song became #1 in the nation and anyone who was anyone flocked to the "Pep" to dance the dance in the club that made it famous. (The band followed the hit record by recording "Doin' the Twist at the Peppermint Lounge" live at the club–it was not nearly as popular.) The club no longer exists.

The Rat

528 Commonwealth Avenue
Boston, Massachusetts

For over 20 years, from the 1970s through the 1990s, The Rat (full name, The Rathskellar) was the premiere underground rock 'n' roll club in Boston. The Cars started out here, and the cavern-like club also hosted Blondie, the Ramones, The Jam, Squeeze, and many other cutting-edge bands back in the 1970s and 1980s. The Rat closed its doors for good in 1997, ending one of punk and new wave's most dominant venues. Today, there's a hotel at the location.

Red Rocks Amphitheatre

18300 W. Alameda Parkway
Morrison, Colorado
303-295-4444

Famed Red Rocks Amphitheatre is a rock structure in Red Rocks Park near Morrison, Colorado (west of Denver), where concerts are given in an open-air amphitheatre. There is a large, tilted, disc-shaped rock behind the stage, a huge vertical rock angled outwards from stage right, several large boulders angled outwards from stage left and a seating area for up to 9,450 people in between. It was created by the workers of the Civilian Conservation Corps under the New Deal Act. One of the notable performances given at Red Rocks was by the rock group U2, who released two tracks from a Red Rocks concert on their 1983 live album, *Under a Blood Red Sky*, and a full concert-length video of the same appearance, segments of which were frequently shown on MTV. A steady rain, the large lighted torches surrounding the stage, and the natural wonder of the Red Rocks setting all provided a dramatic atmosphere for U2's music, and the video helped expand U2's American following.

A two-volume album, *Carved in Stone,* features live performances by various artists at Red Rocks, including R.E.M., Ben Harper, Coldplay, The Allman Brothers Band, and Phish, with proceeds going towards a fund for preservation of the park and amphitheatre. The amphitheatre was also the starting and finishing line of the reality TV show *The Amazing Race* season 9.

Rendezvous Ballroom

Between Washington and Palm Avenues
(Along what is now Ocean Front Boulevard)
Balboa, California

Originally built in 1928, the Rendezvous Ballroom was a huge, two-story dancehall that over the years hosted Artie Shaw, Ozzie Nelson, Benny Goodman, Guy Lombardo, Bob Crosby, Tommy Dorsey, Stan Kenton, and many other music legends of the day. But it was in the late 1950s and early 1960s that a musical revolution began at this spot, because that's when seminal surf guitarist Dick Dale and his group the Del-Tones began playing here. Their numerous appearances at the ballroom are considered by many to be what became the birth of true "Surf" music (Dale's sound even inspired a dance–"The Surfer Stomp"). In 1966, the Rendezvous Ballroom burned to the ground and today a plaque can be found at the site.

"Rock Around the Clock"

HofBrau Hotel
Corner of Oak and Atlantic Avenues
Wildwood, New Jersey

It was here in 1954 where Bill Haley & the Comets first performed "Rock Around the Clock," which, in the eyes of many Wildwood residents, makes this the birthplace of rock 'n' roll. After all, the song is considered to be one of the first true rock 'n' roll records and so Haley's history here certainly counts for something. The band played here regularly from 1950–1955 and there is a plan afoot today to erect a permanent historical marker on the site of the HofBrau Hotel. Wildwood had another brush with rock 'n' roll history at the now defunct Rainbow Club in July of 1960, when a 19-year-old named Chubby Checker (born Ernest Evans) walked onto the stage and first did his

version of "The Twist," a song written and recorded by Hank Ballard two years earlier. Less than a month later, on August 6, 1960, Checker performed "The Twist" on Dick Clark's nationally televised Saturday evening program, and launched a national craze. The single rocketed to number one during the autumn of 1960, remaining on the charts for four months. It hit number one again in late 1961; the only record ever to enjoy two stays at the top more than a year apart.

The Roxy

9009 Sunset Boulevard
West Hollywood, California
310-278-9457

Elmer Valentine and Mario Maglieri, who later brought in partner and manager Lou Adler, in a building previously occupied by a strip club owned by Jerry Lewis, founded the Roxy in the early 1970s. (Adler was actually responsible for bringing the stage play *The Rocky Horror Show* to the United States, and it opened its first American run at The Roxy Theatre in 1974, before it was made into the movie *The Rocky Horror Picture Show* the next year.) Hundreds of famous and yet-to-be-famous acts such as Tori Amos, Foo Fighters, Guns N' Roses, Dire Straits, Al Stewart, and David Bowie have played this highly prestigious venue. The small On the Rox bar above the club has hosted a wide variety of debauchery in its history; it was a regular hangout for John Lennon, Harry Nilsson, Alice Cooper, and Keith Moon during Lennon's "lost weekend" in 1975, and in the 1980s hosted parties arranged by "Hollywood Madam" Heidi Fleiss. Frank Zappa and The Mothers of Invention recorded most of their celebrated *Roxy and Elsewhere* album during December 1973 at the Roxy and the theater remains open (and thriving) today.

The Scene

301 West 46th Street
New York, New York

In the late 1960s, this was arguably New York City's most popular rock 'n' roll hangout. For several months in 1968, Jimi Hendrix was a constant attraction here, jamming with Clapton, Jeff Beck, Jim Morrison and others while recording *Electric Ladyland* at the Record Plant recording studio. The original building was torn down several years ago.

Shelley's Manne-Hole

1608 Cahuenga Boulevard
Hollywood, California

For 14 years (1960-1974), the famous Los Angeles jazz club Shelley's Manne-Hole was located here. Drummer Shelly Manne ran the place, which featured headliners such as Miles Davis, Bill Evans, and John Coltrane. A manhole at the site commemorates the former club.

Springsteen, Bruce

Harvard Square Theater
10 Church Street
Cambridge, Massachusetts

In 1974, Boston-area rock music critic Jon Landau reviewed a concert at the Harvard Square Theater for *The Real Paper.* In his piece, Landau started by bemoaning the lack of passion and soul in the current music scene, and how he had become bored with something that, at one time, had been so vital and relevant. But then he got to writing about the concert, in which a skinny, scruffy, 20-something beach rat from Asbury Park, New Jersey, gave him reason to believe. Landau's words crackle and resonate even today:

"But tonight there is someone I can write of the way I used to write, without reservations of any kind. Last Thursday, at the Harvard Square Theatre, I saw my rock 'n' roll past flash before my eyes. And I saw something else: I saw rock 'n' roll future and its name is Bruce Springsteen. And on a night when I needed to feel young, he made me feel like I was hearing music for the very first time."

Rolling Stone magazine picked-up Landau's quote of seeing the future of rock 'n' roll and the legend of "The Boss" was born. Landau went on to become Springsteen's manager and co-producer; today, the site is a movie theater.

The Starwood

8151 Santa Monica Boulevard
West Hollywood, California

The Starwood was popular during the 1970s and 1980s. Many punk bands and heavy metal bands, including Van Halen, DEVO, X, AC/DC, and The Go-Gos started their careers or played here regularly over the years. The Starwood had been a popular nightclub called PJ's in the 1960s, which typically attracted a large number of celebrities. (During its stint as PJ's, The Standells and Trini Lopez recorded live albums here.) In the early 1970s, PJ's was bought by alleged organized crime figure Eddie Nash, and became The Starwood. It closed in 1982 after a mysterious fire. Today it's the site of a mini-mall.

Stone Pony

913 Ocean Avenue
Asbury Park, New Jersey
732-502-0600

A Jersey shore rock 'n' roll landmark for years, back in the early '70s, Bruce Springsteen played here frequently, as did Southside Johnny and other locals.

Surf Music

Bel Air Club
312 Catalina Avenue
Redondo Beach, California

Thought to be the birthplace of surf music, this is where a band called The Belairs played regularly in 1961 to the beach crowd. Their catchy instrumentals caught on, especially a tune called "Mr. Moto," which became a local hit and eventually inspired The Beach Boys. An office is now located at the site.

Tad Gormley Stadium

City Park
New Orleans, Louisiana

Tad Gormley Stadium is a multipurpose outdoor stadium located in City Park in New Orleans. It has been used for football, track & field, and soccer. It played host to the U.S. Olympic Track & Field Trials for the 1992 Summer Olympics. Its most frequent use is for high school football, which attracts a large following in the South. In recent years, Tulane University has played its homecoming football game at Gormley so that fans could tailgate before and after the game—something which is not possible at their regular home stadium, the Louisiana Superdome. The experiment met with a good deal of success, generating sellout crowds when the Superdome would normally have been sparsely populated. Many people became familiar with the stadium during Hurricane Katrina when iconic images of the flooded stadium were sent all over the world. But its place in rock 'n' roll history was secured when both The Beatles and the Rolling Stones played here in 1966.

The T.A.M.I. Show

Santa Monica Civic Auditorium
1855 Main Street
Santa Monica, California
310-393-9961

Filmed in a single day (October 29, 1964) near the ocean in Santa Monica, this rarely seen 1964 concert film represents one of rock 'n' roll's seminal concert events—one of the first major "package" performances that fused together all of music's most primal forces of the day.

Featuring outstanding performances by James Brown (featuring two go-go dancers named Teri Garr and Toni Basil), Marvin Gaye, Chuck Berry, Lesley Gore, The Beach Boys, the Rolling Stones, The Supremes, Jan and Dean, Gerry and the Pacemakers, Smokey Robinson and the Miracles, Leslie Gore and Billy J. Kramer, and the Dakotas, the concert was documented by television cameras and kinescoped onto film by director Steve Binder.

The title stood for "Teenage Awards Music International" and the show had a huge influence on how other directors (such as D.A. Pennebaker at Monterey Pop) would soon document rock 'n' roll on film.

Texas International Pop Festival

Dallas International Motor Speedway
Lewisville, Texas

This track, which closed down in 1973, was located on Interstate 35 East just north of Dallas. Over Labor Day weekend, 1969 (just two weeks after Woodstock), 120,000 fans converged on the small town of Lewisville for the Texas Pop Festival. They were treated to performances by a diverse range of artists including B.B. King, Canned Heat, Chicago, Delaney & Bonnie & Friends, Freddie King, Grand Funk Railroad, Herbie Mann, Incredible String Band, James Cotton Blues Band, Janis Joplin, Johnny Winter, Led Zeppelin, The Nazz, The Quarry, Rotary Connection, Sam & Dave, Santana, Shiva's Headband, Sly & the Family Stone, Space Opera, Spirit, Sweetwater, Ten Years After, and Tony Joe White.

Thee Image

18330 Collins Avenue
Miami, Florida

Today it's a deli, but back in the 1960s it was a premier rock 'n' roll venue hosting such soon to be legends as Led Zeppelin, Frank Zappa, and the Grateful Dead. It was closed down due to community pressure in 1969, after the infamous Doors show in which Jim Morrison supposedly exposed himself (which happened at the Dinner Key Auditorium in Florida).

Toronto Rock and Roll Revival

Varsity Stadium
277 Bloor Street West
Toronto, Canada

According to Ringo Starr, it was John Lennon's first-ever solo performance–the famed Plastic Ono Band concert here at Toronto's Varsity Stadium on September 13, 1969–that proved to be the end of The Beatles' career. With the exception of the famous rooftop concert at Apple Headquarters, this was Lennon's first live appearance since 1966. After the concert, Lennon returned to London with his mind made up to quit. Starr is quoted as saying "After (John Lennon's) Plastic Ono Band's debut in Toronto we had a meeting in Saville Row where John finally brought it to a head. He said: 'Well, that's it lads, let's end it.'"

The show, billed as The Toronto Rock and Roll Revival, also featured The Doors, Chuck Berry, Little Richard, Bo Diddley, Alice Cooper, and others, and for Lennon, resulted in the album *Live Peace in Toronto* and the single "Cold Turkey." *Rolling Stone* magazine called the show "The second most important event in rock 'n' roll history" (the first being Woodstock, which had taken place the previous month).

US Festival

Glen Helen Regional Park
San Bernardino, California

This was the site for the massive 1982 and 1983 festivals put on by Apple Computer's Steve Wozniak. The shows featured dozens of acts, including U2, The Clash, the Talking Heads, the Grateful Dead, the Police, the B-52's, Ozzy Osbourne, Van Halen, the Stray Cats, Stevie Nicks, and David Bowie. The park is located just off I-15 about an hour east of Los Angeles, and is a great place for fishing, camping, hiking, and more.

U2

Corner of 7th Street and Main Street
Los Angeles, California

This is the L.A. rooftop where U2 taped the music video for the song "Where the Streets Have No Name" in 1987. They actually performed on the roof of a row of stores located right at the corner of 7th Street and Main Street, near the Skid Row section of downtown, before the cops broke it up.

U2

Justin Herman Plaza—The Embarcadero
1 Market Street
San Francisco, California

If you saw the 1989 movie *Rattle and Hum* you'll remember this. On the second leg of the 1987 Joshua Tree Tour, U2 had the idea to stage a "Save the Yuppies" free concert

at this site. On November 11, about 20,000 people spontaneously gathered here to see U2 and during the tune "Pride (In the Name of Love)" singer Bono spray-painted the slogan "Rock 'n' Roll Stops the Traffic" onto a sculpture/waterfall next to the impromptu stage.

Valley Music Center

20600 Ventura Boulevard
Woodland Hills, California

Today it's a Jehovah's Witness center, but it used to be a legendary California concert hall. Back in the 1960s, the Valley Music Center was a vital haven for the fertile Southern California music scene, including The Doors, Buffalo Springfield, The Byrds, and Tina Turner.

Violent Femmes

Oriental Theatre
2230 N. Farwell Avenue
Milwaukee, Wisconsin
414-276-8711

The Oriental Theatre was built and opened in 1927 as a movie palace. The themes of the decor are East Indian, with no traces of Chinese or Japanese artwork and is said to be the only movie palace to incorporate East Indian artwork. The Oriental Theatre is also the world record holder for showings of the *The Rocky Horror Picture Show*. It has played as a midnight film since January 1978! In 1980, the band The Pretenders were booked to play here and before the show, Pretenders singer/guitarist Chrissie Hynde discovered a local group playing in front of the Oriental. She arranged for them to open on the rest of The Pretenders' upcoming tour and the rest was history. That's how the Violent Femmes, perhaps Milwaukee's most famous band, was discovered.

Wattstax Concert

Los Angeles Memorial Coliseum
3911 South Figueroa Street
Los Angeles, California

Wattstax was a memorable August 1972 concert held at the Los Angeles Memorial Coliseum. Its purpose was to benefit the neighborhood of Watts some seven years after the Watts riots, and the concert drew an overwhelmingly African-American crowd of 100,000 and turned into a memorable black-pride event.

A documentary was filmed of the show and remains one of the great (if rarely-seen concert films). The show (hosted by Richard Pryor) featured R&B legend Rufus Thomas, the Bar-Kays, the Dramatics, the Emotions, Isaac Hayes, Albert King, Little Milton, Mel and Tim, the Staple Singers, Johnny Taylor, Carla Thomas, Kim Weston, and others.

Watkins Glen

Route 16 and Meade's Hill Road
Watkins Glen, New York

On July 28, 1973, the largest rock 'n' roll concert ever presented was held at the Raceway in Watkins Glen, New York. Over 600,000 people attended the single-day affair. It was estimated that 12 hours before the show was scheduled to begin, traffic had been blocked for over 100 miles. And Watkins Glen was simply a presentation of three enduring rock and roll bands—the Grateful Dead, The Band, and The Allman Brothers.

The day before the concert, all three bands played short one-to-two-hour sets for the 150,000 people that had already arrived. Then, on the day of the concert, the Dead played for five hours, The Band for three hours, and The Allman Brothers for four hours. To close the show, everyone got on stage for a 90-minute jam.

Whisky a Go-Go

8901 Sunset Boulevard
West Hollywood, California
310-652-4202

It's been called the first real American discothèque and it's one of the most famous rock 'n' roll landmarks in America. It was first opened January 11, 1964, at the site of an old bank building that had been remodeled into a short-lived club called the Party, by a former Chicago policeman, Elmer Valentine. The Whisky a Go-Go opened with a live band led by Johnny Rivers and a short-skirted female DJ spinning records between sets from a suspended cage at the right of the stage. When the girl DJ danced during Rivers' set, the audience thought it was part of the act and the concept of Go-Go dancers in cages was born. Rivers rode the Whisky-born "go-go" craze to national fame with records recorded partly "live at the Whisky." The Miracles recorded the song "Going to a Go-Go" in 1966 (which was covered in 1982 by the Rolling Stones), and Whisky a Go-Go franchises sprang up all over the country.

In 1966, the Whisky was one of the centers of the Sunset Strip police riots. The club was harassed repeatedly by the City of Los Angeles, which once ordered that the name be changed; claiming "whisky" was a bad influence.

The Whisky played an important role in many musical careers, especially for bands based in Southern California. The Byrds, Buffalo Springfield, and Love were regulars, and The Doors were the house band for a while—until the debut of the controversial "Oedipal Section" of the song called "The End" got them fired. Frank Zappa's Mothers of Invention got their record contract based on a performance at the Whisky and Jimi Hendrix came by to jam when Sam & Dave headlined. Otis Redding recorded his album *Live at the Whisky* here in 1966.

Many British performers made their first headlining performances at the Whisky, including The Kinks, The Who, Cream, Led Zeppelin, Roxy Music, and Oasis. The Whisky was a focus of the emerging new wave and punk rock movements in the late 1970s, and frequently presented local acts as diverse as The Germs (which recorded its first album there), The Runaways, X, Mötley Crüe, and Van Halen while playing host to early performances by the Ramones, The Dictators, the Misfits, Blondie, Talking Heads, Elvis Costello, XTC, The Jam, Japanese doo-wop musical group Rats & Star, including a famous sex offender Masashi Tashiro, among others.

The Whisky fell on hard times once the first flush of punk rock lost steam, and closed its doors in 1982. It reopened in 1986 as a "four-wall," a venue that could be rented by promoters and bands. Although a few booths remain on the perimeter, the interior has mostly been transformed into a bare, seatless space where the audience is forced to stand throughout the performances. Against this new economic backdrop, a number of hard rock and metal bands, including Guns N' Roses and Metallica, rose to prominence in the 1980s.

During the early 1990s, the Whisky hosted a number of Seattle-based musicians who would later be dubbed "the godfathers of grunge," including Soundgarden, Nirvana, Mudhoney, The Melvins, and 7 Year Bitch.

Today, almost 50 years on, the Whisky remains an important part of rock 'n' roll history along Sunset Strip.

The Who

Brooklyn Fox Theater
Intersection of Flatbush and Fulton
Brooklyn, New York

On March 25, 1967, The Who made their United States debut here in Brooklyn, as part of a Murray the K Rock and Roll Festival. After a series of shows throughout the week, the band returned during the summer for a more extended tour of the east and south. The vintage Brooklyn Fox Theater, which had been built in 1928, was torn down in 1970.

Winterland

2000 Post Street (at Steiner)
San Francisco, California

On Thanksgiving Day in 1976 (and all through the night), The Band held its farewell concert at the venue where it had played its first live performance—Winterland in San Francisco. Joining them that night were Joni Mitchell, Bob Dylan, Van Morrison, Neil Young, Eric Clapton, and many others. The concert and other festivities were filmed by Martin Scorsese and released a year-and-a-half later as *The Last Waltz*.

There's not a trace of the historic venue that hosted this landmark show, nor the hundreds of others that took place there—including many of the selections used on *Frampton Comes Alive*, recorded on June 13, 1975, and the last performance ever given by the Sex Pistols in 1978. At the Post Street entrance to the apartment complex at the site, however, you will find a Winterland photo exhibit, paying homage to what once happened at the location. Winterland closed on New Year's Eve 1978 with a show starring the New Riders of the Purple Sage, the Blues Brothers, and the Grateful Dead.

Wollman Rink

Central Park
New York, New York
212-439-6900

Wollman Rink was built in 1949, when Kate Wollman donated $600,000 for its construction. In the early 1990s, it was purchased by Donald Trump, who now runs it. It has been a success from the day it opened—over 300,000 skaters glided across the ice in its first year of operation. In use the year round, the summer months find hundreds of in-line skaters taking lessons or perfecting more advanced skills.

Thirty years ago, Wollman Rink was also the site of a very popular music series. Beginning in 1967 and continuing through the early '70s, the F & M Schaefer Brewing Co. sponsored concerts in Central Park. The concerts offered something for everyone. At $2.00 for first-come/first-served orchestra seats, the shows were popular and usually sold out. Hundreds would spend the day in line at the Wollman Rink to socialize and get the best seats. Over the years, some of the acts to appear there included Bruce Springsteen, The Allman Brothers, Dave Brubeck, The Byrds, and Billy Joel. Sadly, pressure from the neighborhood eventually forced the shows to the west side piers and much of the appeal was gone.

Woodstock

Hurd and West Shore Roads, outside Bethel, New York
Directions: Drive north on Hurd Road off 17B. To get to 17B, drive west from
the New York State Thruway on Highway 17. The turn for 17B comes up just as
you pass through Monticello. Once you get into the town of Bethel, look for the
Bethel County Store—the Hurd Road turnoff is a quarter-mile past the store
(look for a white farmhouse that stands on the south side of the road at the
intersection). Drive up Hurd Road until you hit West Shore Road and you'll be
able to locate the marker.

A concrete marker sits at the spot where the stage stood for the original, legendary
Woodstock "Music and Art Fair," three days of peace and love that took place on
August 15-17, 1969, at Max Yasgur's farm. This seminal event was documented both on
film and record. Among the performers were: The Band; Creedence Clearwater Revival;
Crosby, Stills & Nash; the Grateful Dead; Jimi Hendrix; Jefferson Airplane; Janis Joplin;
Santana; Sly & The Family Stone; The Who; and Neil Young (Young performed a few
songs with Crosby, Stills & Nash and later joined the group). Woodstock festivals in the
1990s were held in the nearby town of Saugerties on the Winston Farm at the intersection of Routes 212 and 32.

Youth Opportunities Center

9027 N. Figueroa
Los Angeles, California

The infamous Watts Acid Test was held here on February 12, 1966. The hall was rented
to hold a "happening" that was a precursor to future concerts. Kool-Aid spiked with
LSD (the drug was legal at the time) was handed out to over 600 people who danced
and freaked out for hours. As a bonus, the Grateful Dead, who had been living in Los
Angeles at the time, performed for the crowd.

The Song Remains the Same: Music, Film, and TV Recording Sites

American Bandstand Studio

WFIL
4601 Market Street (46th and Market)
Philadelphia, Pennsylvania

The old WFIL Studio was the home of the original *Bandstand* and then *American Bandstand* from 1952-1963, arguably the show's most influential years. Built in 1947-48,

it is notable as one of the first buildings in the United States designed specifically for television broadcasting, and was placed on the National Register of Historic Places on July 28, 1986. Today, it's an "incubator" building for small businesses.

American Graffiti

Petaluma, California
Petaluma Visitors Program
1-877-273-8258

The movie was inspired by the small town of Modesto, where filmmaker George Lucas grew up, and featured an excellent collection of 1950s rock 'n' roll, including Chuck Berry, Buddy Holly, Bill Haley among many others. But this is the town where the film was primarily shot. You can take a walking tour of the town's many movie sites with a guide from the tourist information office at 799 Baywood Street. A few points along the way:

The main drag used in the movie is Petaluma Boulevard North, between D Street and Washington Street.

Richard Dreyfuss gets drafted into the Pharaohs gang in front of the Old Opera House, 149 Kentucky Street.

The used car lot where Dreyfuss is made to chain the axle of the police car is still a vacant lot. It's located along the McNear Building, 15-23 Petaluma Boulevard North.

American Sound Studio

827 Thomas Street (at Chelsea Street)
Memphis, Tennessee

From 1967 to 1970, 120 Top 20 songs were recorded at the studio that was once located here. Dusty Springfield, Bobby Womack, and Elvis all worked here (this is where the King recorded "Suspicious Minds," "Kentucky Rain," and "In the Ghetto"), and it was also here that the Box Tops recorded "The Letter," the biggest-selling single of 1967-68. The original structure has been torn down—today there is an auto parts store at this location.

Big Pink

2188 Stoll Road
Saugerties, New York

This is the house where Bob Dylan recovered from his accident and invited The Band to hang out and play with him. In addition to *The Basement Tapes*, the sessions also resulted in The Band's debut album, *Music from Big Pink*. The singles, "The Weight" and "This Wheel's on Fire" became instant classics.

The Brill Building

1619 Broadway
New York, New York

"The Brill Building sound" came out of the stretch along Broadway between 49th and 53rd Streets. The building—named after the Brill Brothers, whose clothing store was first located at the street level corner and who would later buy the place—contained 165 music businesses in 1962, including many of the songwriting teams who would help craft the sounds of the 1960s. Jerry Leiber and Mike Stoler worked here, writing many of Elvis's hits, plus Phil Spector, Doc Pomus, and Mort Shuman. And of course, the famous Aldon staff hired by Don Kirshner, which included Carole King, Gerry Goffin, Neil Sedaka, Barry Mann, Cynthia Weil, and Howard Greenfield. This was the group who wrote such hits as "The Loco Motion," "One Fine Day," "Up on the Roof," and "Will You Still Love Me Tomorrow?" Though these names have moved on, the building still houses some music companies today.

Capitol Records

1750 Vine Street
Hollywood, California

According to legend, this famous landmark building was designed to resemble a stack of records. Capitol Records was the first major record company based on the West Coast, and over the years has promoted such acts as The Beatles, the Beach Boys, Pink Floyd, Frank Sinatra, Bob Seger, Duran Duran, Bonnie Raitt, Robbie Robertson, Steve Miller, and Tina Turner. Inside the lobby you'll see an incredible array of gold records, spanning the

entire history of rock 'n' roll and the impressive roster of recording artists that have been represented on the Capitol label. Interestingly, the blinking light atop the tower spells out the word "Hollywood" in Morse code. In 1992 it was changed to read "Capitol 50" in honor of the label's fiftieth anniversary. However, it has since returned to spelling "Hollywood."

Charles, Ray

2107 West Washington Boulevard
Los Angeles, California

This building housed both the office and recording studios of the late legendary singer, Ray Charles. Since 1963, Charles had operated out of here and recorded, in addition to his own music, songs and albums by Stevie Wonder, Billy Preston, and Quincy Jones. Charles, who passed away in 2004, crafted a brilliant career as a singer, pianist, and composer. His songs combined gospel, blues, pop, country, and jazz. Blind since age seven, he paved the way for such artists as Elvis Presley and Aretha Franklin among many others. Charles won 12 Grammy Awards, and his hits over the years include "Georgia on My Mind," "Drown in My Own Tears," and "I Got a Woman."

Clapton, Eric

461 Ocean Boulevard
Highway (A1-A)
Golden Beach (20 miles north of downtown Miami, Florida)

461 Ocean Boulevard was the name of Eric Clapton's 1974 "comeback" album. It's the address of the posh beach house Clapton stayed in while recording the disc nearby, and he liked the place so much, he used it as the name of the album. Though the house is on private property, you can still get a good view of it from the beach.

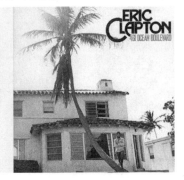

Dazed and Confused

**Bedichek Middle School
6800 Bill Hughes Road
Austin, Texas**

Richard Linklater's 1993 spot-on nostalgic homage to high school life in the mid-1970s was centered here at this real middle school in Austin, the director's hometown. The movie, which featured a killer rock 'n' roll soundtrack with such '70s rockers as Aerosmith, Deep Purple, and Alice Cooper, also included early performances by (among others) Matthew McConaughey (his first movie), Parker Posey, and Ben Affleck.

Fleetwood Mac

**Sound City
15456 Cabrito Road
Van Nuys, California
818-787-3722**

In late 1974, when Mick Fleetwood was looking for a studio to record the next Fleetwood Mac album, he went to Sound City on a recommendation, liked the sound, and hired engineer Keith Olsen to produce and engineer the LP. When Fleetwood first came down to hear what the studio sounded like, Olsen put on a song called "Frozen Love" from the Buckingham Nicks album, which had been recorded there. Fleetwood decided to hire Lindsey Buckingham and Stevie Nicks based on the experience, and within two years the "new" Fleetwood Mac had the number one album in the country. (Nirvana also recorded *Nevermind* here, and Dennis Wilson brought a singer named Charles Manson to cut demos here in the late '60s.)

Freed, Alan

WJW
One Playhouse Square Building
1375 Euclid Avenue
Cleveland, Ohio

Seminal disc jockey Alan Freed (who popularized the term "rock 'n' roll") began broadcasting his *Moondog Rock 'n' Roll Party* over WJW radio in 1951. The station's 50,000-watt power made the show's influence enormous and helped bring many early rock 'n' roll records to a huge audience. A small plaque near the building's entrance acknowledges the history, even though the radio station is long gone.

Geldof, Bob

WRAS Radio Studios
Georgia State University
Atlanta, Georgia
404-651-2240

Boomtown Rats singer Bob Geldof was being interviewed at this college station when he read a wire report about a young California girl who went on a shooting rampage because "She didn't like Mondays." Geldof was so impacted by the story that he returned to his hotel room and penned a song by that name, "I Don't Like Mondays." It became the biggest hit in the band's history.

Glory Days

Maxwell's
1039 Washington Street
Hoboken, New Jersey
201-653-1703

Remember the popular *Glory Days* video from the Springsteen album *Born in The U.S.A.*? This is the famed New Jersey bar that was used for the musical performance part of the video. The baseball scenes were shot at a place called Miller Stadium in West New York, New Jersey.

Gold Star Recording Studios

6252 Santa Monica Boulevard
Hollywood, California

The reason Brian Wilson of The Beach Boys wanted to record here was because he knew it was where Phil Spector had created his famous "Wall of Sound" approach to recording: the dense, layered, echo-filled sound that surrounded songs like "He's a Rebel," "Be My Baby," "Baby, I Love You," and "You've Lost That Loving Feeling" to

name a few. The result was *Pet Sounds*, the dynamic 1967 album that supposedly pushed The Beatles to up the ante with *Sergeant Pepper's Lonely Hearts Club Band.* Small and lacking air conditioning, the main recording studio at Gold Star sat on the southeast corner of Santa Monica and Vine, but was razed in the mid 1980s to make room for the mini-mall that's there now.

Holly, Buddy

Norman Petty Studios
1313 West Seventh Street
Clovis, New Mexico

The Norman Petty Studios on 7th Street is known worldwide as the place where Buddy Holly recorded the smash hit, "Peggy Sue," as well as 18 other hits in just 15 months. In his studios, Petty mixed songs for other stars, including Roy Orbison. Clovis' own

Fireballs also recorded "Sugar Shack," the number one song in 1963, at Norman Petty Studios. Studio tours are available year round by contacting:
Kenneth Broad
Box 926
Clovis, New Mexico
505-356-6422

Little Richard

J & M Studios
523 Gov. Nichols Street
New Orleans, Louisiana

Legendary recording engineer Cosimo Matassa owned several recording studios around the Big Easy. In the one that was located at this site, Little Richard recorded some of the most influential records in rock 'n' roll history: "Tutti Frutti," "Lucille," and "Good Golly Miss Molly." The structure is now a condominium.

"Louie Louie"

142 West 54th Street
Los Angeles, California

The is the actual house where R&B singer Richard Berry wrote the classic garage band anthem, "Louie Louie" in 1955. He recorded it himself in 1956, but it wasn't until The Kingsmen cut it in 1963 that the song became widely known. (Note—Berry had sung lead on The Coasters classic song, "Riot in Cellblock Number 9.")

"Louie Louie"

Northwest Recorders
415 S.W. 13th Street
Portland, Oregon

The Kingsmen had formed in Portland in 1960 and consisted of Lynn Easton on drums, Mike Mitchell on guitar, Don Gallucci on keyboards, Bob Nordby on bass, and guitar player and lead singer Jack Ely. By the time they recorded "Louie Louie," they ranged in age from 17 to 20. On a Friday night in April 1963, The Kingsmen performed at an outdoor concert and did a marathon version of the song. The following morning, they went to a small recording studio in Portland called Northwest Recorders to lay down the tracks. Paul Revere & The Raiders recorded the tune in the same studio the same month, but it was The Kingsmen's version that was destined for greatness. The building is no longer used as a studio, but a plaque commemorates its importance.

Album Covers

Though the majority of classic 1960s to 1980s album covers (back when there were album covers) featured either original artwork and graphics or shots taken in a studio, there were still a fair number that were photographed in public places:

America's Greatest Hits

Crossroads of the World
6671 Sunset Boulevard
Hollywood, California

Remember *America's Greatest Hits* from 1975? It featured "Horse With No Name," "Sister Golden Hair," and "Tin Man" to name a few. If so, then you'll probably recognize the Crossroads of the World center from the album cover illustration. Considered to be L.A.'s first modern shopping mall, Crossroads was built in 1936. The centerpiece building resembles a miniature ocean liner, an Art Deco facade complete with portholes, railings, life preservers, and decks. An outdoor village of small, European-style bungalows surrounds the "ship," and rising above it all is a central 30-foot Streamline Modern tower, topped by an 8-foot, revolving globe of the Earth. Once a retail shopping center, today the Crossroads of the World is a quiet office complex.

Beach Boys–*Surfin' Safari*

Paradise Cove (just north of Malibu on Pacific Coast Highway)
Malibu, California

On a chilly morning in 1962, The Beach Boys posed here on this stretch of California beach for the cover of their first album. (The site is open to the public, but there is a charge for parking.)

Album Covers

The Beastie Boys–*Paul's Boutique*

99 Rivington Street
New York, New York

Highly varied lyrically and sonically, 1989's *Paul's Boutique* did not sell as well as the previous *Licensed to Ill*, but it managed to secure the Beastie Boys' place as critical favorites in the then still-dormant field of popular hip hop. This LP ranks among the great hip-hop recordings of the era. In honor of the photo site, the restaurant located here is actually called Paul's Boutique.

Browne, Jackson–*Late for the Sky*

215 South Lucerne Street
Hollywood, California

Jackson Browne's third album, 1974's classic *Late for the Sky*, had its title track featured in Martin Scorcese's film *Taxi Driver*. The album also boasted other Browne standards "For a Dancer" and "Farther On." The house featured on the cover is in the upscale Hancock Park section of Los Angeles.

Album Covers

The Clash–*London Calling*

The Palladium
126 East 14th Street
New York, New York
212-473-7171

A famous concert venue and then disco in the '80s and '90s, it was here that the famous cover of The Clash's 1980 album *London Calling* was photographed. The picture, which shows bassist Paul Simonon smashing his guitar onstage, is considered to be one of the most definitive in rock 'n' roll.

Creedence Clearwater Revival–*Willy and the Poor Boys*

3218 Peralta Street
Oakland, California

This is where Creedence shot the cover of their fourth album, 1970s *Willy and the Poor Boys.* The art direction was an effective representation of the smash single, "Down on the Corner."

Crosby, Stills & Nash–*Crosby, Stills & Nash*

North of 809 Palm Avenue
West Hollywood, California

The house where famed rock photographer Henry Diltz shot CSN's 1969 debut album cover is long gone from this site. The album featured "Suite: Judy Blue Eyes," "Marrakesh Express" and "Guinnevere" among others. Interestingly, after the album cover was shot, it was pointed out that the singers were posed as Nash, Stills and Crosby. When they returned to re-shoot, the house had been demolished, so they settled for the photo they had.

Album Covers

The Doors–*Strange Days*

150-158 East 36th Street between Lexington and Third Avenues
New York, New York

This dark, 1967 classic featured the bluesy "Love Me Two Times" and the dramatic "People Are Strange." A mysterious,  surreal cover, it was photographed in this New York City courtyard known as Sniffen Court. (The original mid-18th century stables in the courtyard were converted to housing in the 1910s.)

Dr. John–*Dr. John's Gumbo*

Farmer John Company
Soto Street and Vernon
Vernon, California

Dr. John and his band cook through a dozen New Orleans classics on this 1972 gem, featuring the tunes of Professor Longhair, Huey Smith, Earl King, and Ray Charles. The cover was shot in front of the huge mural adorning the wall of The Farmer John Company (also seen in the movie *Carrie*).

Album Covers

The Eagles–*Hotel California*

Beverly Hills Hotel
9641 Sunset Boulevard
Beverly Hills, California
310-276-2251

The Beverly Hills Hotel (one of the most famous hotels in the world) served as the cover for the Eagles' Grammy-winning 1976 masterpiece, *Hotel California.* To get the shot of the "mission bell," a cherry picker was used (making it hard to imagine the angle when you stand in front of the hotel). The inside photo of the band in the hotel "lobby" was actually shot inside the Lido Apartments, located in Hollywood at 6500 Yucca Street.

Huey Lewis and the News–*Sports*

2 A.M. Club
382 Miller Avenue
Mill Valley, California
415-388-6036

"The Heart of Rock & Roll," "Heart and Soul," "I Want A New Drug"–these were the songs that launched Huey Lewis and the News on a national scale in 1983. The cover of their smash album *Sports* was shot at this popular Mill Valley bar, the 2 A.M. Club

Album Covers

King, Carole–*Tapestry*

8815 Appian Way
Los Angeles, California

This was the house where Carole King lived while recording *Tapestry*, then one of the bestselling albums in history. The famous cover of the album was taken sitting next to one of the windows in this house.

Led Zeppelin–*Physical Graffiti*

96 St. Mark's Place
New York, New York

This old brownstone served as the cover for the band's 1975 album, *Physical Graffiti.* If you compare the building to the album cover, you will notice that the only difference is that the third floor was removed from the final photo. Located in the lower right hand corner of the building is the "Physical Graffiti" used clothing store (named after the record came

out). This is also the building where Keith Richards sat with a bunch of Rastafari waiting for Mick Jagger in the Rolling Stones' 1981 video, "Waiting on a Friend."

Album Covers

McCartney, Paul–*Run Devil Run*

Miller's Rexall Drugs
87 Broad Street
Atlanta, Georgia

When Paul McCartney was passing through Atlanta, he saw Miller's Rexall Drugs, and the store inspired the title of his 1999 album. McCartney had been in town with two of his children. (His daughter Heather was unveiling her household creations at a trade show at the Americas Mart Atlanta.) After wandering into this funkier district of town, McCartney saw a bottle of bath salts called "Run Devil Run" in a Rexall shop window. He thought it was a good title for a song–then it became the name of the album (and inspired the album cover art as well).

Pink Floyd–*Wish You Were Here*

Warner Brothers Studios
4210 West Olive Avenue
Burbank, California

Considered by many to be the ultimate Pink Floyd effort, 1975's *Wish You Were Here* is a thematic LP dedicated to Pink Floyd's original frontman, Syd Barrett, who'd burned out years before. The famous cover photo was shot on the lot at Warner Brothers Studios in Burbank, with a guy who was actually on fire (not a photo after-effect). Though the studio is private, VIP tours are offered and while on the tour it is possible to view this location.

Ronstadt, Linda–*Livin' in the U.S.A.*

Irv's Burgers
8289 Santa Monica Boulevard
West Hollywood, California

The inner sleeve of Linda Ronstadt's 1978 smash LP *Livin' in the U.S.A.* featured the singer sitting here at Irv's Burgers.

Album Covers

Simon & Garfunkel–*Wednesday Morning 3 A.M.*

Fifth Avenue and 53rd Street Subway Station
New York, New York

Released in October 1964, *Wednesday Morning, 3 A.M.* was Simon & Garfunkel's first album. An all-acoustic record, it set the table for the huge success the pair would find in just a year.

Spirit–*The Family That Plays Together*

Sunset Highland Motel
6830 Sunset Boulevard
Hollywood, California

The classic 1968 release from this popular California band featured the FM staple "I Got a Line on You." The cover was shot at the Sunset Highland Motel, just across from Hollywood High School. (On January 2, 1997, Spirit guitarist and bandleader Randy California–born Randy Craig Wolfe–drowned off the coast of Molokai, Hawaii.)

The Sweet–*Desolation Boulevard*

8852 Sunset Boulevard
Hollywood, California

The Sweet shot the cover of this 1975 album near the front of a Los Angeles rock 'n' roll club called The Central. Today it's the site of the Viper Room, where River Phoenix died.

The Youngbloods–*Elephant Mountain*

Elephant Mountain
Marin County, California

Released in April 1969, this was the third Youngbloods' LP and their first after the departure of founder Jerry Corbitt. Produced by Charlie Daniels, the album featured an eclectic mix of jazz, blues, country, and rock from the group who sang the smash hit "Get Together." The cover featured the scenic landscape of Northern California's Elephant Mountain.

Martin, Dean/Rolling Stones

The Hollywood Palace
1735 Vine Street
Hollywood, California
213-462-3000

Opened in 1927, the Hollywood Palace is where Groucho Marx filmed his TV quiz series *You Bet Your Life.* It was also the site of the *Merv Griffin Show*, and for a TV variety show called, appropriately enough, *The Hollywood Palace* (hosted by Jimmy Durante), which showcased a weekly cavalcade of superstars. But it was also here that Dean

Martin insulted the Rolling Stones on their first American national TV appearance. After the Stones played, a guy in a suit was shown bouncing on a trampoline. Martin slurred, "This is the father of the Rolling Stones. He's been trying to kill himself ever since."

Media Sound

311 West 57th Street
New York, New York
212-307-7228

Today, it's Le Bar Bat Restaurant, but this former Baptist church was once Media Sound Recording Studios, where the Rolling Stones recorded *Tattoo You,* where John Lennon recorded *Walls and Bridges,* where Lou Reed cut *New York* and where Marc Bolan/T. Rex recorded *Electric Warrior* (which featured the single, "Bang a Gong").

MTV

Unitel Video
515 West 57th Street
New York, New York

This was where MTV was launched on August 1, 1981. Today, they've moved downtown a bit to 1515 Broadway, where their state-of-the-art, "open-faced" complex is visible from all over Times Square.

Partridge Family House

Warner Bros. Ranch
Burbank, California

Remember *The Partridge Family*? It was a memorable TV show about a widowed mother and her five children, living in a small fictional town in Northern California. In the pilot episode, the musical family records a pop song in their garage. Through the marketing efforts of the 10-year-old son Danny, the song becomes a hit, and the family begins touring the country in a colorful school bus, performing their music in various types of venues. The episodes would often contrast their suburban life with the adventures of a show-biz family "on the road." The series originally ran from September 25, 1970, until August 31, 1974, on the ABC television network, as part of the Friday night lineup with *The Brady Bunch*. It had several subsequent runs in syndication.

The story was inspired by, and loosely based on the Cowsills, a real singing family in the late '60s. In fact, in its early development the Cowsill children were approached to be featured on the show, though that idea was quickly discarded. The show starred Shirley Jones as mother Shirley Partridge and David Cassidy (Jones's real life stepson) as her son Keith. The remaining Partridge children were played by Susan Dey as Laurie, Danny

Bonaduce as Danny, Jeremy Gelbwaks (later replaced by Brian Forster) as Chris, and Suzanne Crough as Tracy Partridge. Dave Madden played Reuben Kincaid, who was their manager and family friend. Today, the Partridge Family house on the Warner Ranch still stands, and nearby is the soundstage where interiors for the show were filmed.

The Record Plant

321 West 44th Street
New York, New York

This recording studio is a virtual rock 'n' roll museum, having been the site where Bruce Springsteen cut *Born to Run* and *Darkness of the Edge of Town,* and also where Hendrix recorded *Electric Ladyland* in 1968. On the night John Lennon was murdered in 1980, he had just left a mixing session from this studio.

"Rock Around the Clock"

Pythian Temple Studios
135 West 70th Street
New York, New York

In April of 1954, Bill Haley and the Comets entered a recording studio here and recorded the seminal rock 'n' roll classic, "Rock Around the Clock," which held down the number one spot for eight weeks and went on to sell 45 million copies worldwide. Haley,

who performed on the revival circuit throughout the 1960s and '70s, did get to see his signature song become a U.S. hit for the second time in 1974 when "Rock Around the Clock" appeared on the soundtrack for both the George Lucas film *American Graffiti* and the hit TV show *Happy Days.*

When Haley recorded his landmark tune, this building was a meeting hall for the Knights of Pythias, and Decca records used the building's ballroom as a recording studio. The building still maintains its odd, temple-like appearance, but it is now a condo. Haley died from a heart attack at his home in Harlingen, Texas, on February 9, 1981.

Rock 'n' Roll High School

El Segundo High School
640 Main Street
El Segundo, California

Rock 'n' Roll High School was the classic 1979 film produced by Roger Corman, directed by Allan Arkush, and featuring the Ramones. (The film also starred P.J. Soles, Vincent Van Patten, and Clint Howard. Darby Crash of the punk band The Germs also played an extra in this film.)

The main character, Riff Randall (P.J. Soles), is known as the biggest Ramones fan at Vince Lombardi High School. She waits in line for three days to get tickets to see the Ramones, hoping to meet Joey Ramone so she can give him a song she wrote for the Ramones, "Rock N' Roll High School." The Ramones like it so much they help her take over her high school, and make it a Rock 'n' Roll High School.

In addition to several songs by the Ramones, the soundtrack for the film includes songs by Brian Eno, the Paley Brothers, Paul McCartney & Wings, Nick Lowe, Fleetwood Mac, Devo, Alice Cooper, and Chuck Berry, among others. The movie was shot at various locations around Southern California in addition to El Segundo High School, including the Mayan Theater (1038 Hill Street, Downtown Los Angeles), Mira Costa High School (701 S. Peck Avenue, Manhattan Beach), and the Roxy Theater in Los Angeles (9009 W. Sunset Blvd., Los Angeles).

Running On Empty

Of all the concept albums in the 1970s, Jackson Browne's *Running On Empty* was one of the most unique. Recorded live in (among other places) hotel rooms, on buses, and in rehearsal halls, it strung together an earthy motif of road-as-metaphor songs that took the listener inside the intimate circle of a traveling musician. Here are two of the "public" places where he recorded songs for the album.

"The Road"
Recorded in room 301 of the Cross Keys Inn
5100 Falls Road
Baltimore, Maryland
410-532-6900

"Cocaine" & "Shakey Town"
Recorded in room 124 of the Holiday Inn (now a
Comfort Inn)
3080 S. Route 157
Edwardsville, Illinois
618-656-4900

Saturday Night Fever

Criteria Studios
1755 NE 149th Street
Miami, Florida

This Miami studio has recorded many classic songs, like James Brown's "I Feel Good," Derek & the Dominoes' "Layla," and Brook Benton's "Rainy Night in Georgia." But it was the Bee Gees' *Saturday Night Fever,* also recorded here, that became one of the biggest selling records in history.

School of Rock

Buckley Country Day School
2 I.U. Willets Road
Roslyn, New York

Many of the school interiors from the 2003 film *School of Rock,* starring Jack Black, were shot here at this school on Long Island.

Sea-Saint Studios

3809 Clematis Avenue
New Orleans, Louisiana

This is one of the Big Easy's most famous recording studios, opened by Allen Toussaint in 1973. The Pointer Sisters, Albert King, Dr. John, and many others have recorded here over the years, and in the early 1970s Paul McCartney and Wings recorded their classic *Venus and Mars* album here. More recently, Lenny Kravitz and Michelle Shocked worked here.

Sigma Sound Studios

212 North 12th Street
Philadelphia, Pennsylvania
215-561-3660

When engineer Joe Tarsia took over this studio in 1968, it all but marked the birth of the sound known as "Philadelphia Soul." The Stylistics, O Jays, Delfonics, the Spinners, Harold Melvin and the Blue Notes, and many others all created early 1970s magic here (David Bowie even recorded *Young Americans* at Sigma). The studio continues as a force today, though TSOP (The Sound of Philadelphia, as it was called) has yet to be equaled in terms of commercial impact. The studio has since changed its name to Sigma Sound House.

Sunset Sound

6650 Sunset Boulevard
Hollywood, California
323-469-1186

When musician Tutti Camarata opened his studio in 1958, his main client was Walt Disney (and many soundtracks were cut here.) But once the 1960s kicked in, rock 'n' roll took over and this unpretentious little building near the intersection of Cherokee and Sunset became enormously popular for musicians seeking a recording studio. Led Zeppelin recorded their second and fourth albums here, the latter of which included "Stairway to Heaven." The Doors did the majority of their recording here, and the Rolling Stones cut *Beggars Banquet* here. Other famous recordings include James Taylor's "Fire and Rain," Janis Joplin's "Me and Bobby McGee," Michael Jackson's "Beat It," and hundreds of others.

Synchro Sound

330 Newbury Street
Boston, Massachusetts

Today it's a phone store, but back in the 1980s this was the site of Synchro Sound, the famed studio of the Boston-based band The Cars, where much of their material in the 1980s was recorded as well as records for many other bands, including Romeo Void. Before it was called Synchro Sound, it had been Intermedia studios, the place where another Boston band, Aerosmith, recorded their first smash hit, *Dream On.*

This is Spinal Tap

Raymond Theatre
129 North Raymond Avenue
Pasadena, California
818-541-9522

This classic 1921 vaudeville theater (also used in *Pulp Fiction*) is where many of the concert scenes from this 1984 "Rockumentary" were shot by Rob Reiner. (From the Stonehenge production "extravaganza" to the stage pods, one of which trapped bassist Derek Smalls, played by Harry Shearer). From 1979 through 1991, the Raymond Theatre was known as the live music venue Perkins Palace, and many memorable concerts were presented here, from Fleetwood Mac to Van Halen.

Thriller Video

1345 Carroll Avenue
Glendale, California

In the 1982 music video *Thriller*, Michael Jackson is chased by ghouls through a neighborhood of old Victorian homes, and this is the main house that was used.

The Village Recorder Studios

1616 Butler Avenue
West Los Angeles, California
310-478-8227

This former Masonic Temple (built in 1922) has played host to some of rock 'n' roll's most important recordings, including the Rolling Stones' *Goat's Head Soup*, Eric Clapton's *After Midnight* (as well as his Grammy Award-winning "Tears in Heaven,") most Steely Dan records (including *Aja*), and works by Rikki Lee Jones, Bob Dylan, the Red Hot Chili Peppers, and many more. It was also here in 1978 that Studio D was famously renovated for Fleetwood Mac's legendary recording of *Tusk*. (Eric Clapton was also photographed here for his first solo album.)

Wally Heider's Studio

245 Hyde Street
San Francisco, California
415-441-8934

Wally Heider was one of the most renowned recording engineers in history, and here at the site of his former studio he recorded many artists including the Jefferson Airplane (*Volunteers*); Crosby, Stills, Nash and Young (*Deja Vu*); Creedence Clearwater Revival (*Green River* and other albums); and the Grateful Dead (*American Beauty*). Other artists to record here were Moby Grape, James Brown, Paul Simon, Merle Haggard, Journey, the Dead Kennedys, The Pointer Sisters, and Herbie Hancock. The building that housed Wally Heider's Studio is still a top quality recording studio, today called Hyde Street Studios.

Walker, Jerry Jeff

New Orleans Jail
730 South White Street
New Orleans, Louisiana

Singer/songwriter Jerry Jeff Walker was cooling off here one night in 1967 after being picked up for disorderly conduct. Good thing, too, because during that night he wrote the classic song, "Mr. Bojangles," which became a huge hit for the Nitty Gritty Dirt Band.

"We Are the World"

A&M Studios (now Henson Productions)
1416 North La Brea Boulevard
Hollywood, California

The concept for "We Are the World" came from a group of British artists known as "Band Aid," who had gotten together in late 1984 to record a song called "Do They Know It's Christmas?" Given that song's success, singer Harry Belafonte got together Lionel Ritchie, Michael Jackson, and producer Quincy Jones to come up with an American anthem.

Jackson and Ritchie spent just two hours writing the song, which they wanted to record right after the American Music Awards. Immediately after the award show, 45 artists arrived here to record. The result was 21 lead vocal performances from the likes of Paul Simon, Billy Joel, Tina Turner, Huey Lewis, Bruce Springsteen, Bob Dylan, Daryl Hall, and many more. The song went on to sell 7.5 million copies in the U.S. alone, and raise more than $50 million.

Sweet Home Chicago:
Blues and Jazz Shrines

Antone's

213 W. 5th Street
Austin, Texas
512-320-8424

Antone's

11th anniversary celebration

JIMMY ROGERS
SUNNYLAND SLIM
PINETOP PERKINS
HUBERT SUMLIN
MATT "GUITAR" MURPHY
MEMPHIS SLIM
ANGELA STREHLI
...AND MORE

JULY 8 - 15

A true blues palace, this may be Austin's most famous music venue, which is saying a lot. Live blues is featured seven nights a week and Jimmy Vaughan, Joe Ely, and Charlie Saxton are among the legends who have performed here. Antone's also supports some of Austin's most promising up-and-coming artists.

Blues Alley

Clarksdale, Mississippi

Blues Alley is the name for Clarksdale's Historic Blues District. It is here that you'll find Clarksdale Station, the newly renovated passenger depot of the old Illinois Central Railroad and, just about a hundred yards away, the Delta Blues Museum.

The station is extremely significant to the history of the blues. After all, this is where many famous blues musicians such as Muddy Waters boarded the train to Chicago, seeking jobs and a potential career in music. The Delta Blues Museum houses a collection of memorabilia from B.B. King, Sonny Boy Williamson, Bessie Smith, and Muddy Waters, along with many other exhibits. The Delta Blues Museum is located at 1 Blues Alley (662-627-6820).

Bobbysoxers

Paramount Theater
Broadway Avenue and 43rd Street
New York, New York

Bandleader and clarinetist Benny Goodman had been on a grueling coast-to-coast tour that had been mostly unsuccessful until he reached the Palomar Ballroom in Los Angeles. There, he found "his" audience, one that went completely wild over his "swing" sound, setting off a worldwide sensation.

Goodman brought the orchestra back to New York's Paramount Theater, and just like out west, the audience went wild—dancing up a frenzy in the aisles. "Bobbysoxers" had been born, and with them, the "jitterbug" dance craze. Goodman became known as the "King of Swing" for the rest of his storied career.

Enter Frank Sinatra. The skinny, wavy-haired kid in the bow tie started out singing on a Major Bowes amateur radio broadcast. His career gained momentum in the Big Band era, under Henry James and Tommy Dorsey, then took off like wildfire at the Paramount Theater in New York, where he opened on December 31, 1942.

Bobbysoxers went crazy, screaming in delight, jitterbugging in the aisles, fainting, and eventually spilling out into Times Square, causing such havoc that a riot squad had to be called.

Central Avenue

From Downtown to 103rd Street
Los Angeles, California

During its heyday in the 1940s, Central Avenue was to L.A. what 52nd Street was to New York: a hotbed of jazz joints, dance halls, and nightclubs. Along this sprawling avenue, one could see everyone from Charlie Parker to Duke Ellington to hundreds of other musicians, singers, and entertainers.

Though much of the area has fallen into decline, the landmark Dunbar Hotel retains much of its old glory at 4225 Central Avenue (corner of 42nd Street; 323-234-7882). Beginning in the 1920s, the Dunbar, which was specifically built for black patrons to combat racist practices of other hotels, was like a second home for many out-of-town musicians. Ellington, Basie, Billie Holiday—they all played here and they all stayed here.

Chess Records

2120 South Michigan Avenue
Chicago, Illinois
312-808-1286

This is one of the most famous addresses in rock 'n' roll history. After settling into this two-story building in 1957, the Chess Bothers (Polish-Jewish immigrants Leonard and Phil) continued the tradition they had started 10 years previously of recording the jazz players who performed at the brothers' nightclubs. Only now they had a permanent address and a real recording studio, as opposed to the various rented storefront offices they'd been using.

Over the years, many classic records were cut at Chess. Chuck Berry recorded "Johnny B. Goode" there on February 29, 1958, and Bo Diddley, Muddy Waters, Howlin' Wolf, Willie Dixon, Ramsey Lewis, James Moody, and many other blues greats recorded here.

British blues bands like the Rolling Stones and the Yardbirds treated Chess like Mecca—the Stones even cut a song called "2120 Michigan Avenue" in homage. After years of being used as a dance theater, today it's been restored and tours are available.

John Coltrane

Birthplace

**Hamlet Avenue at Bridges Street
Hamlet, North Carolina**

A plaque here marks the birthplace of legendary jazz saxophonist and composer John Coltrane (1926–1967). Coltrane began playing tenor saxophone as a teen and worked with numerous big bands before coming into his own in the mid-1950s. He became a major stylist while playing as a sideman with Miles Davis. Coltrane made a number of influential recordings, among them the modal-jazz classics "My Favorite Things" (1961) and "A Love Supreme" (1964).

Childhood Home

**200 South Centennial Street
High Point, North Carolina**

John Coltrane (1926–1967) grew up in North Carolina. The commemorative marker at the corner of Centennial Street and Commerce Avenue is located near his boyhood home on Underhill Street.

"Blue Train" House

**1511 North 33rd Street
Philadelphia, Pennsylvania**

In 1952, after returning home from the Navy and with funds provided by the GI Bill of Rights, John Coltrane, saxophonist, family man, and native of Hamlet, North Carolina purchased this three-story brick row house. The house was situated within the area known by locals as Strawberry Mansion, a working-class neighborhood populated at that time by families of diverse ethnic backgrounds. The 26-year-old Coltrane bought the house for himself, his mother, his aunt, and his cousin, and it is here where he composed the legendary "Blue Train" and several other tunes.

Cotton Club

644 Lenox Avenue at 142nd Street
Harlem, New York

This was the location of the most famous nightclub in Harlem, the fabled Cotton Club. The actual building was torn down in the 1950s to make way for a housing project. The posh club was home to everyone from gangsters to celebrities throughout the 1920s and into the mid-1930s, at which time the club was moved to West 48th Street after the Harlem race riots. It was bandleader Duke Ellington's home base for four years and Cab Calloway's for three, and played host to famous black artists from Louis Armstrong to Ethel Waters.

Davis, Miles

312 West 77th Street
New York, New York

This red townhouse is a former Russian Orthodox church and was jazzman Miles Davis's home from the early 1960s through the early 1980s. He recorded several classic albums while living here, including *Miles Smiles* and *Bitches Brew*. He left in the early 1980s after becoming involved with actress Cicely Tyson (whom he eventually married).

Ellington, Duke

2129 Ward Place Northwest
Washington, D.C.

A plaque on the office building that's here marks it as the spot where the great Edward Kennedy "Duke" Ellington was born on April 29, 1899. The innovative composer, bandleader, and pianist would become recognized as one of the greatest jazz composers and performers in the world. Nicknamed "Duke" by a boyhood friend who admired his regal air, the name stuck and became forever associated with the finest creations in big band and vocal jazz.

His genius for instrumental combinations, improvisation, and arranging brought the world exquisite works like "Mood Indigo," "Sophisticated Lady," and the symphonic suites "Black, Brown, and Beige: a Tone Parallel to the History of the Negro in America" and "Harlem: a Tone Parallel to Harlem."

A Great Day in Harlem

17 East 126th Street
Harlem, New York

Jean Bach's documentary *A Great Day in Harlem* told the story of a day in 1958 when many of America's greatest jazz artists were gathered at 10 A.M.–an ungodly hour for musicians who had played until dawn that very morning–to this stoop for a photograph. Amazingly, many showed up, and the photograph, taken by Art Kane and featuring Dizzie Gillespie, Charles Mingus, Thelonious Monk, Marian McPartland, Art Blakey, Milt Hinton, Count Basie, Sonny Hawkins, Lester Young, and dozens of other old lions and upcoming stars assembled on and around the steps of a nondescript brownstone in Harlem, became famous the world over.

Esquire published the photo in its January 1959 issue. As well, the photo was also a key object in Steven Spielberg's film, *The Terminal*. The film starred Tom Hanks as Viktor Navorski, who came to the United States in search of Benny Golson's autograph to complete his father's collection of autographs by the jazz musicians pictured in the classic 1958 photo.

Billie Holiday

First New York Apartment

108 West 109th Street
New York, New York

When Billie Holiday first arrived in New York during the Depression she moved into this five-story apartment building with her mom. While living here, their place became a sort of crash pad for all kinds of hand-to-mouth musicians on whom the Holidays took pity.

Also while living here, Holiday discovered that her future was not as a dancer, but as a singer. She failed a dance audition at a club called Pod's and Jerry's (at 168 West 132nd Street), but a piano player there asked if she could sing. Sing she did, and that's where she first started appearing before an audience.

Last New York Apartment

26 West 87th Street
New York, New York

This was Billie Holiday's last New York apartment, where she lived during the final year of her life. By now she was a sad and lonely singer, whose career had all but dried up. Her health was poor, and on May 31, 1959, she collapsed and fell into a coma. She was rushed to the hospital and treated for drug addiction and alcoholism. While she was there, police found heroin in her room (many believe it was planted by a "well-wisher"). Her condition deteriorated and she died in the hospital on July 17th.

Metropolitan Hospital

1901 First Avenue
New York, New York

The great jazz singer Billie Holiday died here (under police guard) in room 6A-12 on Friday, July 17, 1959. She was just 44 years old. Holiday is buried in St. Raymond's Cemetery in the Bronx, right beside her mother.

Jazz is Born I

Congo Square (now called Armstrong Park)
Located off North Rampart Street, near the intersection of St. Philip Street
New Orleans, Louisiana

In the early 1800s, this area was known as Congo Square and was the only legal place where slaves could get together on Sunday afternoon. On those days, they would gather to play drums, gourds, banjo-like instruments, marimbas, and such European instruments as the violin, tambourine, and triangle—creating what many consider to be the origins of American jazz music. Today, Congo Square has become a part of Armstrong Park, a Jazz Historical Park named for legendary trumpeter Louis Armstrong, who was born in New Orleans in 1900.

Jazz is Born II

Storyville
Iberville Street between Basin Street and Claiborne Avenue
New Orleans, Louisiana

Some music experts theorize that this was the true birthplace of jazz. For about 20 years at the turn of the century, this was New Orleans's legal red-light district, and many early jazz players were employed in this area at local clubs. All but shut down in 1917, this area can be located by looking for the Iberville Housing Project.

Robert Johnson

Johnson, Robert

**109 Young Street
Greenwood, Mississippi**

On the night of Saturday, August 13, 1938, blues legend Robert Johnson was playing guitar in a juke joint located on the outskirts of Greenwood, Mississippi—in the back room of a place called the Shaples General Store at Three Forks. (The store, which is gone now, was located where Highways 82 and 49E cross today.) Legend says this is when Johnson was poisoned by a jealous husband with either strychnine or lye.

In the middle of the night, Johnson was supposedly taken to a house in nearby Greenwood, where his condition worsened. Three days later, on August 16th, he died at the house that stood at this address (a new house now stands in its place). Johnson was buried in the Mt. Zion churchyard before being re-interred in the nearby Mt. Payne graveyard.

Johnson, Robert

**The Crossroads
Clarksdale, Mississippi
Intersection of Highways 61 and 49**

This is the legendary crossroads where, according to the myth, in the dark Mississippi night seminal blues artist Robert Johnson traded his soul to the devil for fame and guitar-playing genius.

Robert Johnson

Johnson, Robert

Gunter Hotel
205 East Houston Street
San Antonio, Texas
210-227-3241

The Blue Bonnet hotel at the southeast corner of Pecan and St. Mary's Streets was torn down in 1988. For many years, it was believed that legendary blues guitarist Robert Johnson made several landmark recordings in a studio in the building in the 1930s. However, it eventually was determined his recordings were made in the Gunter Hotel and

a memorial marker in the hotel lobby commemorates the Robert Johnson sessions. (Johnson's only other recording site took place in Dallas, Texas, at 508 Park at a building that is still unmarked today).

Johnson, who died at the age of 27 in 1938, recorded only twice, for a total of 29 songs. His first recordings, and the largest body of his recorded work, took place at the Gunter from November 23-27, 1936. Songs included in those sessions were "Terraplane Blues," "Cross Road Blues," "Sweet Home Chicago," and "I Believe I'll Dust My Broom." Johnson's influence is cited as primary in the musical careers

of numerous artists, and he was inducted into the Rock and Roll Hall of Fame in 1986.

Leadbelly

414 East 10th Street
New York, New York

Famed bluesman Leadbelly (Huddie Ledbetter) lived in this building throughout the 1940s. While residing here, he entertained the likes of many legendary musicians including Woody Guthrie and Pete Seeger. Leadbelly had become a monumental figure in the history of folk music. He was "discovered" by the influential father-son team of folk-rock historians John and Alan Lomax while in prison in Louisiana, where he was recorded on portable equipment.

It is claimed by Alan Lomax that the state governor, O.K. Allen, pardoned Leadbelly after Allen heard his recordings, which supposedly included an appeal by song directed to Allen. Leadbelly subsequently toured extensively but ended up back in prison in 1939, convicted of assault. (He served four separate prison terms for his violent behavior.) It was after this last prison term that Leadbelly moved to this apartment in 1940.

Minton's

Cecil Hotel
210 West 118th Street
Harlem, New York
212-864-5281

Bebop music is thought to have been "born" here in the early 1940s when Thelonious Monk, Fats Waller, Charlie Parker, Dizzy Gillespie, Kenny Clarke, and others were allowed to improvise by the club owner. Sessions were often after other gigs in the late hours, so they rapidly become a favorite of top jazz musicians. Legend has it that Fats Waller coined the musical term "Bop" when describing improvisational riffs by the younger musicians. The playhouse now includes a housing unit for the elderly.

Charlie Parker

Birdland

1678 Broadway Avenue (near 52nd Street)
New York, New York

The original location of the club that jazz legend Charlie Parker opened in 1949 was in the basement of the building at this address. Parker's problems with drug addiction forced him to ultimately be banned from the club that bore his name, and one night he even showed up in his pajamas after having snuck out of a nearby hospital where he was attempting to detox.

Camarillo State Mental Hospital

California State University, Channel Islands
One University Drive
Camarillo, California

Until 1997, this was the Camarillo State Mental Hospital, where jazz legend Charlie Parker spent six months in 1947. The brilliant sax player had suffered a breakdown that, coupled with heroin and alcohol abuse, led to his confinement at the hospital. Parker was released from Camarillo in late January 1947. He eventually died in New York City on March 12, 1955, at the age of just 36.

Dewey Square

Adam Clayton Powell Boulevard and 118th Street
New York, New York

This small, triangle-shaped park is where Charlie Parker sat and created a musical work called "Dewey Square." Today, the park is called A. Philip Randolph Triangle.

Charlie Parker

New York Home

151 Avenue B
New York, New York

From 1950 to 1954, this was the home of the bop saxophonist Parker, his friend Chan, and their two sons. Parker is honored with a building plaque. He is also remembered with the Charlie Parker Jazz Festival held every summer in Tompkins Square Park.

Rodgers, Jimmie

Hotel Taft
61 Seventh Avenue
New York, New York

Singer Jimmie Rodgers, known as "The Singing Brakeman" and "America's Blue Yodeler" died here at the Hotel Taft. Also thought of as "The Father of Country Music," the 35-year-old singer had suffered from complications due to TB when, numbed by morphine and alcohol, he succumbed to the disease on May 26, 1933. The list of those whom Rodgers influenced directly is very long and includes Gene Autry, Bill Monroe, Ernest Tubb, Hank Snow, Hank Williams, Johnny Cash, Merle Haggard and many others. While the hotel is long gone, a TGI Friday's restaurant occupies the site.

Smith, Bessie

G.T. Thomas Hospital (now the Riverside Hotel)
615 Sunflower Avenue
Clarksdale, Mississippi

Bessie Smith, known as the Empress of the Blues, died here in 1937 after an infamous auto accident on Highway 61, outside of town. She was in a car driven by her companion (and Lionel Hampton's uncle) Richard Morgan. In the accident, Smith was critically injured. A doctor arrived and ordered that she be taken to a "colored" hospital in Clarksdale. However, she had lost a lot of blood and ended up dying at the hospital—she was just 43 years old.

Shortly after her death, John Hammond wrote in *Down Beat* magazine that she might have died because she was initially refused entrance to a white hospital and her treatment was delayed while she was taken to a black hospital. Although Hammond later recanted his story, playwright Edward Albee went ahead and wrote the play *The Death of Bessie Smith*, which forever branded the story in the public's mind.

Tin Pan Alley

**28th Street between 6th Avenue and Broadway
New York, New York**

Tin Pan Alley is where music publishers would peddle songs to artists and producers from the nearby theaters. This important stretch was the center of music publishing at the beginning of the 20th century, when the music business was the sheet music business. The publishers on the street all hired "pluggers" to play songs for prospective customers; the din from all their pianos playing at once gave the street its nickname. The street is now a center for clothing and accessories wholesalers.

Tutwiler Train Station

**Tutwiler, Mississippi
(about 15 miles down Highway 49 from Clarksdale)**

A plaque here and a commemorative mural near the foundation of the old train station mark where W. C. Handy made his remarkable blues discovery in 1902 or 1903. Handy wrote later of falling asleep while waiting for a late night train and being awakened by the sound of a lone figure playing a guitar, using only the edge of his pocketknife as a slide and singing about the place "where the Southern crosses the Dog."

W.C. Handy

The W.C. Handy House

Issaquena Street
Clarksdale, Mississippi

W.C. Handy lived in Clarksdale from 1903 to 1905, and it was during these formative years that he collected many blues songs. Though he was by no means a Delta bluesman, Handy is referred to by many as the "Father of the Blues" because of the love and attention he gave the music, and also because he helped bring blues music to the world.

Handy was a student of music as a child, playing the cornet, and later travelling the South with dance bands, playing minstrel and tent shows. Handy had heard something akin to the blues as early as 1892, but it was while waiting for an overdue train in Tutwiler, Mississippi, in 1902 or 1903 that he heard a shadowy bluesman playing slide guitar and singing about "goin' where the Southern crosses the Dog," (which referred to the junction of the Southern and the Yazoo and Mississippi Valley railroads farther south near Moorhead). Handy called it "the weirdest music I had ever heard," but from that moment on the seed had been planted—it was the true "Birth of the Blues."

W.C. Handy left Clarksdale and settled in Memphis, Tennessee, around 1909, using Beale Street's Pee Wee's Saloon as his headquarters. His greatest contributions to blues music were his compositions "Memphis Blues," "St. Louis Blues," "Yellow Dog Blues" and "Beale Street Blues." Handy died in New York City in 1958 and is today honored with the annual W.C. Handy Awards—the Blues Foundation's equivalent to the Grammys. (His house is no longer located at this vacant site.)

W.C. Handy

W.C. Handy House II

352 Beale Street
Memphis, Tennessee
901-522-1556

This is the W.C. Handy house, which was originally located at 659 Jennette Place. It was here that the Father of the Blues wrote such classics as "Yellow Dog Blues" and "Beale Street Blues." Items that belonged to Handy are featured in this turn-of-the-20th-century frame house, which is open Monday through Saturday 10:00 A.M.-5:00 P.M. in summer; hours vary the rest of the year.

"Where the Southern Crosses the Dog"

Train station
Moorehead, Mississippi

The actual site the bluesman was singing about is located here in the tiny town of Moorehead, where the two railroad lines that were prominent in the Delta at the turn of the century meet. The Southern and the Yazoo and Mississippi Valley (known as the Yellow Dog) railroads cross at right angles here in Moorehead, and some blues experts say that *this* was actually the crossroads where Robert Johnson made the deal to sell his soul—not the more famous crossroads where Highways 61 and 49 meet in Clarksdale. A sign commemorates the exact spot "where the Southern crosses the Dog," a spot which was later often referred to in blues lyrics and made famous by W.C. Handy in his song "Yellow Dog Blues."

DON'T FEAR THE REAPER: HOMICIDES, SUICIDES, AND A BAD MOON RISING

Ace, Johnny

City Auditorium
615 Louisiana Street
Houston, Texas

Johnny Ace was a promising black R&B singer in the early 1950s. During his short career, Ace recorded several other hit "heart ballads" including "Pledging My Love," "Cross My Heart," "The Clock," "Saving My Love For You," and "Please Forgive Me." He accidentally shot and killed himself while playing Russian roulette backstage on Christmas Day 1954. His last words, to Willie Mae "Big Mama" Thornton, were: "I'll show you that it won't shoot."

Ace's recordings continued to gain popularity after his death, and he was immortalized in the song "The Late Great Johnny Ace" by Paul Simon. Demolished in the summer of 1963, City Auditorium is now the site of another popular theater, Jones Hall.

Allman, Duane

Bartlett Street and Hillcrest Avenue
Macon, Georgia

It was almost dusk on October 29, 1971, when guitarist Duane Allman, trying to avoid a flatbed truck, crashed his motorcycle and died at this intersection. Just about a year later, Allman Brothers Band bassist Berry Oakley died in a similar accident just two blocks south of Allman's crash site.

Belushi, John

Chateau Marmont Hotel
Bungalow #3
8221 Sunset Boulevard
Hollywood, California
800-242-8328

Built in 1929, this hotel has been host to many major stars of Hollywood and visiting celebrities from all over the world. And it was here that comic actor John Belushi died from a drug overdose. The last day of his life, Belushi had stopped at the Guitar Center to pick up a guitar that had been custom-made for Les Paul. After that, he started drinking at a club above the Roxy Theater called On the Rox. Lastly, he visited the Rainbow Bar & Grill, where he had a bowl of lentil soup. Then it was back to bungalow 3 at the Chateau Marmont.

Belushi was with Catherine Smith by now, and he had her inject him with a speedball—a combination of heroin and cocaine. Belushi overdosed, but Smith thought he had just passed out, so she left for a while, only to return to find pandemonium had broken out after Bill Wallace—one of Belushi's friends—had discovered his body. They tried frantically to resuscitate him, but were unsuccessful. John Belushi was pronounced dead the morning of March 5, 1982.

Catherine Smith was released after questioning, but then gave an interview to the *National Enquirer,* admitting that she had injected John Belushi with the speedball. She was re-arrested and later served time in prison for the administration of the deadly combination of drugs.

Bono, Sonny

Heavenly Ski Resort
Immediately west of the Nevada border, south of Stateline
and South Lake Tahoe.
800-2HEAVEN

On January 5, 1998, the 62-year-old congressman and former pop star was killed after skiing into a 40-foot pine tree. Bono, who was on vacation with his wife and two kids, skied off the main trail of the Upper Orion run into the tougher-to-navigate wooded area.

Buckley, Tim

Santa Monica Hospital
2021 Arizona Avenue
Santa Monica, California

It was in the emergency room here where 28-year-old singer/songwriter Tim Buckley died at 9:42 P.M. on June 29, 1975. At first, authorities suspected that Buckley had suffered a heart attack, but then the county coroner's ruled his death was due to a heroin/morphine overdose (combined with alcohol). Ten days later, Richard Keeling, a research assistant in the music department at UCLA, was arraigned on charges of second-degree murder. According to reports, Keeling allegedly furnished Buckley with the lethal dose of drugs. Under California law, this constitutes grounds for a murder indictment.

Cline, Patsy

Mount Carmel Road (2.2 miles west of Camden)
Camden, Tennessee
877-584-8395

Thirty-year-old country singing star Patsy Cline had traveled to Kansas City to do a benefit concert for a popular disk jockey who had died there. Returning to Nashville in a private plane piloted by her manager, Randy Hughes, they encountered bad weather and crashed in a remote, wooded area near Camden, Tennessee, on March 5, 1963. Both were killed in the crash, as were country performers Cowboy Copas and Hawkshaw Hawkins. The crash site (about a three-mile hike off the main highway, 641 North) is marked with a commemorative plaque honoring the four victims.

Chapin, Harry

Near Exit 40
Long Island Expressway
Long Island, New York

On July 18, 1981, fans waited in Eisenhower Park's Lakeside Theater (located in East Meadow with entrances on Hempstead Turnpike at East Meadow Avenue and at the intersection of Merrick and Stewart Avenue), for a free concert by the popular troubadour Harry Chapin. But instead of hearing hits like "Cats In the Cradle" or "Taxi," fans were told by security that there wouldn't be a show that night because Chapin had been killed on his way to the venue, the victim of a fiery collision between his car and a tractor-trailer on the Long Island Expressway.

Chapin had been driving west in his blue Volkswagen Rabbit when he veered into the path of the truck. Chapin, historically a bad driver whose license had been revoked after several suspensions, was pulled alive from the wreckage but died soon after from massive internal bleeding.

Cobain, Kurt

171 Lake Washington Boulevard East
Seattle, Washington

On the morning of April 8, 1994, an electrician arrived at Kurt Cobain's house in Seattle and spotted what he thought was a mannequin lying on the floor of a small cottage/greenhouse above the garage. Upon closer examination, he realized that what he saw was the body of a young male with a shotgun on his chest. The police arrived and a body, dressed in jeans, a shirt, and Converse trainers, was removed for identification. Fingerprints confirmed that it was Kurt Cobain, Nirvana's much tormented frontman.

In 1996, Cobain's former wife Courtney Love announced that she was tearing down the garage/greenhouse where Kurt killed himself to discourage fans from visiting.

Cooke, Sam

Hacienda Motel (now Polaris Motel)
9137 South Figueroa Street
Los Angeles, California

Popular soul singer Sam Cooke ("You Send Me," "Wonderful World," "Another Saturday Night") was shot to death at the site of the former Hacienda Motel in December of 1964 by a motel manager armed with a .22 pistol. Cooke had taken a young woman to the seedy motel, and after the shooting she claimed that he had tried to rape her. However, evidence suggests that she may have been a prostitute who may have tried to rob Cooke (leading to Cooke's panic and subsequent chase). When Cooke broke down the door of the manager's office, where he mistakenly believed the woman had gone, the shocked manager shot and killed him.

Crash, Darby

137 North Fuller Avenue
Hollywood, California

Darby Crash, lead singer of seminal Los Angeles punk band The Germs, died here on the morning of December 7, 1980. He and his girlfriend Casey both left suicide notes and took supposedly lethal doses of heroin. But while Darby died, Casey survived. The death was largely under-reported due to the fact that the very next day John Lennon was shot outside his New York City apartment.

Croce, Jim

Natchitoches Regional Airport
450 Wallenberg Drive
Natchitoches, Louisiana (off Interstate 49)
318-352-9513

Known for hits such as "Bad, Bad Leroy Brown," and "Time in a Bottle," singer/song-writer Jim Croce had just finished a show at Prather Coliseum, the basketball arena at Northwestern State University, on the evening of September 20, 1973. Croce's small private plane crashed immediately after takeoff from runway 17, hitting the trees just east of the runway and killing Croce and five members of his entourage.

Originally, Croce was to have spent the night in Natchitoches and have flown to Dallas the next day, but there was a last minute change of plans and Croce ended up leaving immediately after the show. Today, a plaque commemorating Croce's last concert can be found in the Student Union at Northwestern State University.

Denver, John

Located east of Point Pinos at the northern tip of Monterey Peninsula, between Asilomar Avenue and Acropolis Street, off Ocean View Boulevard in the Pacific Ocean.
Monterey, California

The folk rock troubadour had moved to the Carmel area not long before October 12, 1997, the day he crashed his small, "experimental" craft into the sea. Planning a trip down south, he was actually giving the secondhand plane a test run when the accident

occurred. The experts suspect that Denver accidentally adjusted a rudder which caused a nosedive that he was too low to correct. Many of Denver's fans gather nearby to honor the anniversary each year, and also to help clean up the beach in honor of the ecology-minded singer.

Entwistle, John

Hard Rock Hotel
4455 Paradise Road
Las Vegas, Nevada
800-851-1703

John Entwistle, the quiet, rock steady bassist (and co-founder) of The Who died here of an apparent heart attack on June 27, 2002. He was just 57. Entwistle was in Vegas for an exhibit of his artwork, which was to be followed by a Who performance at the Joint, on June 28th, the opening night of the group's U.S. tour. "The Ox" as he was nicknamed contributed tracks to The Who including "Boris the Spider" and "Whiskey Man." He also had a prolific solo career in the early-1970s, releasing *Smash Your Head Against the Wall* in 1971, which was quickly followed by *Whistle Rhymes* a year later and *Rigor Mortis Sets In* (1973), *Mad Dog* (1975), and *Too Late the Hero* (1981). Entwistle's final release was 1999's live album, *Left for Live*. Today, the hotel has yet to reveal the exact room where he died, as to not attract undue attention by fans of Entwistle.

Fuller, Bobby

1776 North Sycamore Avenue
Hollywood, California

This was the apartment of Bobby Fuller, the singer who (as lead vocalist of The Bobby Fuller Four) recorded the hit song "I Fought the Law (and the Law Won)." On July 18th, 1966, just five months after hitting the Top 10, Fuller died from carbon monoxide poisoning in his car while parked just outside of this building. Police labeled the 22-year-old's death a suicide.

Garcia, Jerry

Serenity Knolls
145 Tamal Road
Forest Knolls, California
415-488-0400

On Monday, August 7, 1995, Jerry Garcia, lead guitarist and vocalist for the Grateful Dead, drove up this road in West Marin and checked himself into this substance treatment center after telling friends and bandmates that he was going to Hawaii. A week

earlier, he had checked out of the Betty Ford Treatment Center after staying two weeks of a proposed month-long stay.

When a counselor at the facility made a routine bed check at 4:23 A.M. on Wednesday, August 9th, they discovered he had died in his sleep. Paramedics were called but were unable to revive him. Jerome John "Jerry" Garcia was pronounced dead, just eight days after his 53rd birthday.

Gaye, Marvin

2101 South Gramercy Place
Los Angeles, California

This is the family home where legendary Motown singer Marvin Gaye was shot to death by his minister father, Marvin Gaye, Sr., during an argument at their home in April 1984. The father pleaded guilty to voluntary manslaughter, but received only five years' probation.

Just before his death, Gaye's career had recently turned around but the resurgence brought with it an increased reliance on cocaine. He returned to the U.S. and moved in

with his parents in an attempt to regain control of his life. But the return only exacerbat-
ed his troubles; he and his father quarreled
bitterly and constantly, and Gaye threatened
suicide on a number of occasions. Finally, on
the afternoon of April 1, 1984—one day before
his 45th birthday—Gaye was shot after a final
argument and died on the lawn in front of the
house after staggering outside.

George, Lowell

Marriott-Twin Bridges
333 Jefferson Davis Highway
Arlington, Virginia

The blues/rock band Little Feat was formed in 1970 by two alumni of Frank Zappa's Mothers of Invention: innovative slide guitarist Lowell George and bassist Roy Estrada. The group disbanded in 1978 after several near hits and critically acclaimed albums, including the popular live set *Waiting for Columbus*. Lowell George then recorded a solo album, *Thanks I'll Eat It Here*, and went out on the road to promote it in 1979. But excess caught up with the overweight, overindulgent George, who succumbed to a heart attack on June 29, 1979. The hotel where he died (the very first Marriott to be opened) was demolished in 1990. George had performed the night before in Washington at the Lisner Auditorium, located on the campus of The George Washington University at 730 21st Street, NW. Ironically, this is where Little Feat's *Waiting for Columbus* had been recorded.

Graham, Bill

Highway 37 between Sears Point and Vallejo
Near Vallejo, California

On October 25, 1991, the famed concert promoter Bill Graham was killed here in a helicopter crash. Graham, who was 60 at the time, made a name for himself in the 1960s by promoting shows at San Francisco's Fillmore Auditorium and New York City's Fillmore East, and later in the '70s and '80s by promoting "mega-tours" for bands such as the Rolling Stones. Graham (and two others) died when his Bell 206B helicopter hit an electrical transmission tower and crashed during heavy rain and high winds.

Hardin, Tim

625 North Orange
Hollywood, California

Tim Hardin was a gentle, soulful 1960s singer/songwriter who had achieved more recognition through covers of his songs from other singers, such as Rod Stewart ("Reason to Believe"), Nico ("Eulogy to Lenny Bruce"), Scott Walker ("Lady Came From Baltimore"), Fred Neil ("Green Rocky Road" has been credited to both him and Hardin), and, of course, Bobby Darin, who made Hardin's "If I Were a Carpenter" a Top 10 hit in 1966. Beleaguered by a heroin habit from early in his career, Hardin died of a drug overdose at this house on December 29, 1980.

Hathaway, Donny

Essex Hotel
160 Central Park South
New York, New York
212-247-0300

In 1979, soul singer Donny Hathaway tragically fell 15 stories to his death at this posh hotel. Hathaway was probably best know for his duets with Roberta Flack, including "Where Is the Love?" and "The Closer I Get To You." (He also sang the theme to TV's *Maude*.) He reportedly suffered from bouts of depression, and was hospitalized on more than one occasion.

On January 13, 1979, Hathaway and his manager returned to his hotel room after having dinner with Flack. Later that night, Hathaway's body was discovered below his 15th-floor window. The hotel room door was locked from the inside, and there was no sign of foul play. The window's safety glass had been removed and laid on the bed. It appeared that Hathaway had jumped to his death.

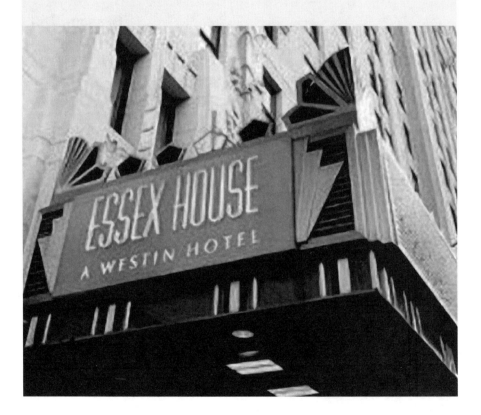

Holly, Buddy

Off State Road 20, north of Clear Lake, Iowa
Directions: Take Interstate 35 (the main road) to Clear Lake. From I-35, take Highway 18 west into town. Turn onto a road marked S28 going north from 18 (there's a gas station on the northeast corner of the intersection). Drive 5½ miles on S28 and turn right onto 310th Street. Turn immediately onto Gull Avenue, a gravel road. Drive north on Gull ½ mile and stop at 315th Street. Park. Walk to the west past the sign marking 315th Street into the cornfield. Walk west on the north side of the wire fence for half a mile. Four oak trees (one for each victim) mark the exact site of the crash, where a memorial also sits.

"The Winter Dance Party Tour" planned to cover 24 cities in a short three-week time frame, and Buddy Holly would be the biggest headliner. Waylon Jennings, a friend from Lubbock, Texas, and Tommy Allsup would go as backup musicians. Ritchie Valens, probably the hottest of the artists at the time, the Big Bopper, and Dion and the Belmonts rounded out the list of performers. It was the dead of winter and the tour bus had heating problems when they arrived at the Surf Ballroom in Clear Lake, Iowa, on February 3, 1959. They were cold and tired. So harsh were the conditions, that Buddy had decided to charter a plane for himself and his guys.

Dwyer Flying Service was called and charged $36 per person for a single engine Beechcraft Bonanza. At the last minute, Waylon Jennings gave his seat up to the Big Bopper, who was ill and had a hard time fitting comfortably in the bus. When Buddy learned Jennings wasn't going to fly, he said, "Well, I hope your old bus freezes up." Jennings said, "Well, I hope your plane crashes." Allsup flipped Valens for the remaining seat and Valens won.

The plane took off just after 1:00 A.M. from Clear Lake and never got far from the airport before it crashed, killing all onboard. At the next tour stop in Moorhead, Minnesota, the rest of the performers looked for local talent to fill in, deciding the show must go on. They found a 15-year-old singer named Bobby Vee, which was the start of his career.

Hoon, Shannon

440 St. Charles Avenue
New Orleans, Louisiana

The tour bus for the band Blind Melon had been parked here on October 21, 1995, when pal and fellow Hoosier Axl Rose of Guns N' Roses discovered singer Shannon Hoon's dead body on-board. The bus was in the lot next to the Hotel InterContinental and it is suspected that drugs were responsible for the 28-year-old's death.

Jam Master Jay

24/7 Recording Studio
90-10 Merrick Boulevard
Queens, New York

On October 30, 2002, legendary hip-hop DJ Jam Master Jay (born Jason Mizell), of the seminal rap group Run-DMC, was shot and killed while working in his 24/7 Recording Studio. The crime was a brutal, execution-style murder that stunned music fans around the world. According to police, two men entered the second floor of the building about 7:30 P.M. and committed the murder. Jay was just 37 and left behind a wife and three sons. To date, nobody has been arrested in connection with the case.

Joplin, Janis

Landmark Hotel (now the Highland Gardens Hotel)
Room 105
7047 Franklin Avenue
Hollywood, California
323-850-0536

This is where Janis Joplin accidentally overdosed on October 4, 1970. She died in her room at the Landmark Hotel in Los Angeles, having scored a particularly pure batch of heroin. Her sad, lonely death followed that of Jimi Hendrix, who'd died just two weeks earlier. (Jim Morrison would die within a year.) Janis was cremated and her ashes were scattered along the Marin County coastline of California. The album she was recording at the time, *Pearl*, was released after her death. Although Janis Joplin's career lasted only a few years, she has been hailed as the greatest white female blues singer who ever lived.

Lennon, John

The Dakota Apartments
One West 72nd Street
New York, New York

John Lennon was killed by Mark David Chapman on December 8, 1980, as he returned to his New York apartment from a recording session. At almost 11:00 P.M. that night, Lennon's limo pulled up outside the Dakota and doorman Jose Perdomo left his post to open the car doors for Lennon and his wife, Yoko Ono. Yoko got out first, followed closely by her husband. As Yoko passed him, Chapman said "Hello." As Lennon passed, Chapman pulled a snub-nosed .38 revolver from his pocket, dropped into combat stance, and said, "Mr. Lennon?" As Lennon turned, Chapman fired five shots, four of which hit Lennon.

Mortally wounded, Lennon staggered up the steps into the Dakota's front lobby and collapsed; he died later that evening at Roosevelt Hospital, after losing 80% of his blood. After shooting Lennon, Chapman took *The Catcher in the Rye* out of his pocket and tried to read it as he paced the sidewalk and waited for the police to come get him.

Though Chapman's lawyer initially entered a plea of insanity, Chapman later changed the plea to guilty. He was sentenced to 20 years to life in prison, a sentence which he is serving in New York's Attica prison. Chapman was denied parole at his first parole hearing in October of 2000.

Lynyrd Skynyrd

Off Highway 568, near Gillsburg, Mississippi.

Near dusk on October 20, 1977, while flying from Greenville to Baton Rouge, the plane carrying southern rock legends Lynyrd Skynyrd crashed, killing singer/songwriter Ronnie Van Zant, guitarist Steve Gaines, backup singer Cassie Gaines (Steve's sister) and road manager Dean Kilpatrick. Pilot Walter Wiley McCreary and co-pilot William John Gray, both from Dallas, also died.

The aircraft had become low on fuel and both engines quit before the twin engine Convair 240 (built in 1947) could reach McComb Airport, so a forced landing was made in a wooded area. The swamp where the plane crashed is eight miles from McComb Airport. In all, 20 other members of the band and road crew were injured, many critically. The actual crash site is a good distance from the nearest road, so a track had to be cut from the thick forest. Today, the track has grown over, so the site is nearly impossible to reach.

Nelson, Rick

Near FM Road 990, outside DeKalb, Texas
Directions: Take Highway 82 east of out DeKalb and cross the train tracks to FM Road 1840. FM Road 990 will come up in about half a mile and you make a right onto it. From there, the crash site is about 400 yards west of 990, a half-mile from the intersection of 1840 and 990.

Rick Nelson was the all-American kid on *Ozzie & Harriet* and had several major hits in the late 1950s and early 1960s, such as "Hello Mary Lou," "It's Late," "Poor Little Fool," and "Travelin' Man." In 1972, he hit the Top 20 with "Garden Party."

While on tour on December 31, 1985, Rick Nelson's plane went down due to a fire that started in a faulty heating unit. The rumors of a fire caused by freebasing coke were entirely incorrect, yet still persist. The fire began in the rear of the plane, and the fumes quickly spread throughout the plane causing the crash. Rick Nelson was only 45 years old. The pilot and co-pilot survived, but Nelson, his fiancée, and five other people perished when the DC-3 hit the ground.

Notorious B.I.G.

6060 Wilshire Boulevard
Los Angeles, California

It was here outside the Petersen Automotive Museum, the site of a Soul Train awards party on March 9, 1997, where rapper Notorious B.I.G. (real name Christopher Wallace, also known as Big E. Smalls) was gunned down and killed by a drive-by shooter shortly after midnight while sitting inside his Chevrolet Suburban. It has been reported recently that Smalls may have supplied the gun that killed rival rapper Tupac Shakur in Las Vegas the year before he himself was murdered (as well as possibly putting a one-million-dollar bounty on Shakur's head). However, the Smalls family disputes the charges leveled by *Los Angeles Times* Pulitzer Prize-winning journalist Chuck Phillips.

Pappalardi, Felix

30 Waterside Plaza
New York, New York

This is where Felix Pappalardi, the famed producer of the rock supergroup Cream in the '60s and bass player in the group Mountain, was shot dead by his wife and collaborator, Gail Collins. Police charged his wife in the slaying after receiving a call from her at about 6 A.M. When police arrived at the apartment, they said they found the musician lying on the bed in his underwear, a single bullet in his neck. Pappalardi, 41, was pronounced dead at the scene. A .38-caliber two-shot derringer was lying nearby, police said. Mrs. Pappalardi apparently called her attorney after notifying police of the shooting.

Parker, Charlie

Stanhope Hotel
995 Fifth Avenue
New York, New York
212-774-1234

On the night of March 12, 1955, while visiting his friend, the "jazz baroness" Nica de Koenigswarter, legendary sax player Charlie Parker died here at this luxury hotel of pneumonia. Though he was only 34 years old, the coroner estimated Parker's age to be 64 due to the wear and tear on his drug-and-alcohol ravaged body. Parker was a revolutionary giant among jazz musicians of the time, but it would take the general population years to discover his musical genius.

Parsons, Gram

Joshua Tree Inn
61259 29 Palms Highway
Joshua Tree, California
760-366-1188

Room 8 is the destination for many music afi-
cionados from the world over. While registered
in this room on September 18, 1973, musician
Gram Parsons (a veteran of The Byrds and The
Flying Burrito Brothers), died at the age of 26
after too much tequila and morphine. Parsons
had just finished his "Fallen Angels" tour featuring his duet partner, Emmylou Harris.

On the peach-colored wall of the room hangs
the same mirror and picture that hung there back in 1973. Also, a journal is kept on a
bedside table for the scores of fans who come to pay homage. Yvo Kwee, the owner,
says that the mirror sometimes rattles inexplicably around 4:00 A.M. and the back door
sometimes opens itself.

A few miles from the inn is one of the most bizarre landmarks in
rock 'n' roll. It seems that after Parsons died his road manager
and pal Phil Kaufman and an accomplice hijacked Parsons's body
from LAX where it was on its way to New Orleans. The two drove
back out to Joshua Tree National Park, up to a landmark called
Cap Rock (where, it has been reported, Parsons used to get high
with his musical soulmate Keith Richards and look for UFOs) and

lit Parsons's body on fire, as
per an earlier agreement he
had made with Parsons.

Kaufman and his accomplice were eventually charged
with misdemeanor theft for stealing the coffin and
fined just over $1,000. Though he never achieved
great commercial success, Gram Parsons still has a
small but intense following. Some of these fans laid a
plaque at Cap Rock, featuring the words "Safe at
Home" (the name of one Parsons's songs). The site
continues to draw people from all over the world. The
road leading to the west entrance of Joshua Tree
State Park is located just down the street from the
Joshua Street Inn. The number at the park is 760-
367-5500, and Cap Rock is located about 10 miles in
from the park's west entrance.

Presley, Elvis

Graceland
3734 Elvis Presley Boulevard
Memphis, Tennessee
1-800-238-2000

Where the King lived . . . and died. Even though you're not allowed to see the bathroom where it all ended, you can tour the mansion (which even houses the famous pink Cadillac.) Located on 14 acres, it features a pool room, "jungle room," trophy building, and much more. Don't forget to pay respects in the Meditation Garden. (In 1976, it was reported that Bruce Springsteen was escorted away by Graceland security guards after trying to climb over the main gates and meet Elvis, who was still alive at the time.)

Redding, Otis

Lake Monona (The memorial is located in the
William T. Evjue Rooftop Garden, part of the Monona Terrace)
Madison, Wisconsin

This was where the plane carrying soul singer Otis Redding and his backup band the Bar-Kays crashed on the afternoon of December 10, 1967. They were traveling from Cleveland to do two shows in Madison that evening when the plane went down on its approach to Madison Airport. No cause was ever uncovered, though witnesses heard the engine sputtering.

A memorial to Redding was erected on the western shore of Lake Monona that consists of three benches and a plaque in Law Park on John Nolan Drive. Supposedly, if you sit on the middle bench and face east, you're facing the part of the lake where the plane down.

Rhoads, Randy

Flying Baron Estates
31017 Airway Road
Leesburg, Florida

On March 18, 1982, the Ozzy Osbourne band played what would be their last show with Randy Rhoads at the Civic Coliseum in Knoxville, Tennessee. On the way to Orlando they were to pass by the Flying Baron Estates, where tour bus driver Andrew C. Aycock owned a home. They stopped there to get some spare parts for the bus and the next morning Aycock took out a red and white 1955 Beechcraft Bonanza F-35 that was parked at a neighboring estate and started giving rides. With Randy Rhoads and a woman named Rachel Youngblood onboard, the plane "buzzed" the band's tour bus several times. Then, the plane's left wing struck the left side of the band's tour bus, hit a nearby pine tree, and crashed into a mansion, killing all on board.

Selena

Days Inn
901 Navigation Boulevard
Corpus Christi, Texas
866-231-9330

On March 31, 1995, the popular Tejano singer Selena (Selena Quintanilla-Perez) was shot and killed by Yolanda Saldivar, 34, the former president of the Selena fan club. After holding police at bay for nine hours, she finally gave up and admitted that she had shot her onetime friend. Selena was just 23 years old.

According to testimony from the trial, Selena was meeting with Saldivar to discuss allegations that Saldivar had embezzled money from her when the shooting occurred. The defense argued that Saldivar had accidentally fired the shot that killed Selena, while the prosecution maintained that the shooting was deliberate. Saldivar was eventually found guilty and sentenced to life in prison. If you're interested in searching for room 158, where the murder occurred, forget it—the hotel renumbered the entire floor.

Shakur, Tupac

**On Flamingo Road, just east of Las Vegas Boulevard,
near the intersection of Koval Lane
Las Vegas, Nevada**

Though the popular gangsta rap star Tupac Shakur had made headlines over a series of run-ins with the law, none got more attention than the gangland-style hit that ended up taking his life on September 13, 1996. After leaving the Tyson/Seldon fight at the MGM Grand Hotel in Las Vegas (he was videotaped getting into an altercation on the way out), the BMW Shakur was riding in with record executive Suge Knight was stopped on Flamingo Road near the Strip. Based on eyewitness accounts, two men jumped out of a Cadillac and blasted 13 rounds into the BMW, hitting Shakur four times (Knight suffered a minor head wound). Shakur died several days later as a result of the wounds suffered in the ambush.

Shannon, Del

**15519 Saddleback Road
Canyon Country, California**

This is the home where singer Del Shannon committed suicide. Shannon's first big hit had been "Runaway" in 1964. It charted at number one for four straight weeks. He had hits such as "Keep Searchin' (We'll Follow the Sun)" and "Hats Off to Larry," but nothing matched the unbridled success of "Runaway." On February 8, 1990, Shannon shot himself in the head with a .22 caliber rifle. He had apparently been suffering from depression.

Smith, Elliot

**Lemoyne Street
Silverlake, California**

On October 21, 2003, musician Elliot Smith fatally stabbed himself here in his apartment after arguing with a girlfriend, Jennifer Chiba. She told police that she and Smith were arguing when she locked herself in the bathroom. Then, after hearing a scream, she opened the bathroom door and found Smith standing with his back to her. When he turned around, she observed a kitchen knife in his chest. She then pulled the knife out of his chest and saw "two cuts" before he walked away and collapsed. Chiba called 911 at 12:18 P.M. and performed CPR and first aid with a dispatcher's help until the paramedics arrived shortly after. Elliot Smith died at County-USC Medical Center 78 minutes later. The singer had been battling depression, drugs, and alcohol for years, and had attempted suicide once before in 1997. During his lifetime, Elliott released five full-length albums as a solo artist as well as a number of singles. Elliott was nominated for an Academy Award for "Miss Misery," his musical contribution to the Academy Award winning movie, *Good Will Hunting*.

Thunders, Johnny

St. Peter's Guest House
Room 37
1005 St. Peter Street
New Orleans, Louisiana
504-524-9232

Though over the years there were always many rumors that he had died, this was actually the last stand for the heroin-addled guitar slinger Johnny Thunders. He died here on April 23, 1991. The former New York Doll had thought about moving to New Orleans, finding some new musicians, and maybe starting a new band, but he never got the chance to complete his plan. Thunders checked into room 37 of the St. Peter Guest House in the late hours of the 23rd of April, and the following morning he was dead. Apparently, he had scored heroin upon arriving and dealt himself a lethal shot, dying overnight.

Tiny Tim

Women's Club of Minneapolis
410 Oak Grove Street
Minneapolis, Minnesota

It was here at the Women's Club of Minneapolis that singer Tiny Tim suffered a fatal heart attack in November of 1996. The quirky cult figure, who became famous for singing "Tiptoe Through the Tulips" and for getting married on *The Tonight Show,* had suffered a heart attack the month before but had recently resumed performing. During a benefit concert here, Tim (real name Herbert Khaury) told his wife Susan Khaury during the performance that he felt ill. She was trying to help him back to their table when he collapsed. He died later at the local hospital.

Vaughan, Stevie Ray

Alpine Valley Resort
East Troy, Wisconsin (85 miles northwest of Chicago)
1-800-227-9395

Guitar hero Stevie Ray Vaughan was killed in a post-gig helicopter crash in East Troy, Wisconsin, on August 27, 1990. He was 35. Vaughan and three members of Eric Clapton's entourage perished when their helicopter crashed into a ski slope about a mile from the Alpine Valley Music Theatre, where they'd just finished playing a concert.

Wilson, Dennis

Basin C at Dock 1100
Maruesas Way
Marina del Rey, California

This is where Beach Boys' drummer Dennis Wilson died at the age of 39 in a drowning accident off of a friend's boat. With his brothers and Mike Love, Dennis helped The Beach Boys turn out such hits as "California Girls," "Fun, Fun, Fun" and "Wouldn't It Be Nice." Apparently, on December 28, 1983, Wilson had too much to drink, decided to go swimming, and subsequently drowned.

Wilson, Jackie

Latin Casino
2235 Marlton Pike
Cherry Hill, New Jersey

Specializing in Vegas-style floor shows, this onetime nightclub hosted everyone from Sinatra to Diana Ross. On September 25, 1975, while onstage at the Latin Casino, Jackie Wilson had the heart attack (with brain damage occurring) that eventually led to his death in 1984. The Latin Casino was torn down soon after Wilson's death and it's now the site of a car manufacturer's office building.

Knockin' on Heaven's Door: R.I.P.

Author's Note: Within this chapter, you will notice that the length of the entries varies quite a bit. Obviously, Jimi Hendrix deserves more space than, say, Shannon Hoon. However, because an artist like Hendrix is covered in several places throughout the book, I chose not to go into great detail about Hendrix's life within this chapter. Conversely, someone like Hoon, who only appears in one more spot in the book, gets more space here than one might expect.

Allman, Duane
November 20, 1946–October 29, 1971

Rose Hill Cemetery
1071 Riverside Drive
Macon, Georgia
478-751-9119

Guitarist Duane (Howard) Allman was a seminal member of The Allman Brothers Band along with his brother Gregg, Richard "Dickey" Betts, Jai Johanny "Jaimoe" Johanson, Claude Hudson "Butch" Trucks, Jr., and the late Raymond Berry Oakley, III. Allman was known for his inventive slide guitar playing, as featured on such bluesy classics as "Statesboro Blues," "Trouble No More," "Done Somebody Wrong," and "Drunken Hearted Boy." Allman was killed in a motorcycle accident on October 29, 1971.

Anderson, Pink
February 12, 1900–October 12, 1974

Lincoln Memorial Gardens
Cannons Campground R
Spartanburg, South Carolina
864-582-1249

Blues musician Pinkney "Pink" Anderson was famous for helping spearhead the blues guitar style known as the Piedmont blues back in the late 1920s. However, most people are familiar with his first name only because Pink Floyd co-founder Syd Barrett supposedly came up with the name Pink Floyd by combining "Pink" with another blues legend: Floyd Council (see below under "C").

Ball, Ernie
1927–September 9, 2004

San Luis Cemetery
2 Higuera Street
San Luis Obispo, California
805-543-7053

As any guitar player knows, Ernie Ball was the foremost pioneer in the development and manufacturing of guitar strings. For over 40 years, everyone from the Rolling Stones to Eric Clapton to Slash used Ball's strings and instruments. He was a self-made man, starting out with a small store in California's San Fernando Valley and going on to build a company that made more than $40 million per year. According to British music writer Mo Foster, in the 1950s, Ball was the first industry figure to notice and exploit the trend

for electric guitarists to buy lighter gauge banjo strings to replace the heavier gauge guitar strings—which were then the standard—in order to improve playability. This led to his development of the so-called "slinky" string sets, which became his trademark. He is also credited as the developer of the first modern acoustic bass guitar, introduced under the Earthwood label in 1972. Ernie Ball died on September 9, 2004, in San Luis Obispo.

Ballard, Hank
November 18, 1927–March 2, 2003

Greenwood Cemetery
1173 Cascade Road SW
Atlanta, Georgia
404-753-2128

R&B legend Hank Ballard was first discovered back in the early 1950s by the famed writer-producer named Johnny Otis. Within 10 years, Ballard had amassed a mind-boggling 22 hit singles on the rhythm and blues charts, including the million-selling "Work With Me Annie" in 1954. But we remember Ballard for his biggest hit, 1958's "The Twist," which he wrote and sang. However, it was only released on the "B" side of another record and it was Chubby Checker who, one year later, made the song famous. Ballard died of throat cancer in 2003.

Bloomfield, Michael
July 28, 1944–February 15, 1981

Hillside Memorial Park
6001 West Centinela Avenue
Culver City, California
310-641-0707
Plot: Courts of the Book Mausoleum. Sanctuary of Meditation, Crypt 314,
third row from the bottom on the left.

Michael Bloomfield came from a well-off family on Chicago's North Side. Interestingly, the Bloomfield fortune was made possible by his father's unique invention—the sugar holder with a flapper lid! Michael was a 1960s session musician made most famous through his work with Bob Dylan during his first explorations into the "electric Dylan" phase. Bloomfield's sound was a major part of Dylan's sound, as featured especially on the *Highway 61 Revisited* album (which included "Like a Rolling Stone").

Bloomfield's playing bridged a deep blues influence with rock and folk, and in 1965, he joined the Paul Butterfield Blues Band. His work on the band's self-titled debut, and the subsequent record *East-West*, brought him universal acclaim. Bloomfield's complicated solos were always at the forefront of his playing and influenced many young players of the day. On February 15, 1981, Bloomfield was found dead of a heroin overdose in San Francisco in his parked car. According to his friends, the size of the dose that killed him meant that he probably did not drive to this spot and overdose. Instead, it seemed that the lethal dose had been administered somewhere else and he had been driven to this spot to avoid complications for his drug-ingesting comrades. In any event, the official cause of death was ruled an accidental drug overdose.

Bolin, Tommy
August 1, 1951–December 4, 1976

Calvary Cemetery
1821 Jackson Street
Sioux City, Iowa
712-255-7933

Tommy Bolin began playing in bands around Sioux City before heading off to Boulder, Colorado, in his late teens. He had played in a band called American Standard before joining Ethereal Zephyr, a band named after a train that ran between Denver and Chicago. When record companies became interested, the name was shortened to Zephyr.

In 1973, Bolin became Joe Walsh's replacement in the James Gang and played on their next two records. The year 1975 saw the release of Bolin's first and highly anticipated solo record, *Teaser*. Bolin also took part in Deep Purple's *Come Taste the Band* album as lead guitar player. The Deep Purple world tour that followed allowed Tommy to show-case one song per night from *Teaser*.

During this period, it had become apparent that he had a heroin addiction. A bad fix before a show in Japan rendered his left arm partially paralyzed for a brief period. Erratic shows became the norm for this lineup and their singer, David Coverdale, walked off the stage after a show in Liverpool, and Deep Purple was no more.

In 1976, Bolin began to record *Private Eyes*, his second solo record. Tragically, Bolin's tour for *Private Eyes* would be his last. The cost of keeping a band on the road and his heavy drug addiction forced him into the role of supporting act. His legendary final show, in which he opened for Jeff Beck on December 3, 1976, encored with a barn-burning rendition of the classic tune "Post Toastee." He even posed for a famous photo with Jeff Beck after the show.

In one account of his last hours, Bolin was found unconscious shortly following the performance. The management, who by some reports did not want any more negative publicity about the tour, had him taken to his room with his girlfriend to look after him. (In other accounts, his death followed a night of hard partying that had involved beer, champagne, cocaine, and, finally, heroin.) By morning, Bolin's condition had deteriorated. His girlfriend feared for his life and called for an ambulance. When paramedics arrived, Tommy Bolin was pronounced dead. He was just 25 years old.

Buchanan, Roy
September 23, 1939–August 15, 1988

Columbia Gardens Cemetery
3411 Arlington Boulevard
Arlington, Virginia
703-527-1235
Plot: Section C (second to last row) on Azalea Avenue

In 1953, at the age of 13, soon-to-be-legend Roy Buchanan bought his very first Fender Telecaster and soon left his northern California home for fame and fortune in Los Angeles. By 1955, Roy was leading his own rock 'n' roll band, The Heartbeats, and soon he'd work his way eastbound, finally hooking up with rockabilly legend Dale Hawkins. Throughout the 1960s, Buchanan honed his craft and in 1971, thanks to accolades from John Lennon, Eric Clapton, Merle Haggard, and an invitation to join the Rolling Stones, Roy "broke" nationally as the result of an hour-long public television documentary. Entitled "The Best Unknown Guitarist in the World," the show won Roy a contract with Polydor and thus started a decade of worldwide touring. Roy's diverse career featured many phases including worldwide tours with Lonnie Mack, The Allman Brothers, and many other blues/rock guitar icons. Sadly, Buchanan committed suicide in Virginia in 1988. He was just 48 years old.

Buckley, Jeff
November 17, 1966-May 29, 1997

Memorial marker overlooking the Sumatran Tigers at the Memphis Zoo
Memphis Zoo
2000 Prentiss Place
Memphis, Tennessee
901-276-9453

Born in California's Orange County on November 17, 1966, Jeff Buckley emerged in New York City's avant-garde club scene in the 1990s as one of the most unique musical artists of his generation. His first commercial recording, the four-song EP *Live At Sine*, was released in December 1993 on Columbia Records in the United States and Big Cat Records in the United Kingdom and Europe. After wrapping up a tour in 1996,

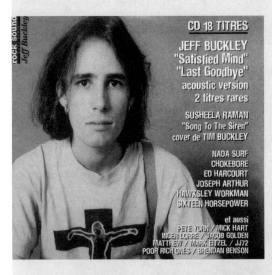

Buckley started writing for a new album to be called *My Sweetheart the Drunk*. In 1997, he moved to Memphis, Tennessee and started recording demos. He went into the studio again, recruited a band, and plans for the new album looked hopeful.

On May 29, 1997, as the band's plane touched down on the runway to join him in his Memphis studio, Buckley went swimming in the Wolf River, a tributary of the Mississippi River. His friend Keith Foti remained ashore and, after moving a radio and guitar out of reach of the wake from a passing tugboat, looked up to see that Jeff was gone. Despite a notable rescue effort mounted that night, Buckley remained missing, and the search was called off the next day. His body was spotted a week later by a tourist on a riverboat marina and brought ashore. An autopsy confirmed that Buckley had taken no illegal drugs before his swim and that a drug overdose could be ruled out as the cause of his death.

As for the plaque at the zoo, while in Memphis prior to his death, Jeff had visited the zoo quite a bit. He was especially enamored with the snow leopards and the butterfly exhibit and was even planning to volunteer some of his time there. That's why two brass memorial plaques, which were made possible by contributions from fans all over the world, were unveiled in the zoo at the Sumatran tiger exhibit on September 18, 1998.

Burnett, Chester "Howlin' Wolf"
June 10, 1910-January 10, 1976

Oak Ridge Cemetery
4301 W. Roosevelt Road
Hillside, Illinois
708-344-5600
Plot: Section 18, right by the road

Chester Burnett (Howlin' Wolf) was named after the 21st President of the United States (Chester Arthur) and it was a chance meeting with Delta blues legend Charley Patton that changed his life forever. Legendary blues singer Howlin' Wolf would go on to become one of the most influential artists in history, penning and recording such Chicago blues classics as "I Ain't Superstitious," "The Red Rooster," "Shake for Me Back Door Man," "Spoonful," and "Wang Dang Doodle." One of the bands most influenced by him was the Rolling Stones, whose cover of "The Red Rooster" became a number-one record in England.

At the height of the British Invasion, the Stones came to America in 1965 for an appearance on ABC-TV's rock music show, *Shindig*. Their main stipulation for appearing on the program was that Howlin' Wolf would be their special guest. With the Stones sitting respectfully at his feet, the Wolf performed a storming version of "How Many More Years," and was seen on his network-TV debut by an audience of several million. Wolf never forgot the respect the Stones paid him, and he spoke of them highly right up to his final days. After his death, a life-size statue of him was erected in a Chicago park.

Carpenter, Karen Anne
March 2, 1950-February 4, 1983

Forest Lawn-Cypress
4471 Lincoln Avenue
Cypress, California
1-800-204-3131
Plot: Ascension Mausoleum, Sanctuary of Compassion

Karen Carpenter is best remembered for her singing partnership with her older brother, Richard, as The Carpenters. Born in New Haven, Connecticut, she moved with her family to Downey, California, in 1963. Eventually, Richard put together an instrumental trio, with Richard playing the piano, Karen on the drums, and friend Wes Jacobs on the bass and tuba. In 1966, their group won first place in the Hollywood Bowl Battle of the Bands, and garnered a recording contract with RCA Records.

The Carpenters' debut album, *Offering*, was released in November of 1969 and featured their first single, a ballad version of The Beatles' "Ticket to Ride," which peaked nationally at #54. "Close To You," which would become Karen and Richard's breakthrough recording, took just six weeks to reach number one; it remained there for four consecutive weeks. The song was the first of 17 Top 20 singles—10 of them Gold—for the duo that have now become standards, including "Superstar," "Rainy Days and Mondays,"

"Sing," "Top of the World," and "Yesterday Once More." From "Close To You" in 1970 to "A Kind of Hush" in 1976, Karen and Richard had a string of 16 consecutive Top 20 hits. Over the following years, the Carpenters became one of the most popular groups in history, selling nearly 100 million units worldwide. Sadly, Karen died unexpectedly at her parents' home on February 4, 1983, from heart failure, the result of years of suffering with anorexia nervosa.

Carr, Eric
July 12, 1950-November 24, 1991

Cedar Hill Cemetery
5468 Route 9W
Newburgh, New York
845-562-0505

Following two albums that alienated many fans (1979's *Dynasty* and 1980's *Unmasked*), and a falling-out with original drummer Peter Criss over his drug abuse problems and general unreliability, the band KISS held open auditions for a new drummer and discovered Eric Carr. At the time of his audition, Carr (then Paul Caravello) was cleaning stoves for a living, while playing drums in a variety of bands. After joining KISS, he changed his name to Eric Carr, and adopted the persona of "The Fox," with his makeup design reflecting the character. Carr is often cited by fans as a favorite among drummers in the band's history, for his intense playing style and trademark timing, which was extremely different from the soft-by-comparison, jazz-influenced technique of Criss. Eric was also part of the band's well-publicized removal of their stage makeup in 1983. Carr died of cancer in 1991.

Cash, Johnny
February 26, 1932-September 12, 2003

Hendersonville Memory Gardens
353 East Main Street
Hendersonville, Tennessee
615-824-8605

Johnny Cash, of course, was the singer/songwriter who was known as "The Man in Black" for his trademark wearing of all black clothing. Contrary to his songs and outlaw image, he never spent time in prison (except to visit). The legendary Cash was known for his deep and distinctive voice and the boom-chick-a-boom or "freight train" sound of his Tennessee Three backing band. He started all his concerts with the simple introduction "Hello, I'm Johnny Cash."

Much of Cash's music, especially that of his later career, was steeped in sorrow, moral tribulation, and redemption. His signature songs include "I Walk the Line," "Folsom Prison Blues," "Ring of Fire," and "Man In Black." He also recorded several humorous songs, such as "One Piece at a Time," "The One on the Right Is on the Left," and "A Boy Named Sue"; bouncy numbers such as "Get Rhythm"; and various train-related songs, such as "The Rock Island Line." He sold over 50 million albums in his nearly 50-year career and is generally recognized as one of the most important musicians in the history of American popular music. Cash's wife, country singer June Carter, is buried alongside him.

Chapin, Harry
December 7, 1942–July 16, 1981

Huntington Rural Cemetery
555 New York Avenue
Huntington, New York
631-427-1272

Singer, songwriter, and social activist Harry Chapin originally wanted to become a filmmaker, and his socially conscious folk-rock ballads showed a distinct flair for storytelling. His signature song, the six-minute opus "Taxi" (1972), reveals the bittersweet observations of a taxi cab driver, while "W. O. L. D." (1973) describes the life of a disc jockey. "Cat's in the Cradle" (1974), Chapin's only number one hit, is about a businessman who realizes too late how he sacrificed his relationship with his son for his job, and it remains a classic today. Chapin died in a car accident en route to one of his own concerts on Long Island.

Charles, Ray
September 23, 1930–June 10, 2004

Inglewood Park Cemetery
720 E. Florence Avenue
Inglewood, California
310-412-6500
Plot: Mausoleum of the Golden West, Eternal Love Corridor, Crypt A-32

What can be said of Ray Charles Robinson, the pioneering American pianist and soul musician? Frank Sinatra called him "the only true genius in the business." When Ray was five, his 4-year-old brother George drowned in an outside washing tub. Not long after this event, Ray began to lose his sight and was totally blind by the age of seven. In 1965, Charles was arrested for possession of heroin, a drug to which he had been addicted for 17 years. It was his third arrest for the offense, but he avoided prison time after kicking the habit in a clinic in Los Angeles. He spent a year on parole in 1966.

After the 1960s, Charles's releases were hit-or-miss, with some big hits and critically acclaimed work, and some music that was panned by fans and critics alike. He focused largely on live performances, although his version of "Georgia On My Mind," a Hoagy Carmichael song originally written for a girl named Georgia, was a hit and soon was proclaimed the state song of Georgia on April 24, 1979, with Charles performing it on the floor of the state legislature. This act was significant in that it symbolized to many the move away from segregation and racism. He also had success with his unique version of "America the Beautiful."

Ray Charles died at age 73 on June 10, 2004, at 11:35 A.M. of acute liver disease at his home in Beverly Hills, California, surrounded by family and friends. His final album, *Genius Loves Company,* released two months after his death, consists of duets with various admirers and contemporaries; the album won eight Grammy Awards. In August 2005, the United States Congress honored Charles by renaming the former West Adams Station post office in Los Angeles the Ray Charles Station.

Clark, Gene
November 17, 1944–May 24, 1991

Saint Andrews Cemetery
3530 N. 1000 West
Tipton, Missouri

Guitarist Gene Clark was co-founder of the famed folk rock group The Byrds. He was born here in Tipton, Missouri, but spent his formative years growing up in Kansas City. He joined the New Christy Minstrels in the early 1960s before co-founding The Byrds. After enjoying a huge success as The Byrds' lead songwriter, Clark embarked on a solo career until his premature death in 1991.

Cochran, Eddie
October 3, 1938–April 17, 1960

Forest Lawn-Cypress
4471 Lincoln Avenue
Cypress, California
1-800-204-3131

Eddie Cochran was a popular rockabilly guitarist, singer, and songwriter whose most famous song was "Summertime Blues." Cochran's start goes back to 1956, when he was hired to appear in the musical comedy film *The Girl Can't Help It.* He agreed and sang a song called "Twenty Flight Rock" in the movie, delivered with an attitude and stance that can be regarded as the earliest germ of punk rock seen decades later. In 1957, Cochran had his first big hit, "Sittin' in the Balcony," but it was "Summertime Blues" (co-written with Jerry Capeheart), that became an important influence on music in the late 1950s, both lyrically and musically. Cochran's brief career included only a few more hits, such as "C'mon Everybody," "Somethin' Else," "My Way," "Weekend," "Nervous Breakdown," and his posthumous U.K. number one hit "Three Steps to Heaven." Cochran was killed in a car crash while he was on tour in Britain.

Collins, Albert
October 1, 1932–November 24, 1993

Paradise Memorial Gardens
6200 S. Eastern Avenue
Las Vegas, Nevada
702-736-6200

Albert Collins was the famed blues guitar player known by his nickname "The Master of the Telecaster." His 1960 album *Frosty* sold over one million copies and his career began to grow as his music was being played on blues radio stations all over the United States. In 1978, his Grammy-nominated album *Ice Pickin'* won Best Blues Album of the Year from the Montreaux Jazz Festival. His guitar playing genius was recognized by the

music world in 1983, when he won the W. C. Handy Award for his album *Don't Lose Your Cool,* which also won the award for best blues album of the year. In 1985, Collins shared a Grammy for the album *Showdown!,* which he recorded with Robert Cray and Johnny Copeland. The influential and highly respected Albert Collins died of lung cancer in 1993.

Cooke, Sam
January 22, 1931-December 11, 1964

Forest Lawn Memorial Park
1712 S. Glendale Avenue
Glendale, California
1-800-204-3131
Plot: Garden of Honor, right side
(private area, not accessible to the general public)

The charismatic Sam Cooke was a popular and influential American gospel, R&B, soul, and pop singer, as well as a songwriter and an entrepreneur. In fact, today, musicians and critics alike recognize him as one of the true founders of soul music. Major hits like "You Send Me," "Chain Gang," "Wonderful World," and "Bring It On Home To Me" are among some of his very best work and remain popular today.

Sam Cooke was also among the first modern black performers and composers to attend to the business side of his musical career, and founded both a record label and a publishing company as an extension of his careers as a singer and composer. Cooke also took an active part in the civil rights movement, paralleling his musical ability to bridge gaps between black and white audiences.

Cooke died at the age of 33 under mysterious circumstances on December 11, 1964, in Los Angeles. Though the details of the case are still muddy, he was shot to death by Bertha Franklin, the manager of the Hacienda Motel who claimed that Cooke had threatened her, and that she killed him in self-defense. The verdict was justifiable homicide, though many believe that crucial details did not come out in court, or were buried afterward.

Council, Floyd
September 2, 1911–May 9, 1976

White Oak AME Zion Cemetery
712 Wall Street
Sanford, North Carolina

Floyd Council was an American blues musician who began his musical career on the streets of Chapel Hill in the 1920s with his two brothers, Leo and Thomas. According to a 1969 interview, Floyd stated he had recorded 27 songs over his career, seven of them backing Blind Boy Fuller. Floyd moved to Sanford, North Carolina, where he died of a heart attack in 1976.

But why do we remember his name? Because Roger "Syd" Barrett derived the name "Pink Floyd" by juxtapositioning the first names of Pink Anderson and Floyd Council. He had read about the players in a liner note by Paul Oliver for a 1962 Blind Boy Fuller LP: "Curley Weaver and Fred McMullen, Pink Anderson or Floyd Council—these were a few amongst the many blues singers that were to be heard in the rolling hills of the Piedmont, or meandering with the streams through the wooded valleys."

Croce, Jim
January 10, 1943–September 20, 1973

Haym Salomon Memorial Park
200 Moores Road
Frazer, Pennsylvania
610-644-1100

During the early 1960s, folk singer Jim Croce created several college bands and played at coffeehouses and universities. and later, with his wife Ingrid, performed as a duo in the mid-1960s to early 1970s. Croce got his first substantial gig at a rural bar and steak house in Lima, Pennsylvania, called the Riddle Paddock. There, Croce developed his magical rapport with audiences and built his musical repertoire to over 3,000 songs.

In 1972, Croce signed a three-year record deal with ABC Records releasing *You Don't Mess Around with Jim* and *Life & Times* in the same year. The hit singles "You Don't Mess Around with Jim," "Operator (That's Not the Way It Feels)," and "Time in a Bottle" (written for his newborn son, A. J. Croce) helped the former album reach number one on the charts in 1974. Croce's biggest single "Bad, Bad Leroy Brown," hit number one on the U.S. charts in the summer of 1973, selling two million copies.

Croce was killed in a small commercial plane crash on September 20, 1973, in Natchitoches, Louisiana, just before the release of his album, I Got a Name. He was just 31 years old. The posthumous release included the hits, "I Got a Name," and "I'll Have To Say I Love You in a Song."

Danko, Rick
December 29, 1942–December 10, 1999

Woodstock Cemetery
Rock City Road
Woodstock, New York

Rick Danko was probably best known as a member of The Band. At the age of 17, he booked himself as the opening act for Ronnie Hawkins, an American rockabilly singer whose group, The Hawks, was considered to be one of the best in Canada. (Among those already in the group were drummer Levon Helm, who had joined Hawkins in 1957 before Hawkins ventured north, and lead guitarist Robbie Robertson, who had joined in 1960.) Hawkins, impressed by Danko, asked him to join The Hawks as rhythm guitarist.

Danko agreed. Playing a circuit that stretched in an arc from Ontario to Arkansas, they became known as "the best damn bar band in the land." By 1965, they met the legendary blues harmonicist and vocalist Sonny Boy Williamson, and planned a collaboration with him as soon as he returned to Chicago.

Around the same time, however, Bob Dylan hired them as his backing group and so that was that. Through May of 1966, Dylan and The Band traveled across America, Australia, and Europe, playing new versions of Dylan classics. After the final shows in England, Dylan retreated to his new home in Woodstock, New York, and The Hawks joined him shortly thereafter. It was Danko who had found the pink house on Parnassus Lane, just off of Stoll Road. He, Garth Hudson, and Richard Manuel (two other members of The Band) quickly moved in, with Robertson ensconcing himself nearby.

The music that the group had been performing with Dylan was moved to the basement of the hangout quickly dubbed "Big Pink." The sessions, which began in May 1967, ended in October 1967. The resulting music can be heard on the classic album, *The Basement Tapes*. By the end of 1999, a lifetime of abuse had left Danko in horrible shape—physically huge—and barely recognizable. On December 10, 1999, just before turning 57 and only days after the end of a brief tour of the Midwest, Danko died in his sleep.

Fender, Leo
August 10, 1909–March 21, 1991

Fairhaven Memorial Park
1702 Fairhaven Avenue
Santa Ana, California
714-633-1442
Plot: Lawn Section J

Clarence Leonidas Fender is the famous founder of Fender Electric Instrument Manufacturing Company, now known as Fender Musical Instruments Corporation. His guitar, bass, and amplifier designs from the 1950s continue to dominate popular music more than half a century later, played in the hands of everyone from Keith Richards to Eric Clapton. In fact, Marshall and many other amplifier companies have used Fender instruments as the foundation of their products. Fender and inventor Les Paul are often cited as the two most influential figures in the development of electric instruments in the 20th century.

Freed, Alan
December 15, 1922–January 20, 1965

Ferncliff Cemetery and Mausoleum
Secor Road
Hartsdale, New York
914-693-4700
Plot: Unit 8, Alc S-T, Columbarium B, niche 2

Alan Freed, also known as "Moondog," was the famed American disc jockey who became internationally known for promoting African-American rhythm and blues music on his radio shows in the United States and Europe under the name of "rock and roll" (and for the many live concerts he staged). Many of the top African-American performers of the first generation of rock 'n' roll (such as Little Richard and Chuck Berry) salute Alan Freed for his pioneering attitude in breaking down racial barriers among the youth of 1950s America, because Freed took chances nobody else would take. Sadly, his career was destroyed by the payola scandal that hit the broadcasting industry in the early 1960s.

In 1962, after KDAY refused to allow him to promote rock 'n' roll stage shows, Freed moved to WQAM in Miami, Florida, but that association lasted only two months. He died in a Palm Springs, California, hospital in 1965 at the age of 43, suffering from uremia and liver cirrhosis, which was brought on by alcoholism. Shortly before this he had begun working at a radio station in Palm Springs, California. He was initially interred in the Ferncliff Cemetery in Hartsdale, New York, but his ashes were later moved to their present location in the Rock and Roll Hall of Fame on March 21, 2002.

Fuller, Bobby
October 22, 1942–July 18, 1966

Forest Lawn Hollywood Hills
6300 Forest Lawn Drive
Los Angeles, California
323-254-7251
Plot: Sheltering Hills, L-362, space 4

Born in Baytown, Texas, Robert Gaston Fuller spent most of his youth in El Paso, Texas, where he idolized Buddy Holly, a fellow West Texan. Fuller came to Los Angeles in 1964 with his band The Bobby Fuller Four and was signed to Mustang Records by producer Bob Keane, noted for discovering Ritchie Valens and producing many surf music groups. Fuller's first Top 40 hit was a tune he wrote called "Let Her Dance" and his second hit "I Fought the Law" reached number four on *Billboard* (and was written by Sonny Curtis, a former member of Holly's group The Crickets).

Just as "I Fought The Law" became a Top 10 hit, Bobby Fuller was found dead in a parked automobile near his Los Angeles home. The police considered the death an apparent suicide, however many people still believe Fuller was murdered. He was found with multiple wounds all over his body and covered in gasoline leading many to speculate that the perpetrators fled before they could set the car on fire.

Gibb, Andy
March 5, 1958–March 10, 1988

Forest Lawn Hollywood Hills
6300 Forest Lawn Drive
Los Angeles, California
323-254-7251
Plot: Court of Remembrance, 2534, outside and facing the Serenity section

Born Andrew Roy Gibb, the youngest of the Bee Gee boys began playing at tourist clubs around Spain's coastal island of Ibiza, and later back in his homeland of Britain on the Isle of Man as a young teenager. The idea of his joining the Bee Gees was often discussed, but the age gap between him and his elder brothers (more than 11 years younger than Barry, slightly more than eight years younger than twins Robin and Maurice) nullified the idea.

But it didn't keep him from becoming a pop idol. In the United States, Gibb became the first male solo artist to chart three consecutive number one singles on the *Billboard* Hot 100. In July of 1977, he had his first major hit, "I Just Want to Be Your Everything," a tune penned by his brother Barry, just as his million-selling first album *Flowing Rivers* broke into the U.S. Top 20. The album's second single "(Love Is) Thicker Than Water" broke in early 1978 amidst the commercial explosion caused by his brothers' contributions to the *Saturday Night Fever* soundtrack, replacing "Stayin' Alive" at the top of the U.S. charts, and then succumbing to "Night Fever" when it reached the summit in mid-March. Back then, the Gibb brothers all but owned the world.

Despite his impressive accomplishments, the pressures of his newfound fame consumed Gibb, and eventually drug addiction took over. His family convinced him to seek treatment at the Betty Ford Clinic in the mid-1980s and then Gibb toured with a stage show of his greatest hits and covers, also appearing in guest-starring roles on several television situation comedies. On March 7, 1988, Andy Gibb was rushed to the John Radcliffe Hospital in Oxford complaining of stomach pains. Three days later, on the morning of March 10, 1988, Andy Gibb died at age 30 of myocarditis—a sudden inflammation of the heart muscle caused by a viral infection. While his years of alcohol and cocaine abuse did not directly result in his death, they did aggravate his condition.

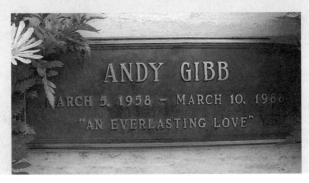

Hatfield, Bobby
August 10, 1940–November 5, 2003

Pacific View Memorial Park
3500 Pacific View Drive
Corona del Mar, California
949-644-2700

Robert Lee "Bobby" Hatfield was one half of The Righteous Brothers singing duo. He was born in Beaver Dam, Wisconsin, and moved with his family to Anaheim, California, when he was four. There, Hatfield played baseball and briefly considered going pro, but his passion for music won over. He would soon meet up with his singing partner, Bill Medley, while going to California State University, Long Beach. The pair began singing as a duo in 1962. Their first single was "Little Latin Lupe Lu"; their first hit was "You've Lost That Lovin' Feelin'," produced by Phil Spector in 1964. Follow-up hits included "(You're My) Soul and Inspiration" and "Unchained Melody."

The duo broke up in 1968 but made a big comeback with "Rock And Roll Heaven" in 1974. They were then inducted into the Rock and Roll Hall of Fame in March 2003 by one of their biggest fans, Billy Joel. Hatfield died in a Kalamazoo, Michigan hotel, apparently in his sleep. In January 2004, a toxicology report concluded that an overdose of cocaine had precipitated a fatal heart attack.

Hendrix, Jimi
November 27, 1942–September 18, 1970

Greenwood Memorial Park
350 Monroe Avenue
Renton, Washington
425-255-1511

Hendrix, of course, was the guitarist best known for his masterful prowess on the electric rock guitar. A gifted singer and songwriter, Hendrix was not merely a rock musician, he was a dynamic presence and performer who changed the course of rock 'n' roll music. His roots were steeped in the blues, R&B, and soul, and he spent many years prior to his superstardom as a backup guitarist in various blues and R&B groups. His debut album *Are You Experienced* was a product of his group the Jimi Hendrix Experience, which he formed in 1967. Hendrix died of drug-related problems while in London in 1970, only four years after he became an international star.

Holly, Buddy
September 7, 1936–February 3, 1959

City of Lubbock Cemetery
2011 E. 31st Street
Lubbock, Texas
806-767-2270

The great Buddy Holly (born Charles Hardin Holley) was one of the first true stars of rock 'n' roll and of course some of his most famous classics are "That'll Be the Day" and "Peggy Sue." Holly jumped into the rock 'n' roll arena from a background in country and western music where he grew up in Lubbock, Texas. He played the guitar and sang, and he had a keen interest in recording studio production techniques; he is credited with being the first to use overdubbing and double-tracking. As we know, he was killed in a plane crash in 1959, along with fellow rockers Ritchie Valens and J.P. "The Big Bopper" Richardson.

Buddy Holly's musical career started in earnest in the fall of 1949, when he met Bob Montgomery at Hutchinson Junior High School. They shared a common interest in music and soon teamed up as the duo "Buddy and Bob." Initially influenced by bluegrass music, they sang harmony duets at local clubs and high school talent shows. His musical interests grew throughout high school while singing in the Lubbock High School Choir.

Holly moved toward rock 'n' roll after seeing Elvis Presley sing in concert in Lubbock in early 1955. A few months later, he actually appeared on the same bill with Presley, also in Lubbock. Holly's transition to rock continued to crystallize after he opened for Bill Haley and the Comets at a local rock show. As a result of his electrifying performance at the show, Holly was offered and signed a contract with Decca Records.

Hoon, Shannon
September 26, 1967–October 21, 1995

Dayton Cemetery
Dayton, Indiana
Plot: far north side, in the new section, in the middle,
at the very back, near the fence

Shannon Hoon (born Richard Shannon) was born and raised in Lafayette, Indiana, and after high school graduation joined a local band named Styff Kytten. Hoon soon left Indiana for Los Angeles in search of stardom and immediately after arriving on the West Coast, met musicians Brad Smith and Rogers Stevens. Together, they formed the band Blind Melon. In California, Hoon was befriended by his sister Anna's high school friend, Axl Rose. In fact, Rose invited Hoon to join him in the studio, where his band Guns N' Roses was recording its albums *Use Your Illusion I* and *Use Your Illusion II*. Hoon ended up singing backup vocals on several tracks, including "Don't Cry." Rose also invited Hoon to appear in the video for "Don't Cry," giving Hoon his first real taste of stardom.

In 1992, Blind Melon released their self-titled debut album. It was produced by Pearl Jam's Rick Parashar and garnered some positive reviews, but ultimately failed to dent the charts. Blind Melon toured, supporting acts like Ozzy Osbourne, Neil Young, Guns N' Roses, and Soundgarden over the course of 1992–1993. As their popularity grew, the members of the band became increasingly involved in drug use, with Hoon being the main offender. In 1993, when the track "No Rain" was released as a single, Blind Melon suddenly became huge "overnight" stars. The quirky video for "No Rain" featured a young, overweight girl in a bee costume (often referred to as the "Bee Girl") and became a huge MTV hit, driving the album multi-platinum.

In 1995, Hoon and his long time girlfriend Lisa Crouse had a daughter, after which Hoon soon entered rehab again. Blind Melon needed to tour to support their album, *Soup*, so Hoon negotiated an early release from his drug rehab program with the stipulation that his drug counselor would accompany him on the road. The counselor, however, was unable to keep Hoon from falling back into his pattern of drug use and was dismissed from the tour less than a month into it. Without the counselor to keep him in check, Hoon's drug use went off the chart.

After a particularly disastrous performance in Houston, Hoon began an all-night cocaine binge. The next day, October 21, 1995, Blind Melon was scheduled to play a show in New Orleans at the famed venue, Tipitina's. When one of the band's roadies went to the tour bus to wake Hoon up for a sound check, he was unable to bring him to. An ambulance was summoned and Hoon was pronounced dead on the scene at the age of 28. The cause of death was attributed to an accidental cocaine overdose.

Hopkins, Sam "Lightnin'"
March 15, 1912-January 30, 1982

Forest Park Lawndale Cemetery
6900 Lawndale Street
Houston, Texas
713-928-5141
Plot: Section 23 (Lawn View), Lot 266, Space 11

Sam "Lightnin'" Hopkins was a country blues guitar legend, from Houston, Texas. He learned the blues from Blind Lemon Jefferson and his older cousin, country-blues singer Alger "Texas" Alexander. Lightnin' Hopkins was a great influence on many local musicians around Houston and Austin in the 1950s and 1960s. His style was developed by playing without a backing band, which led to him playing, in effect, bass, rhythm, lead, percussion, and vocals, all at the same time.

In 1968, Hopkins recorded an album backed by psychedelic rock band the 13th Floor Elevators, and a song named after him was recorded by R.E.M. on their album *Document*. It is also a fact that Jimi Hendrix became interested in blues music listening to Lightnin' Hopkins records with his father. Even though he is not that well-known today, Hopkins was hugely influential and continues to influence young blues players even today.

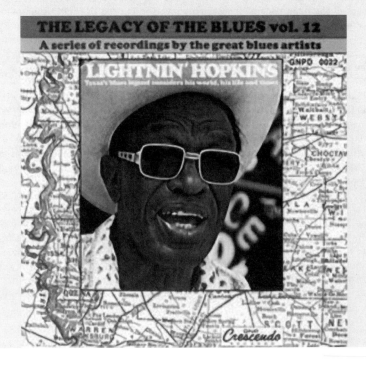

James, Rick
February 1, 1948–August 6, 2004

Forest Lawn Cemetery
1411 Delaware Avenue
Buffalo, New York
716-885-1600

Rick James (James Johnson) was the famed funk and soul musician who worked as a singer, keyboardist, bassist, record producer, arranger, and composer during his long and successful career. One of the most popular artists on the Motown label during the late 1970s and early 1980s, James was renowned for his wild brand of funk music and his trademark cornrow braids, wearing them well before the style became popular. As his career progressed, James was given the unofficial title "The King of Punk-Funk."

In the 1990s, the dark side of James's life began to overpower his music and everything else. In 1991, he, along with future wife, Tanya Hijazi, were accused of holding 24-year-old Frances Alley hostage for up to six days (accounts vary on how long she was actually held), tying her up, forcing her to perform sexual acts, and burning her legs and abdomen with a hot crack pipe during a weeklong cocaine binge.

In 1993, while out on bail for that earlier incident, a coked-up James assaulted another woman, music executive Mary Sauger, at the St. James Club & Hotel in West Hollywood. Sauger claims she met James and Hijazi for a business meeting, but claims the two kidnapped and beat her over a 20-hour period. He was found guilty of both offenses, but was cleared of a torture charge in the crack-pipe incident that could have put him behind bars for the rest of his life.

Serving two years in Folsom Prison, along with losing $2 million in a civil suit to one of the women, did not stop him from writing new songs. He was released in 1995, and dur-

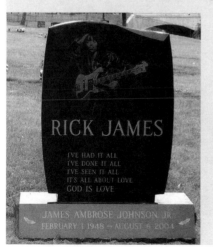

ing interviews for a segment of the VH1 series *Behind the Music,* he spoke openly and in-depth about his life and his battle with drugs for the first time.

James attempted a comeback with a new album and tour in 1997, but suffered a mild stroke during a concert in Denver, Colorado, effectively ending his musical career. On August 6, 2004, Rick James's caretaker found him dead in his Los Angeles home. James had died from pulmonary and cardiac failure with his various health conditions of diabetes, stroke, and a pacemaker being listed as contributing factors.

Johnson, Robert
May 8, 1911-August 16, 1938

Little Zion Cemetery
Grand Street (measure 2.3 miles from the second bridge you go over along
Fulton-Grand St. in Greenwood. Little Zion will be on your left.)
Leflore County, Mississippi

Legendary Robert Johnson is among the most famous Delta blues musicians and arguably the most influential. He is an inductee of the Rock and Roll Hall of Fame. Considered by some to be the "Grandfather of Rock-and-Roll," his vocal phrasing, original music, and guitar style influenced a range of musicians, including Led Zeppelin, Bob Dylan, the Rolling Stones, U2, Jimi Hendrix, and Eric Clapton, who called Johnson "the most important blues musician who ever lived." So where do you start when describing his legend?

Of all the great blues musicians, Johnson was probably the most obscure. We know that he recorded 29 songs and that he died at a young age. However, there are only five dates in Johnson's life that can be incontrovertibly used to define the facts of his life:

On Monday, November 23; Thursday, November 26; and Friday, November 27, 1936, he was in San Antonio, Texas, at a recording session. Seven months later, on Saturday, June 19, and Sunday, June 20, 1937, he was in Dallas at another session. Everything else about his life is conjecture.

In the last year of his life, Johnson is believed to have traveled to St. Louis and possibly Illinois. He spent some time in Memphis and traveled through the Mississippi Delta and Arkansas. By the time he died, at least six of his records had been released.

His death occurred on August 16, 1938, at the approximate age of 27. He died at a little country crossroads near Greenwood, Mississippi. He had been playing for several weeks at a country dance in a town about 15 miles from Greenwood when, by some accounts, he was given poisoned whiskey at the dance by the husband of a woman he had been secretly seeing.

Lopes, Lisa "Left Eye"
May 27, 1971-April 25, 2002

Hillandale Memorial Gardens
6201 Hillandale Drive
Lithonia, Georgia
770-981-1144

Nicole Lopes was a popular rapper also known under the stage name of "Left Eye," and she was a member of the popular R&B and hip-hop group TLC. (She received the name "Left Eye" from a boyfriend because her left eye was larger than her right eye.) In addition to hit songs like "Waterfalls" with TLC, Lopes also did some solo performing. She was considered by some fans as the creative talent behind TLC and, though she sang infrequently, contributed her own self-written raps to many of TLC's popular singles, including "Waterfalls" and "No Scrubs."

Lopes was also a self-taught keyboardist and, by way of a Beethoven piano piece, displayed those talents during her solo spot on TLC's headlining concert performances. She was known for wearing a pair of glasses with a condom in place of the left eye lens, which was one of the ways the group promoted safe sex. Sadly, Lopes died in a car accident in Honduras on April 25, 2002. She had been there doing missionary work, which was something she had a passion for. It is said by those close to her that she had been undergoing a spiritual epiphany and had recently ended a month-long fast prior to her death.

Lymon, Frankie
September 30, 1942-February 27, 1968

Saint Raymonds Cemetery
2600 Lafayette Avenue
Bronx, New York
718-792-2080
Plot: St. Anthony, Range 13, Grave 70

Lymon was a spirited rock 'n' roll/R&B singer, best known as the boy soprano lead singer of a New York City-based classic early rock 'n' roll group called The Teenagers. The group included five boys, all in their early-to-mid-teens. For a 1950s band, the original Teenagers were surprisingly diverse: three members were African-American and the remaining two were Puerto Rican.

Together for only 18 months, Frankie Lymon & the Teenagers are nonetheless renowned for being one of rock music's earliest successes, presented to international audiences by DJ Alan Freed. The group is also noted for being rock's first all-teenaged act. Their first single, 1956's "Why Do Fools Fall in Love," was also their biggest. After Lymon went solo in mid-1957, his career and those of The Teenagers fell into decline. Lymon eventually fell into heroin addiction, and died in 1968, at the age of 25.

Marley, Bob
February 6, 1945-May 11, 1981

Bob Marley Mausoleum
Nine Mile
St. Ann, Jamaica
876-995-1763

Bob Marley (born Robert Nesta Marley) is remembered as a legendary Jamaican singer, songwriter, and guitarist. He may be most famous for having popularized the genre of reggae music outside Jamaica. A faithful Rastafarian, Marley is regarded by many as a prophet of the religion, as well as one of the greatest songwriters of all time.

His best known songs are an influential blend of reggae, rock, and rhythm and blues, and include "I Shot the Sheriff," made famous in 1974 by Eric Clapton (which raised Marley's international profile), "No Woman No Cry," "Exodus," "Could You Be Loved," "Jamming," "Redemption Song" and one of his most famous songs, "One Love." His posthumous album Legend (1984) became the bestselling reggae album ever, with sales of more than 12 million copies.

In July 1977, Marley was found to have malignant melanoma in a football wound on his right big toe. Marley refused amputation, citing worries that the operation would affect his dancing, as well as the Rastafarian belief that the body must be "whole." The decision probably cost him his life.

Soon, the cancer spread to Marley's brain, lungs, liver, and stomach. After playing two shows at Madison Square Garden as part of his fall 1980 Uprising Tour, he collapsed while jogging in NYC's Central Park. The remainder of the tour was cancelled.

Bob Marley played his final concert at the Stanley Theater in Pittsburgh, Pennsylvania, on September 23, 1980. The live version of "Redemption Song" on the album *Songs of Freedom* was recorded at this show. Marley afterwards sought medical help from Munich specialist Josef Issels, but his cancer had already progressed to the terminal stage.

While flying home from Germany to Jamaica for his final days, Marley became ill, and landed in Miami for immediate medical attention. He died at Cedars of Lebanon Hospital in Miami, Florida on the morning of May 11, 1981, at the age of 36. He was buried in a crypt near his birthplace with his Gibson Les Paul, a soccer ball, a marijuana bud, and a Bible. A month before his death, he was awarded the Jamaican Order of Merit.

McKernan, Ronald C. "Pigpen"
September 8, 1945–March 6, 1973

Alta Mesa Memorial Park
695 Arastradero Road
Palo Alto, California
650-493-1041
Plot: Hillview Sec. Bb16, Lot 374

Ronald C. "Pigpen" McKernan was a founding member of the rock band the Grateful Dead. During his tenure with the band, his musical contributions included vocals, keyboards, harmonica, percussion, and guitar.

McKernan was hanging around coffeehouses and music stores when he met guitarist Jerry Garcia. One night Garcia invited McKernan to come up onstage, play his harmonica, and sing some blues. Garcia loved the performance and he knew he wanted McKernan to be the blues singer in all the local jam sessions. While it is believed by many that it was Jerry Garcia who gave McKernan his nickname of "Pigpen," it was actually a high school buddy named Roger who dubbed him Pigpen because of his funky, offbeat approach to life.

Pigpen was a participant in each of the predecessor groups leading up to the formation of the Grateful Dead, beginning with the Zodiacs and then Mother McCree's Uptown Jug Champions. Bob Weir and Bob Matthews were added to the mix and evolved into The Warlocks. Around 1965, Pigpen urged the band to go electric and that represents the actual birth of the Grateful Dead.

Pigpen was the high-energy, charismatic bluesman. He played blues organ as well as harmonica and vocals, and could scat lyrics as well. While his buddies were experimenting with LSD, Pigpen stuck to his booze, Thunderbird wine and Southern Comfort. Pigpen would go on to add more signature tunes to the Dead's repertoire, including such classics as "Turn on Your Lovelight" and "In the Midnight Hour." Soon, though, Pigpen's liver began giving out due to the heavy drinking. His organ playing became less prominent in the band's sound, but he continued to serve as a vocalist along with Garcia and Weir.

By 1971, Keith Godchaux had joined the band on piano, while Pigpen continued playing harmonica, percussion, and the Hammond organ. He vowed to quit drinking so he could still be a part of the band, but sadly, after their "Europe '72" tour, Pigpen's health had deteriorated to the point that he could no longer tour with the Dead. His final concert appearance was June 17, 1972, at the Hollywood Bowl, in Los Angeles. On March 8, 1973, Pigpen was found dead at age 27 of a gastrointestinal hemorrhage at his home.

Melvin, Harold
June 25, 1939–March 24, 1997

Ivy Hill Cemetery
Easton Road
Philadelphia, Pennsylvania
215-248-4533

Melvin was the founder and original lead singer of the R&B band Harold Melvin and the Blue Notes, but he is most famous for discovering Teddy Pendergrass. Pendergrass initially played drums for the band and went on to be lead singer. The popular Philadelphia soul band's hits include "The Love I Lost" and "Wake Up Everybody," and they've seen their songs covered by numerous artists, from Simply Red to Jimmy Somerville.

The Blue Notes were wildly popular throughout the 1970s, but interest waned in the '80s, although Melvin toured regularly with various incarnations of the group. Sadly, in the 1990s Harold Melvin suffered a severe stroke and never was able to recover. He died on March 24, 1997, in his hometown of Philadelphia.

Mizell, Jason "Jam Master Jay"
January 21, 1965–October 30, 2002

Ferncliff Cemetery and Mausoleum
Secor Road
Hartsdale, New York
914-693-4700
Plot: Hillcrest Garden C, Plot 1120

Jason William Mizell, known as Jam Master Jay, was a founder and the DJ of Run-DMC, the highly successful hip-hop group based in Queens. Mizell and the other two members of Run-DMC, the MCs Darryl "DMC" McDaniels and Joseph "Reverend Run" Simmons, were natives of the middle-class black neighborhood of Hollis, Queens. Mizell played bass and drums in several garage bands prior to joining Run-DMC; on all of their albums from *Raising Hell* on, he played keyboards, bass, and live drums in addition to his turntable work.

In 1989, Mizell established the label Jam Master Jay Records, which scored a strong success in 1993 with the band Onyx. He also connected Public Enemy's Chuck D with Def Jam co-founder Rick Rubin. (Def Jam's other founder, Russell Simmons, is the brother of DJ Run.) In the 1990s, Mizell suffered the effects of a bad car accident and a gunshot, mirroring similarly hard times for DJ Run (rape charge) and DMC (alcohol abuse). Sadly, Mizell was shot in the head and killed in a Merrick Boulevard recording studio in Queens at 7:30 P.M. on October 30, 2002.

Mydland, Brent R.
1952–July 26, 1990

Oakmont Memorial Park
2099 Reliez Valley Road
Lafayette, California
925-935-3311

Brent Mydland was the fourth keyboardist in the history of the Grateful Dead. He was with the Dead for 11 years, joining in 1979 after a session with a Bob Weir solo project. Mydland died of a drug overdose after taking a speedball at his home on "My Road" in Lafayette, California, on July 26, 1990, shortly after completing the band's summer tour. He was replaced by Vince Welnick on synthesizers and vocals, and, for a short time, temporary fill-in Bruce Hornsby on grand piano. (Welnick passed away in 2006.)

Nelson, Ricky
May 8, 1940–December 31, 1985

Forest Lawn Hollywood Hills
6300 Forest Lawn Drive
Los Angeles, California
323-254-7251
Plot: Revelation, Lot 3538

Ricky Nelson was one of the first American teen idols. Born in Teaneck, New Jersey, he was the younger son of Ozzie Nelson, the famous big band leader, and Harriet Hilliard Nelson, the band's singer. Along with brother David Nelson, the family starred in the long-running radio and television series *The Adventures of Ozzie & Harriet* from 1944 to 1954 on the radio, and 1952 to 1966 on television. However, David and Ricky Nelson did not join the cast until 1949; for the first five years of the radio show, professional actors played the sons.

Ricky Nelson began his rock 'n' roll music career in 1957. He recorded his debut single, the Fats Domino song "I'm Walkin'," in hopes of impressing a date of his who was an Elvis Presley fan. It seemed to work, because Nelson's first song was a hit, reaching number four on the charts. Soon, each episode of the *Ozzie & Harriet* television show ended with a musical performance by Ricky. From 1957 to 1962, Nelson had 30 Top 40 hits, more than any other artist at the time, except Elvis Presley.

In 1972, Nelson reached the Top 40 one last time with "Garden Party," a song he wrote in disgust after a Madison Square Garden audience booed him when he tried playing new songs instead of just his old hits. In 1985, Nelson joined a nostalgia tour of England. It was a big hit, and it revived some interest in Nelson. He tried to duplicate that effect in the United States, and he began a tour of the South. While on that tour, he died in a plane crash in De Kalb, Texas, in 1985.

Nilsson, Harry
June 15, 1941–January 15, 1994

Pierce Brothers Valley Oaks Memorial Park
5600 Lindero Canyon Road
Westlake Village, California
818-889-0902
Plot: Garden of Gethsemane, Plot 830, Grave H

Harry Edward Nilsson III was a popular American songwriter, singer, pianist, and guitarist, during the 1960s and 1970s. For most of his recordings, he did not use his first name, and was credited only as Nilsson. Despite some spectacular successes, including two Grammy Awards, Nilsson's tendency to make broad musical jumps from one record to the next seemed to hurt him. His most well-known recordings are "Without You," "Everybody's Talkin'" (theme from the movie *Midnight Cowboy*) and "Coconut." Many children remember the work he did on an animated feature called *The Point*. Harry Nilsson died of a heart attack in 1994. Many adults recall that Nilsson was a near-constant companion of John Lennon in the early 1970s during the ex-Beatle's "Lost" period away from Yoko.

Nolan, Jerry
May 7, 1946–January 14, 1992

Mount Saint Mary's Cemetery
17200 Booth Memorial Avenue
Flushing, New York
718-353-1560

Jerry Nolan was an amazing rock 'n' roll drummer who played with both the New York Dolls and The Heartbreakers. In fact, some consider Nolan to be the first punk rock drummer, as his drumming style influenced many others, including Paul Cook from the Sex Pistols. A native of New York City, Nolan joined the New York Dolls in the autumn of 1972 replacing Billy Murcia, who had died of a drug overdose.

After just two albums, Nolan left the Dolls together with Johnny Thunders. The two, along with bassist Richard Hell, formed The Heartbreakers. The band was successful in England but Nolan quit the band soon after it released its only studio album, *L.A.M.F.*, because he felt the album was poorly mixed. Nolan outlived his long-time friend, Johnny Thunders, by only a few months. In late 1991, while Nolan was being treated for bacterial meningitis and bacterial pneumonia, he suffered a stroke and went into a coma from which he never recovered. He spent his final weeks on a life support system.

Oakley, Berry
April 4, 1948-November 11, 1972

Rose Hill Cemetery
1071 Riverside Drive
Macon, Georgia
478-751-9119

Raymond Berry Oakley was bass player and founding member of The Allman Brothers Band along with Gregg Allman, Claude Hudson "Butch" Trucks, Jr., Jai Johanny "Jaimoe" Johannson, Richard "Dickey" Betts, and the late Duane Allman. He was a guiding force in the band, and when The Allman Brothers Band moved to Macon, it was Berry who found a house where they could live, rehearse, celebrate, and withdraw together. He encouraged sit-down family-style dinners at least once a week to breed harmony and felt very strongly that everyone in their extended family give back something to their adopted home. While the constant touring of The Allman Brothers Band limited their civic involvement, it was not uncommon to see stories and photos of their wives and girlfriends in the Macon newspaper recording their involvement with some worthy local cause.

On November 11, 1972, Berry was riding with Kim Payne, a member of the road crew, when he drove his Triumph motorcycle into a curve too fast and hit a Macon City bus. Immediately after the accident Berry said he was fine and refused treatment. Later that evening, he was rushed to the hospital. He had suffered a skull fracture and died soon after. A resolution was passed designating a portion of State Highway 19 in Macon as "Duane Allman Boulevard" and a bridge there as "Raymond Berry Oakley III Bridge" in honor of the two great musicians.

Another Allman Brothers-related site to see in Macon is The Big House museum (located at 2321 Vineville Avenue, phone is 478-742-7486). It's home to the Allman Brothers Band Archives and it's the actual house where the band lived and played during their most productive years in the early 1970s. Many members of the band, their roadies, friends and families hung out here and today the museum offers a chance to totally re-

live the magical legacy of the band. The sleepy Southern town of Macon is imbued with the Allman Brothers, and this is the perfect place to experience the mark the band left here.

Orbison, Roy
April 23, 1936–December 6, 1988

Westwood Memorial Park
1218 Glendon Avenue
Los Angeles, California
310-474-1579
Plot: Section D, 97 [unmarked]

Roy Orbison was a pioneer of rock 'n' roll whose recording career spanned more than four decades. By the mid-1960s, Orbison was internationally recognized for his ballads of lost love, complex melodies, characteristic dark sunglasses, and distinctive use of falsetto, typified in songs such as "Only the Lonely," "In Dreams," "Oh, Pretty Woman," "Crying," and "Running Scared."

Orbison was also a powerful influence on contemporaries such as the Rolling Stones. In 1963, he headlined a European tour with The Beatles. He became lifelong friends with the band, especially John Lennon and George Harrison. (Orbison would later record with Harrison in the Traveling Wilburys.)

Orbison smoked most of his life, and had triple heart bypass surgery on January 18, 1978. On December 6, 1988, at the age of 52, he suffered a fatal heart attack while visiting his mother in the Nashville, Tennessee, suburb of Hendersonville. In 1987, he was inducted into the Rock and Roll Hall of Fame and posthumously in 1989 into the National Academy of Popular Music/Songwriters Hall of Fame.

Parsons, Gram
November 5, 1946–September 19, 1973

Garden of Memories Cemetery
4800 Airline Drive
New Orleans, Louisiana
504-833-3786

Gram Parsons (born Cecil Ingram Connor) was an influential singer, songwriter, guitarist, and pianist. A solo artist as well as a member of both The Byrds and The Flying Burrito Brothers, he is best known for a series of recordings which anticipate the so-called country rock of the 1970s and the alt-country movement that began around 1990. Parsons described his records as "Cosmic American Music." He deeply influenced the Rolling Stones among many others and his death in 1973 remains one of the most controversial in rock 'n' roll history.

Perkins, Carl
April 9, 1932–January 19, 1998

Ridgecrest Cemetery
200 Ridgecrest Road
Jackson, Tennessee
731-427-5844

Carl Perkins was a true pioneer of the rockabilly music that famously evolved at Sun Records in Memphis in the early 1950s. In late 1955, a desperately poor and struggling Perkins wrote the song "Blue Suede Shoes" on an old potato sack. Produced by Sam Phillips, the record was a massive chart success. At the peak of the song's national success, Perkins was involved in a near-fatal car accident and it may have cost him his career. Perkins could only watch as his pal, Elvis Presley, also had success with a cover version of "Blue Suede Shoes" (a follow-up to Elvis's first hit, "Heartbreak Hotel").

Intentionally or not, the Elvis cover stole Perkins's thunder, and he never had another Top 40 hit, even after his move to Columbia Records in 1958. However, many groups including The Beatles, who covered "Matchbox," "Honey Don't," and "Everybody's Trying To Be My Baby," kept his songs in the public eye. Perkins's last album, Go Cat Go!, was released in 1996, and featured new collaborations with Paul Simon, John Fogerty, Tom Petty, and Bono. His last major concert appearance was the "Music for Monserrat" all-star charity concert at Royal Albert Hall on November 15, 1997. Two months later, Carl Perkins died at the age of 65 from throat cancer after suffering several strokes.

Phillips, John
August 30, 1935–March 18, 2001

Forest Lawn-Cathedral City
69855 E. Ramon Road
Cathedral City, California
760-321-0994

John Phillips was the co-founder and leader of the 1960s pop group The Mamas and the Papas. The quartet included Phillips, his wife Michelle Phillips, Denny Doherty, and Cass Elliot. John Phillips wrote and arranged most of the group's hits, including the smashes "California Dreamin'" and "Monday Monday." (The Mamas and the Papas were inducted into the Rock and Roll Hall of Fame in 1998.) Phillips also co-wrote the sentimental 1967 hit "San Francisco (Be Sure To Wear Flowers In Your Hair)," which was recorded by Scott McKenzie.

That same year Phillips helped organize the Monterey Pop Festival, the famous three-day concert that included performances by Jimi Hendrix, Janis Joplin, the Grateful Dead, and The Who. Phillips had his last hit as the co-author of The Beach Boys' 1988 pop chart-topper "Kokomo." In later years, Phillips battled drug and alcohol problems, requiring a liver transplant in 1992.

Phillips, Sam Cornelius
January 5, 1923–July 30, 2003

Memorial Park Cemetery
5668 Poplar Avenue
Memphis, Tennessee
901-767-8930

Samuel Cornelius Phillips was a legendary record producer who played an important role in the emergence of rock 'n' roll as the major form of popular music in the 1950s. He is most notably credited with discovering Elvis Presley, and is associated with several other noteworthy rhythm and blues and rock 'n' roll stars of the day.

Phillips's pivotal role in the early days of rock 'n' roll was solidified by a famed jam session on December 4, 1956, which came to be known as the Million Dollar Quartet. Jerry Lee Lewis was playing piano for a Carl Perkins recording session at Phillips's studio. Johnny Cash was there listening, and Elvis Presley walked in unexpectedly, leading to an impromptu session featuring the four musicians.

In 1986, Sam Phillips was also part of the first group of musicians inducted into the new Rock and Roll Hall of Fame and the Rockabilly Hall of Fame has recognized his pioneering contribution to the genre. In 1987, Phillips was also inducted into the Alabama Music Hall of Fame. He received a Grammy Trustees Award for his lifetime achievements in 1991, in 1998 he was inducted into the Blues Hall of Fame, and in October 2001 he was inducted into the Country Music Hall of Fame. Phillips died of respiratory failure at St. Francis Hospital in Memphis, Tennessee, on June 30, 2003, only one day before the original Sun Studio was designated a National Historic Landmark.

Pickett, Wilson
March 18, 1941–January 19, 2006

Evergreen Cemetery
25 South Alexandria Pike
Louisville, Kentucky
502-366-1481

Singer Wilson Pickett's first major break came when he was invited to join The Falcons in early 1959. The Falcons were one of the first vocal groups to bring gospel into a popular context (thus paving the way for soul music). Pickett's biggest success with The Falcons came in 1962, when "I Found a Love" (co-authored by Pickett and featuring his lead vocals) peaked at #6 on the R&B charts, and at #75 on the pop charts. Pickett's major breakthrough came at Stax Records' recording studio in Memphis, where he recorded his third Atlantic single, "In the Midnight Hour" (1965). Perhaps his best remembered hit, it peaked at #1 R&B, #21 pop. In 1991, Pickett was inducted into the Rock and Roll Hall of Fame, and his music was prominently featured in the film The Commitments, featuring Pickett as an off-screen character. Pickett died of a heart attack on January 19, 2006.

Pitney, Gene
February 17, 1940-April 5, 2006

Somers Center Cemetery
Maple and School Streets
Somers, Connecticut

Gene Francis Alan Pitney was a popular American singer and songwriter who, through the mid-1960s, achieved success on both sides of the Atlantic (he had more than 20 Top 40 hit singles). He was also an accomplished guitarist, pianist, drummer, and skilled sound engineer. In 1961, Gene Pitney released his first solo single, "(I Wanna) Love My Life Away," on which he played several instruments and multi-tracked the vocals, followed by his first big hit, "Town Without Pity" that same year. This tune won the Golden Globe Award for Best Song in a Motion Picture, and was nominated for an Academy Award for Best Song.

Pitney also wrote hit songs for others, including "He's a Rebel" for The Crystals and Vikki Carr, "Today's Teardrops" for Roy Orbison, "Rubber Ball" for Bobby Vee, and "Hello Mary Lou" for Ricky Nelson.

Pitney is also well remembered for his emotional rendition of the title song to the movie *The Man Who Shot Liberty Valance* (1962), which starred Jimmy Stewart, John Wayne, Vera Miles, and Lee Marvin. Pitney's unique vocal delivery of the Burt Bacharach and Hal David song told the story almost as well as the movie itself. Although it was a certified Top 10 hit for Pitney, it was never used in the movie due to a publishing argument.

His 1963 hit, "Mecca," is considered by some to be a precursor to psychedelia in its use of Indian musical influences, two years before The Beatles began incorporating these influences. The use of exotic musical instruments became something of a Pitney trademark, as evidenced by the Mariachi trumpets used in "Lonely Drifters," the ukuleles in "Hawaii," and the gypsy fiddle in "Golden Earrings." The song, "That Girl Belongs to Yesterday," which became a hit for him, was also the first Rolling Stones song to be a hit in the United States, and it was partly Pitney's endorsement of the group that helped them to succeed in America. In 2002, Pitney was inducted into the Rock and Roll Hall of Fame. Pitney died on April 5, 2006, at the age of 66. He was found dead by his tour manager in the Hilton Hotel in Cardiff, Wales, in the middle of a U.K. tour. An autopsy confirmed the singer died of natural causes.

THE BEST OF
GENE PITNEY
18 ORIGINAL HITS

featuring
Mecca, The Man Who Shot Liberty
Valance, If I Didn't Have A Dime,
Twenty Four Hours From Tulsa
plus many more

Preston, Billy
September 2, 1946–June 6, 2006

Inglewood Park Cemetery
720 E. Florence Avenue
Inglewood, California
310-412-6500

William Everett Preston was a multi-talented soul musician from Houston, Texas (though he was raised mostly in Los Angeles). In addition to his successful, Grammy-winning career as a solo artist, the versatile Preston collaborated with some of the greatest legends in the music industry, including The Beatles, the Rolling Stones, Little Richard, Ray Charles, George Harrison, Eric Clapton, Bob Dylan, Sam Cooke, Sammy Davis, Jr., Sly Stone, Aretha Franklin, the Jackson 5, Quincy Jones, and the Red Hot Chili Peppers. He played the electric piano on the "Get Back" sessions in 1969 and is one of several people sometimes credited as the "Fifth Beatle." He is, in fact, the only person to receive label performance credit on any Beatles record. He died in 2006 from chronic kidney failure.

Ramone, Dee Dee
September 18, 1952–June 5, 2002

Hollywood Forever
6000 Santa Monica Boulevard
Hollywood, Los Angeles
323-469-1181

Douglas Glenn Colvin is best remembered as the bassist and founding member of punk rock band the Ramones. Colvin, nicknamed "Dee Dee," wrote or co-wrote many of the Ramones' most popular songs, including "53rd & 3rd," "Commando," "Rockaway Beach," and "Poison Heart." He was the bassist for the band from their formation in 1974 through 1989, when he left to pursue a short-lived career in rap music under the name Dee Dee King. Afterwards, he continued to write songs for the Ramones until 1996, when the band retired. Colvin struggled with drug addiction for much of his life, especially heroin. He'd begun using drugs as a teenager, and continued to use for the majority of his adult life. He died in 2002, in Los Angeles, from heroin toxicity.

Ramone, Joey
May 19, 1951–April 15, 2001

Hillside Cemetery
1401 Woodland Avenue
Lyndhurst, New Jersey
856-438-1612

During his youth, soon to be punk star Jeffrey Hyman (aka Joey Ramone) was considered something of an outcast and had a dysfunctional family life. Growing up on the streets of New York, he was a fan of The Who and the Rolling Stones, among other bands. He took up drums at 13, playing throughout his teen years, and originally was the drummer for the Ramones. Upon Tommy Ramone's suggestion, he switched to vocals. Hyman was said to be the "heart and soul" of the Ramones, and his favorite songs from their repertoire often were the ballads and love songs.

Interestingly, Hyman did not speak to guitarist Johnny Cummings for many years. This animosity began when Cummings "stole" Hyman's girlfriend Linda, whom Cummings later married, supposedly prompting Hyman to write "The KKK Took My Baby Away" for the *Pleasant Dreams* album. They also were strongly averse to each other's politics; Hyman being a left-leaning liberal while Cummings was a staunch conservative. The pair never truly resolved their differences before they died.

Hyman died of lymphoma at New York-Presbyterian Hospital on April 15, 2001. He apparently had had the cancer for a long time though few knew of his condition. Countless memorials, both by fans and the rockers he influenced, followed his passing. When he died, he was listening to the U2 song "In a Little While." This was during U2's Elevation Tour, and from that point on during shows, U2 singer Bono would dedicate the song to Joey.

On November 30, 2003, a block of East 2nd Street in New York City was officially renamed "Joey Ramone Place." It is the street where Hyman once lived with band mate Dee Dee Ramone, and is near CBGB, the onetime club where the Ramones got their start.

Ramone, Johnny
October 8, 1948–September 15, 2004

Hollywood Forever (memorial)
6000 Santa Monica Boulevard
Hollywood, California
323-469-1181

Johnny Ramone (John Cummings) was a co-founder and guitarist of the Ramones. He was known for his fast, high-energy playing style that consisted of quick, double down strokes; aka the "Buzzsaw" style, which became highly influential among other speed-punk bands.

Although never a "closet Republican" (many around him said he was vocal about his opinions), Johnny made his political affiliation known to the world in 2002, when the Ramones were inducted into the Rock and Roll Hall of Fame. After thanking everyone who made it possible—clad in his trademark T-shirt, ripped blue jeans, and leather jacket—Johnny said, "God bless President Bush, and God bless America." This further added to the feud he had going with lead singer Joey.

On September 15, 2004, Johnny Ramone died in his Los Angeles home after a five-year battle with prostate cancer. After his death, his remains were cremated, but a cenotaph was built in Hollywood Forever Cemetery, just several yards away from Dee Dee Ramone's grave.

Rhoads, Randy
December 6, 1956–March 19, 1982

Mountain View Cemetery
570 E. Highland Avenue
San Bernardino, California
909-882-2943

The late Randall William "Randy" Rhoads was rated by *Rolling Stone* magazine as number 85 in The 100 Greatest Guitarists of All Time. His unique neo-classical metal style of playing set him apart from other guitarists of the early 1980s and he influenced a slew of other players. A true classical student of the instrument, while on tour with Ozzy Osbourne, he would often seek out classical guitar tutors for lessons.

On March 19, 1982, Ozzy's band was headed to a festival in Orlando, Florida. They stopped at the bus driver's house in Leesburg, Florida, after driving much of the night. The driver (and sometime pilot), Andrew Aycock, took Rhoads and hairdresser Rachel Youngblood on a plane ride early that morning. During the flight, an attempt was made to "buzz" the tour bus where the other band members were sleeping. They succeeded three times but the fourth time tragedy struck. The right wing clipped the right side of the tour bus by accident, sending the small plane careening into a nearby mansion. Nobody in the mansion was hurt, but Rhoads, 25, was killed instantly, as were Aycock, 36, and Youngblood, 58. It was found later that Aycock had some amount of cocaine in his system; Rhoads's toxicology test revealed no illicit drugs.

Slovak, Hillel
April 13, 1962–June 27, 1988

Mount Sinai Memorial Park
5950 Forest Lawn Drive
Los Angeles, California
818-905-7600
Plot: Maimonides 26, L-4613, Space 1

It was while attending Fairfax High School in Los Angeles that musician Hillel Slovak met future band mates Jack Irons, Anthony Kiedis, and Michael Balzary (also known as Flea), who would soon form the Red Hot Chili Peppers. Hillel and Anthony developed serious heroin habits early in their careers, which is the vice that ultimately led to Hillel's death. He was once fired from the Peppers for a short amount of time because of this addiction. During the European tour supporting *The Uplift Mofo Party Plan* album, more serious drug problems became apparent, and Slovak was found dead of a heroin overdose on June 25, 1988. He was just 26 years old.

Thunders, Johnny
July 16, 1952–April 23, 1991

Mount Saint Mary's Cemetery
17200 Booth Memorial Avenue
Flushing, New York
718-353-1560

Johnny Thunders, born John Anthony Genzale, Jr., was an influential rock 'n' roll guitarist and singer, first with the New York Dolls, the proto-punk glam rockers of the early
'70s. During the late '70s, he was a familiar figure on the New York punk scene, both
with The Heartbreakers and as a solo artist. His screeching, distinctive guitar sound
was highly influential in punk rock and new wave music. After leaving the Dolls in 1976,
he formed The Heartbreakers with Dolls drummer Jerry Nolan, ex-Demons guitarist
Walter Lure, and Television bassist Richard Hell, who left soon after to form Richard
Hell and the Voidoids.

With Thunders leading the band, The Heartbreakers toured America and Britain, releasing one official album, *L.A.M.F.*, in 1977. *L.A.M.F.* remains a punk classic that documents
the important bridge between the U.S. and U.K. punk scenes (just ask the Sex Pistols
or The Clash).

In late 1979, Johnny Thunders began playing in a band called Gang War, along with John
Morgan, Ron Cooke, Philippe Marcade, and former MC5 guitarist Wayne Kramer. They
recorded several demos and performed live several times before disbanding.

After that, Thunders recorded a number of solo albums beginning with the classic *So
Alone* in 1978. Many consider the drug-addled LP Thunders's true masterpiece. During
the early '80s, Thunders re-formed The Heartbreakers for various tours and the group

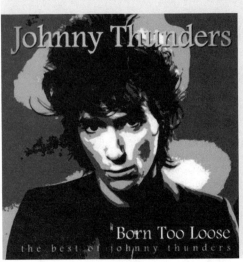

recorded their final album in 1984.
As well, Thunders toured regularly
around the world. Many rumors sur-
round Johnny's death at the St.
Peter House in New Orleans,
Louisiana, in April 1991, but he
apparently died of drug-related
causes. He had arrived in town the
day before to get a new band
together and start up some recording sessions.

Valens, Ritchie
May 13, 1941–February 3, 1959

San Fernando Mission Cemetery
11160 Stranwood Avenue
Mission Hills, California
818-361-7387

Richard Steven Valenzuela, better known as Ritchie Valens, was a pioneer of rock 'n' roll. Born in Pacoima, California, he became the first Mexican-American rock 'n' roll star. A completely self-taught musician, Valens was an accomplished singer and guitarist and in concert, he often improvised new lyrics and added new riffs to popular songs while he was playing. Due to his high-energy performances, Valens earned the nickname "The Little Richard of the Valley."

In May 1958, record executive Bob Keane heard about Valens, so he invited Ritchie to audition at his home in the Silver Lake area of Los Angeles, where he had a small recording studio. Impressed, Keane signed Ritchie to his record company on May 27, 1958.

After several songwriting and demo recording sessions with Keane in his basement studio, Keane decided that Ritchie was ready to record with a full band backing him. The first songs cut at the famed Gold Star studios on one afternoon in July 1958, were "Come On, Let's Go" and "Framed," a Jerry Leiber and Mike Stoller tune. Pressed and released within days of the recording session, the record was a hit. Valens's next record, a double A-side, which was the final record to be released in his lifetime, included the songs "Donna" and "La Bamba."

In early 1959, Valens was traveling the Midwest on a tour dubbed "The Winter Dance Party." Accompanying him were Buddy Holly with a new lineup of The Crickets, Tommy Allsup on guitar, Waylon Jennings on bass, and Carl Bunch on drums; Dion and the Belmonts; J.P. "The Big Bopper" Richardson; and Frankie Sardo. None of the other performers had backing bands, so The Crickets filled in for all the shows.

As has been well documented, Holly, fed up with the conditions on the buses, chartered a small plane for he and The Crickets to get to the next show on time, get some rest, and get their laundry done. After the February 2, 1959, performance at the Surf Ballroom in Clear Lake, Iowa, Holly, Richardson (who begged Waylon Jennings for his seat because he had the flu), and Valens (who had won Tommy Allsup's seat after a coin toss), were taken to Clear Lake airport by the manager of the Surf Ballroom.

The plane, a four-passenger Beechcraft Bonanza, departed into a blinding snowstorm and crashed almost immediately into farmer Albert Juhl's cornfield. The crash killed all three musicians, as well as the 21-year-old pilot, Roger Peterson.

Waters, Muddy
April 4, 1915–April 30, 1983

Restvale Cemetery
11700 S. Laramie Avenue
Alsip, Illinois
708-385-3506

The blues singer and guitarist McKinley Morganfield, better known as "Muddy Waters," is considered to be one of rock 'n' roll's most influential musicians. Though he never enjoyed huge commercial success, Waters inspired the likes of Bob Dylan, Elvis Presley, Eric Clapton, Jeff Beck, and Mick Jagger. His most famous recordings include "Rollin' Stone" (1950), "I Just Wanna Make Love to You" (1954), and "Got My Mojo Working" (1954). His influence is spread over a wide variety of musical genres including blues, rhythm and blues, rock 'n' roll, folk, jazz, and country. Waters also helped Chuck Berry get his first record contract. His 1958 tour of England marked perhaps the first time an amplified, hard-rocking band was heard there, although on his first tour he was the only one plugged in.

The Rolling Stones named themselves after Waters' 1950 song, "Rollin' Stone," also known as "Catfish Blues," which Jimi Hendrix covered as well. One of Led Zeppelin's biggest hits, "Whole Lotta Love," is based upon the Muddy Waters hit, "You Need Love," which was written by Willie Dixon. Dixon wrote some of Muddy Waters's most famous songs, including "I Just Want to Make Love to You" (a big radio hit for the '70s rock band Foghat), "Hoochie Coochie Man," and "I'm Ready." Angus Young of the rock group AC/DC has cited Waters as one of his influences, paying tribute through the band's cover of "Baby Please Don't Go." In 1983, the legendary bluesman passed away in his sleep.

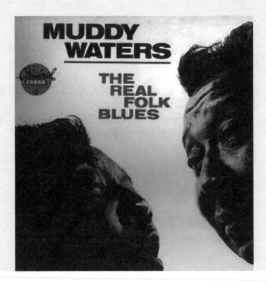

Wells, Mary
May 13, 1943–July 26, 1992

Forest Lawn Memorial Park
1712 S. Glendale Avenue
Glendale, California
1-800-204-3131

Mary Wells was the wonderful 1960s rhythm and blues singer from Motown Records who was best known by her early '60s hits "My Guy," " Two Lovers," "You Beat Me To the Punch," and "The One Who Really Loves You," which all made the Top 10. Her career fluctuated over the years and in 1990, Wells, a longtime smoker, was diagnosed with cancer of the larynx. She immediately began treatment and was forced to sell her house, possessions, and eventually could not afford health insurance. The treatments ravaged her voice, which forced Wells to quit touring.

With no way to continue treatment, Wells's friends Diana Ross, Mary Wilson, and Martha Reeves helped her financially, along with Rod Stewart, Bruce Springsteen, and Bonnie Raitt. In the summer of 1992, Wells was hospitalized for pneumonia at the Kenneth Norris Jr. Cancer Hospital in Los Angeles. Still suffering the effects of her cancer, her weakened immune system could not take the extra strain. Wells died on July 26, 1992, at age of just 49.

Wilson, Carl
December 21, 1946–February 6, 1998

Westwood Memorial Park
1218 Glendon Avenue
Los Angeles, California
310-474-1579

Lead guitarist Carl Wilson was the youngest of the three brothers who made up the core of The Beach Boys. After his elder brother Brian's initial retirement from the stage in 1965, Carl became the de facto leader of the band onstage (interestingly, contracts at that time read that promoters hired "Carl Wilson plus four other musicians"). Soon after, Carl became the band's in-studio leader, helping his brother Brian to produce the bulk of the albums *20/20, Sunflower, Surf's Up*, and others.

In the late 1960s, Wilson also made headlines as a conscientious objector to the Vietnam War, at one point having to let the rest of the band tour the U.K. without him while he was up before the draft board.

During the 1970s, Wilson also produced records for other artists and appeared on many songs as a backing vocalist, most notably Chicago's "Wishing You Were Here," Elton John's "Don't Let The Sun Go Down On Me" (with then former-band mate Bruce Johnston), and David Lee Roth's hit cover version of "California Girls." Wilson died of cancer in 1998.

Zappa, Frank
December 21, 1940–December 4, 1993

Westwood Memorial Park
1218 Glendon Avenue
Los Angeles, California
310-474-1579
Plot: Section D, 100 [unmarked]

Legendary guitarist Frank Zappa was also a studio wizard whose early work with his band The Mothers of Invention displayed exceptional musical knowledge and a biting sense of humor. His radical work earned him a devout cult following, though he did have several hits over the years (including the novelty song "Valley Girl"). After dozens of solo albums, including *Weasels Ripped My Flesh, Apostrophe* and *Shut Up 'N Play Yer Guitar*, Zappa went from being an underground rock star to being a highly regarded composer. With just a high-school education, Zappa was essentially self-taught in music. Funny, literate, and extremely articulate, Zappa always occupied his own unique niche in music.

A legendary workaholic, he created hundreds of recorded and written musical works, spread over some 60 music albums released during his lifetime (plus several posthumous releases). Almost all his compositions were original or collaborative efforts and there is no doubt that he would have produced hundreds more had he lived longer. In addition to his many music albums, Frank Zappa also crafted feature-length and short films, long-format music videos, music video clips, graphic art, album covers, books, and many other works. A true renaissance man in every sense, Frank Zappa died of cancer in 1993. He was 53 years old.

can't BUY ME LOVE: ROCk 'n' ROll Museums, Restaurants, Hotels, and Other Places to Spend Your cash

The Alabama Music Hall of Fame

617 Highway 72 West
Tuscumbia, Alabama
800-239-AMHF

The Alabama Music Hall of Fame exhibits hundreds of items that celebrate and call attention to the extraordinary musical heritage of Alabama. The Alabama Music Hall of Fame was a dream and goal of the Muscle Shoals Music Association—a professional organization of recording studio owners, producers, musicians, songwriters, and other music professionals based in the Shoals area. In 1980, through their efforts, the state legislature created a state agency, the Alabama Music Hall of Fame Board, to honor all of the state's great music achievers and to build a facility in which to showcase these talented individuals and their accomplishments.

In 1987, the citizens of Alabama passed a statewide referendum for the construction of the first part of the project, a 12,500-square-foot exhibit hall-The Alabama Music Hall of Fame. Grand opening ceremonies were held July 26, 1990. The artists who are inducted are not limited to any single style of music, nor are they restricted to just the realm of performance. From performance to song writing, and from management to publishing, Alabamians have contributed in many ways to making the industry of music what it is today.

The American Jazz Museum

1616 E. 18th street
Kansas City, Missouri
816-474-8463

The American Jazz Museum is the premier jazz museum in the United States. Located in the historic 18th & Vine district in Kansas City, Missouri, it preserves the history of Jazz. The museum features exhibits on Charlie Parker, Duke Ellington, Louis Armstrong, and more. Items on display include a saxophone owned by Charlie Parker and various Down Beat awards, rare photos, album covers, memorabilia, and personal items from the

stars of jazz. There are also more than 100 recordings of the greatest jazz ever played, plus films and special collections honoring the impact of jazz on the American experience. The Blue Room is a fully functioning jazz club on site, and the Gem Theatre across the street is a larger venue hosting jazz music.

Armstrong, Louis

34-56 107th Street
Corona, New York
718-478-8274

Louis Armstrong was born in a poor section of New Orleans known as "the Battlefield" on August 4, 1901. When he died in 1971, the man known as Satchmo was widely recog-

nized as a founding father of jazz. Today, you can visit where the legend lived in New York, experiencing many artifacts and mementos related to his illustrious life. As you'll learn, over the years Satchmo entertained millions, from heads of state and royalty to the kids on his stoop in this working-class neighborhood. Guided 40-minute tours of the house leave every hour, on the hour.

Bata Shoe Museum

327 Bloor Street West
Toronto, Canada
416-979-7799

It's shoe-time! Here at this unique shoe museum you'll find over 10,000 shoes ranging from those worn by Chinese women with bound feet to ancient Egyptian sandals to chestnut-crushing clogs. Elton John's famous, early 1970s platform shoes are here as well. Over 4,500 years of history and a collection of 20th-century celebrity shoes are reflected in the permanent exhibition All About Shoes and three other galleries feature special exhibitions. It's a place that's a perfect fit for anyone.

B.B. King's

237 West 42 Street
New York, New York
212-997-4144

Located in the heart of Times Square is the B.B. King Blues Club & Grill, named of course for the famed blues guitarist. Owned by the Bensusan Family, proprietors of the world renowned Blue Note Jazz Club, the club features world-class musical talent and consists of two distinct spaces: the Showcase Room and Lucille's Grill.
In addition to memorable shows by B.B. King himself, the club has hosted many other legends over the years including Gregg Allman and Friends, Brian Wilson, George Clinton & the P-Funk All-Stars, Etta James, Erykah Badu, Macy Gray, Peter Frampton, Better than Ezra, Karl Denson's Tiny Universe, Dr. John, Robert Cray, and many more.

Berklee School of Music

1140 Boylston Street
Boston, Massachusetts
617-266-1400

This legendary music school has produced many famous students over the years (and even lesser known session players, music teachers, etc.) Aimee Mann, Quincy Jones and Melissa Etheridge are just a few of the students that took classes here.

Blueberry Hill

6504 Delmar Boulevard
St. Louis, Missouri
314-727-4444

Blueberry Hill is a restaurant and bar located in the Delmar Loop neighborhood in University City, a suburb of St. Louis, Missouri. Chuck Berry performs here one Wednesday each month downstairs in the Duck Room. Blueberry Hill possesses a wide appeal among St. Louis residents during the day and evening, and becomes a popular twenty-something hangout at night, with many Washington University students visiting throughout the week. The restaurant is decorated with various music memorabilia, figurines, and even centaur statues. The restaurant is famous for its hamburgers and has several themed rooms, such as a karaoke room (lined with jukeboxes) and a darts room, which hosts a weekly league and an annual tournament. The exterior sign has recently been renovated. It now includes three bright marquee screens and a tall neon-accented sign with two '50s-era dancers.

Outside the restaurant is the St. Louis Walk of Fame, the brainchild of Blueberry Hill's owner, Joe Edwards. The St. Louis Walk of Fame, lining the sidewalks on both sides of Delmar, features stars with the names of celebrities that have hailed from St. Louis. On

display at Blueberry Hill is "The Guitar That Rocked the World." It's the Gibson ES-350T on which Chuck Berry wrote, recorded, and performed his great classics such as "Sweet Little Sixteen," "Memphis," "Rock & Roll Music," and "Johnny B. Goode." A large exhibit of Chuck Berry memorabilia forms one of the many displays at Blueberry Hill.

Blues & Legends Hall of Fame Museum

1021 Casino Center Drive
Robinsonville, Mississippi
1-866-618-0088

This great little museum is actually located within the Horseshoe Casino. Admission is free and you simply walk through the casino to get to the museum and it's easy to find. Once there you'll discover some great artifacts that are organized by artist. There is also a great collection of Bill Graham and Family Dog psychedelic concert posters, which showcase many blues artists.

Alice Cooper's Town

101 E. Jackson Street
Phoenix, Arizona
602-253-7337

Alice Cooper's Town is named after legendary rock star and owner Alice Cooper (who is also a big sports fan). And know up front that this is not your typical bar and grill. There's a main dining area (that specializes in BBQ and homestyle cooking), indoor and outdoor bar, a mezzanine, two patios, and a spacious courtyard. The decor at Alice Cooper's Town is something to behold as well: a unique combination of authentic autographed sports and music memorabilia including The Fender Wall of Fame. The guitars in this one-of-a-kind display are rotated regularly and feature signature model Fender guitars from renowned musicians including Eric Clapton, The Who, Black Sabbath, Fleetwood Mac, Mötley Crüe, and the Rolling Stones. The wall surrounding the display is also adorned with autographs from famous celebrities who have visited the restaurant.

Alice Cooper's Town also features a state-of-the-art video and sound system including a monster video wall, a large outdoor scoreboard with a big screen TV, and a live music stage. Alice even opened a second location, at 2217 East Ninth St., Cleveland, just across from Jacobs Field.

Croce's

802 Fifth Avenue
San Diego, California
619-233-4355

In 1985, Ingrid Croce, Jim's widow, opened Croce's Restaurant & Jazz Bar, located in the historic Gaslamp Quarter in San Diego, California, partially as a tribute to her late husband. There's live nightly music, and from time to time the late performer's son A.J. stops in with his friends to jam. The food is good, and this is also a great people watching venue.

Delta Music Museum and Hall of Fame

218 Louisiana Avenue
Ferriday, Louisiana
318-757-9999

The former U.S. Post Office in Ferriday has now been completely renovated and outfit-ted as the fantastic Delta Music Museum. Ferriday is home to entertainers Jerry Lee Lewis and Mickey Gilley, evangelist Jimmy Swaggart, blues trombonist Pee Wee Whittaker, General Claire Chennault, and newscaster Howard K. Smith, and is now also home to the new museum, which was dedicated on March 2, 2002.

Previously known as the Ferriday Museum and housed in a small bank building, the Delta Music Museum is a new addition to the Louisiana Department of State's Historic Museums Program. Inside you'll find many artifacts relat-ed to local bluesmen and Delta musicians, like Aaron Neville, Clarence "Frogman" Henry, and many others.

Duke's Tropicana Coffee Shop

8909 W. Sunset Boulevard
West Hollywood, California
310-652-3100

Long known as a hangout for bands playing the Whisky a Go-Go (which is located right next door), Duke's is a famous rock 'n' roll eatery located right on the Strip. You never know who you'll see eating here, but you always know you'll get one of the best break-fasts in town after a long night. The Doors played their first official club gig here in the early '60s when, it was a nightclub named London Fog. Note—Duke's was originally located nearby at 8585 Santa Monica Boulevard, as part of the legendary Tropicana Motel.

Elvis is Alive Museum

50's Café
Interstate 70, Wright City exit 199
Wright City, Missouri
636-745-3154

When Bill Beeny opened the 50's Café in 1981, his goal was to pull in travelers along Interstate 70 who would enjoy his extensive collection of 1950s celebrity photos and memorabilia. By 1991, the cafe was 99 percent Elvis. After fielding the question "Is Elvis alive?" one too many times, he decided to make the "museum" a reliquary of proof that the King is, in fact, still walking around. He displays government documents, pathology reports, DNA testing results, 3,000 photographs, and transcripts of interviews with Elvis's relatives and former employees—all proving, according to Beeny, that Elvis lives.

Experience Music Project

325 Fifth Avenue North
Seattle, Washington
206-367-5483

One of the most famous guitars of all time is the white Fender Stratocaster Jimi Hendrix played August 18, 1969, at the Woodstock Festival in upstate Bethel, New York. Hendrix and his Band of Gypsies were the final act to come on to the stage at Woodstock as dawn broke at the end of the festival.

Many of the more than 400,000 people who had flocked to Woodstock had already packed up and started home, but those who stayed for that rainy Monday morning show witnessed one of the most talked-about performances in rock history. After all, it was here that Hendrix played his infamous version of the American national anthem, "The Star-Spangled Banner," signifying the close of the '60s and Hendrix's distaste of U.S. involvement in Vietnam.

The guitar was sold at Sotheby's auction house in London in 1990 to an Italian collector, but a few years later, Microsoft billionaire Paul Allen discovered the whereabouts of the guitar and bought it from the collector. The guitar is now owned by Paul Allen who placed it as the central exhibition in Seattle's Experience Music Project, a huge state-of-the-art museum of rock memorabilia. At the museum, you'll also experience over 80,000 other rock 'n' roll artifacts, including early electric guitars, costumes, and handwritten lyrics sheets.

Georgia Music Hall of Fame and Museum

200 Martin Luther King, Jr. Boulevard
Macon, Georgia
888-GA-ROCKS

The Georgia Music Hall of Fame, the state's official music museum, is located in Macon, the city where artists like Little Richard, James Brown, Otis Redding, and The Allman Brothers Band launched their careers. The 43,000-square-foot facility features permanent and changing exhibits that include music, videos, memorabilia, instruments, and performance costumes.

But perhaps some of the most prized artifacts belong to Ray Charles. The museum is the home of a suit that Charles donated himself, along with a reel-to-reel tape deck that was used to record a concert at Atlanta's Herndon Stadium in 1959 that celebrated the fifth anniversary of radio station WAOK-AM. The marathon concert—sort of a black Woodstock—featured top African-American recording stars such as Ray Charles, Ruth Brown, B.B. King, and Buddy Johnson.

The Gibson Guitar Factory

The Beale Street Showcase
145 Lt. George Lee Avenue
Memphis, Tennessee
901-544-7998

Take a complete tour of the Gibson Beale Street Showcase in Memphis. This memorable tour of Gibson's Memphis guitar factory consists of an intimate viewing of the facility as Gibson's skilled craftsmen create some of the finest guitars in the world. It's an opportunity to witness the intricate process of binding, neck-fitting, painting, buffing, and tuning that creates these incredible musical instruments. See and hear how Gibson has helped shape the world of music for over 100 years and how he continues to set the pace for the musical innovations of tomorrow. The tour lasts approximately 45 minutes and in the gift shop you can, of course, buy a guitar.

Gram's Place Bed and Breakfast

3109 North Ola Avenue
Tampa, Florida
813-221-0596

In 1980, Mark Holland founded the Gram Parsons Foundation to share, perpetuate, and educate people about the music of Gram Parsons. After working for four years with John Kravet and Judy Katz, Mark wrote, produced, and directed the first documentary on Gram Parsons (*The Legend of the Grievous Angel*) for public access cable in Tampa.

Gram's Place was established in 1991 after owner Mark Holland took a trip to Amsterdam, Holland. Impressed by the tolerant nature of the people of Amsterdam, and after receiving the Dutch "Gram Parsons Award" created by Henk Korsten of the Netherlands (recognizing Gram Parsons as the official Godfather of Country Rock Music), Mark set out with a dream—to bring all people together through music. This bed and breakfast came next, and today it's a place to celebrate not just the music of Parsons, but of all musicians. This is a funky, low-key place to crash and play music in an environment lovingly maintained by the owners to reflect a spirit of creativity and soul.

Hard Rock Cafe

www.hardrock.com

This chain of casual dining restaurants has become famous worldwide for not just serving up food, but heaps of rock 'n' roll memorabilia as well. It was founded in 1971 by Isaac Tigrett and Peter Morton, and their first Hard Rock Cafe opened near Hyde Park Corner in London, in a former Rolls Royce car dealership's showroom, where in 1979 they began to cover the walls with rock 'n' roll ephemera. The cafe was reportedly named after The Doors' 1970 album *Morrison Hotel*, which was in turn named after a now closed bar in downtown Los Angeles depicted on the back cover of *Morrison Hotel*. The Hard Rock Cafe's motto—Love All, Serve All—was adopted from Tigrett's guru Sathya Sai Baba.

A second location, originally developed by an unaffiliated group and later purchased by Hard Rock International, opened in downtown Toronto in 1978. The chain began global expansion in 1982 when the two agreed to develop their own cafes across the world. Morton (Hard Rock America) opened Hard Rocks in Los Angeles, San Francisco, Chicago, and Houston while Tigrett (Hard Rock International) did so in New York City, Dallas, and Paris, France.

Eventually Tigrett sold his interest to Robert Earl and Mecca Leisure, but Morton opened several more units including Las Vegas, Nevada; San Diego and Newport Beach, California; Sydney and Melbourne, Australia; Honolulu and Maui, Hawaii; and Israel, among many others

Today, there are more than 143 Hard Rock Cafes in over 36 countries, with several more in the works. As well, in 1995, Peter Morton opened the first Hard Rock Hotel & Casino off the Las Vegas strip and it was an overnight sensation.

Harrison, George

Hard Day's Nite Bed and Breakfast
113 McCann Street
Benton, Illinois
618-438-2328

This was once the house of Louise Harrison, George Harrison's sister, and it's where the first Beatle ever stayed in the United States. Louise Harrison lived in the house from 1963 to 1968, and shortly before The Beatles exploded in the U.S., Harrison made a trip here. He wanted to see his sister, but he also needed a break from insane Beatlemania

that had already kicked in overseas. When George took his summer vacation, it is said he spent his time picnicking and performing with a local band, The Four Vests. George left in September and returned to the United States the following February to appear on *The Ed Sullivan Show*.

In 1996, Benton decided to make a parking lot next to Benton Consolidated High School, where the house resides. Three couples came together to buy the house and with the help of Louise, convinced the town that it should survive as a historical site. Today, it lives on as the Hard Day's Nite Bed and Breakfast, replete with a Beatles mini-museum inside. At the Franklin County Jail Museum, one of the rooms is dedicated to George's Benton stay, primarily his visit to the WFRX 1300 radio station in West Frankfort. On display are the turntables that first brought Beatles records to the American airwaves. The museum is located ½ mile off I-57 on Route 14 in Benton (618-932-6159).

Holly, Buddy

Buddy Holly Center
1801 Avenue G
Lubbock, Texas
806-767-2686

The Buddy Holly Gallery features a permanent exhibition on the life and music of Buddy Holly. Artifacts owned by the city of Lubbock, as well as other items that have been loaned to the center, are presented in this exciting exhibition. Included in the display are Buddy Holly's Fender Stratocaster, a songbook used by Holly and his band The Crickets, clothing, photographs, recording contracts, tour itineraries, Holly's glasses, homework assignments, report cards, and much more—including the last guitar he ever played. That's right. The white Fender Stratocaster Holly played for his last show at the Surf Ballroom in Clear Lake, Iowa, on February 2, 1959, is now on display here in Lubbock.

The guitar has an interesting story. In July 1958, New York guitar store Manny's shipped the guitar to Holly while he was on the road. The instrument replaced one that was stolen from the group's station wagon while the band stopped for lunch in East St. Louis, Missouri. After Holly's death, the guitar remained in his family's possession until a private collector purchased it for $125,000. In 1990, actor Gary Busey, who played Holly in *The Buddy Holly Story*, bought the guitar for $242,000, but more recently a deal was made with the city of Lubbock to have it put on display in the museum.

House of Blues

Various Cities
www.hob.com

The House of Blues is a chain of music halls and restaurants opened in 1992 by Hard Rock Cafe founder Isaac Tigrett and his friend and investor Dan Aykroyd. It is a home for live music and Southern-inspired cuisine, and the clubs celebrate African-American culture, specifically blues music and folk art. The charter HOB in Harvard Square, which opened its doors on Thanksgiving Day 1992, has since closed (although the original hands-in-concrete driveway still remains on the property), but plans are in the works to re-open in Boston in a larger venue. Jim Belushi is also closely associated with the enterprise and is present at most openings.

James Cafarelli designed and built all the Houses of Blues except the most recent two. Current locations include: Cleveland, Ohio; Myrtle Beach, South Carolina; San Diego and Los Angeles, California; Chicago, Illinois; New Orleans, Louisiana; two venues on casino property, including Las Vegas, Nevada (at Mandalay Bay) and Atlantic City, New Jersey (at the Showboat Casino); and two venues on Disney property, one at Walt Disney World in Orlando, Florida, and one at Disneyland in Anaheim, California. (Disney was at one time a partial shareholder, according to *DisneyWar* by James B. Stewart.) The Chicago location is adjacent to the House of Blues Hotel.

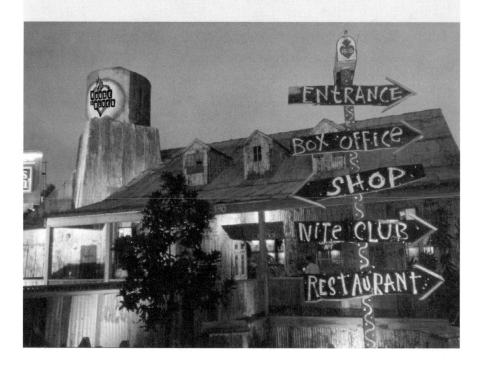

Hula Moon Café

27 Mount Pleasant Street
Rockport, Massachusetts
978-546-5185

This charming little place, with a menu that's part Hawaiian, part Japanese, and part Californian, is owned by David Robinson, the original drummer of the band The Cars.

Kate's Lazy Meadow Motel

5191 Route 28
Mount Tremper, New York
845-688-7200

A rustic modern place in the Catskills, Kate's Lazy Meadow Motel in Woodstock, New York, is owned and operated by Kate Pierson, one of the lead singers and founding members of the band The B-52's. It features stylish, retro chic interiors, 1950s Frigidaires, and atomic-starburst clocks.

Manny's New York

156 West 48th Street (between 6th & 7th Avenues)
New York, New York
212-819-0576

The "original music superstore," Manny's has been a New York institution since they opened their doors in 1935. They quickly became known as the store where the stars shop, a reputation that still holds to this day.

Margaritaville Café

http://www.margaritaville.com/cafe_NO.php

The Margaritaville Café is a chain of themed restaurants owned and operated by singer Jimmy Buffet. There are locations in New Orleans, Key West, Orlando, Las Vegas, Myrtle Beach, Jamaica, and Cancun and each one of them features the frozen concoctions and beach/island theme that is emblematic of so much of Buffet's music. These are places for "Parrotheads" to eat, drink, and celebrate Jimmy Buffett.

Marley, Bob

The Bob Marley Museum
56 Hope Road
Kingston, Jamaica
876-927-9152

The Bob Marley Museum in Kingston is dedicated to the reggae musician Bob Marley. It is located at 56 Hope Road, Kingston 6, and is Bob Marley's former place of residence. It was also home to the Tuff Gong record label, which was founded by The

Wailers in 1970. In 1976, it was the site of a failed assassination attempt on Bob Marley. Inside are many of Marley's personal effects, writings, photographs, and much more.

McCabe's

3101 Pico Boulevard
Santa Monica, California
310-828-4497

McCabe's is a musical instrument store in Santa Monica, California, opened in 1958. They specialize in acoustic and folk instruments: guitars, banjos, mandolins, dulcimers (both hammered and plucked), fiddles, psaltries, bouzoukis, sitars, ouds, ethnic percussion (also electrics and amps). McCabe's, in addition to being a world-class store, is also a famous concert site. Over the years, hundreds of performers have graced the intimate, 100-seat back room, including Beck, REM, Jackson Browne and others. It's one of the most unique, intimate venues in America, and you never know who will show up to play.

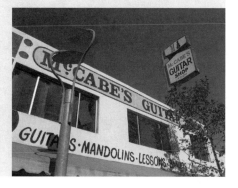

Morrison Hotel Gallery

7517 W. Sunset Boulevard
Los Angeles, California
323-874-2068

Henry Diltz is one of the world's most famous rock 'n' roll photographers, the man who all but defined the genre starting back in the 1960s. For more than 40 years, he's chronicled countless contemporary music icons, creating some of the most famous images ever taken of Jackson Browne; Crosby, Stills & Nash; the Eagles; Joni Mitchell; James Taylor; and many others. Diltz has also shot over 200 album covers, including The Doors' 1970 classic *Morrison Hotel,* which inspired the name of the music-centric gallery venture Diltz co-founded in 2001.

Today, there are three Morrison Hotel Gallery locations and each one of them boasts an impressive array of rock 'n' roll photographs including many by Diltz himself. Morrison Hotel Gallery was co-founded by Henry Diltz and partners Peter Blachley, Richard Horowitz, and Sam Milgrom, and the group also represents the work of other renowned photographers including Jim Marshall, Neal Preston, Danny Clinch, Gered Mankowitz, Bob Gruen, Baron Wolman, and others, so you can imagine what the exhibits are like. These are "must visit" galleries on any rock 'n' roll tour and a rare chance to see some of rock's most famous images up close and personal. The other two locations are at 124 Prince Street in New York City and 1230 Prospect Street in La Jolla, California.

Motown Museum

2648 West Grand Boulevard
Detroit, Michigan
313-875-2264

The Motown sound was born in this old brick house, which is now home to a museum dedicated to the revolutionary musical style. Marvin Gaye, Smokey Robinson, Diana Ross and the Supremes, Stevie Wonder, the Jackson Five—they all got their start here under the orchestration of Motown Records Svengali Berry Gordy, Jr.

Today, this Michigan historic site looks just like it did in the early 1960s. You can see sheet music and the actual studio equipment they used, including the piano played by all the greats. Photographs and gold records adorn the walls alongside the original costumes worn by Motown musicians who have recorded here.

Museum of Iowa Rock and Roll History

Arnolds Park
Lake Okoboji, Iowa
712-332-6540

This is one of the newest museums in the country dedicated to rock 'n' roll, with permanent displays that include a reproduction of the Iowa Great Lakes recording studio, a '60s era radio broadcast booth, vintage recording equipment plus memorabilia from many of the inductees to the hall of fame. The museum is located on the site of the famous Roof Garden Ballroom at Arnolds Park Iowa, which is fitting, as virtually thousands of teenagers and visitors visited the Iowa Great Lakes region during the '50s, '60s, and '70s and packed the historical amusement park at Arnolds Park and the Roof Garden Ballroom.

The Roof Garden opened for operation on June 23, 1923, and during the '30s and '40s, the hottest big bands in the U.S. made the Roof their summer place to play. From Count Basie to Glen Miller to Louis Armstrong to the Dorseys. In the late '50s, the ownership of the Roof Garden passed on to Darlowe Oleson, who brought in The Beach Boys, The Byrds, Jerry Lee Lewis, the Yardbirds, The Monkees, Gene Vincent, Eddie Cochran, The Crickets, and many more. The Roof Garden closed in 1988, but thankfully the museum sits right here on the site.

Museum of Making Music

5790 Armada Drive
Carlsbad, California
760-438-5996

The Museum of Making Music presents visitors with an interactive journey through a century of musical instrument innovations that helped shape American popular music

from the 1890s to the present day. It includes over 500 vintage instruments on display, hundreds of audio and video examples at the push of a button, and an interactive area where visitors can play on a variety of hands-on instruments. The museum also presents a number of special events and educational outreach activities.

National Music Museum

University of South Dakota
414 E. Clark Street
Vermillion, South Dakota
605-677-5306

The National Music Museum, "America's Shrine to Music," was founded in 1973 here on the campus of the University of South Dakota, as the National Music Museum & Center for Study of the History of Musical Instruments. The museum is fully accredited by the American Association of Museums and is recognized as "A Landmark of American Music" by the National Music Council. The museum's renowned collections, which include more than 10,500 American, European, and non-Western instruments from all

cultures and historical periods, are among the world's most inclusive. They include many of the earliest, best-preserved, and historically most important instruments known to survive. The museum's rise to world-class status has attracted international attention, and each year the museum attracts thousands of visitors from all 50 states and around the world.

Ted Nugent's Bowhunter's World
(now called United Sportsman of America)

4133 West Michigan Avenue
Jackson, Michigan
517-750-9060

Rocker/hunter Ted Nugent operates this retail location, which features hunting and fishing gear. Nugent, who started locally with the Amboy Dukes before hitting it big as a solo artist, also publishes a magazine for outdoorsmen.

Orbison, Roy

Orbison Museum
Wink City Hall
205 East Hendricks Boulevard
Wink, Texas
915-527-3622

Singer Roy Orbison spent his youth in this tiny town, located about 54 miles west of Odessa. To honor their native son, a small museum (which includes one of his famous guitars) and a gift shop were created; there are future plans for a plaque and a statue as well. The influential musician died at the age of 52 on December 6, 1988, after suffering a heart attack while visiting his mother in Hendersonville, a suburb of Nashville, Tennessee.

Rock and Roll Hall of Fame and Museum

One Key Plaza
751 Erieside Avenue
Cleveland, Ohio
216-781-ROCK

A stunning piece of daring architecture designed by internationally renowned architect I. M. Pei, the Rock and Roll Hall of Fame and Museum contains equally remarkable interactive exhibits, films, videos, and priceless and poignant artifacts, and serves as the host of the permanent Hall of Fame exhibit. In addition to its permanent exhibits, the museum stages a number of temporary exhibits throughout the year, including large-scale shows that occupy the top two levels of the building. The museum also produces events for the public that include concerts, lectures, panel discussions, film series, and teacher education programs. Here is a list of some of the most important artifacts held at the museum:

- John Lennon's *Sergeant Pepper* costume
- The Everly Brothers' tap shoes
- John Lennon's handwritten lyrics for the Beatle classic,"In My Life"
- Carl Perkins's guitar
- The Supremes' dresses
- Grace Slick's Woodstock outfit
- Kurt Cobain's guitar
- Parts from the plane that Otis Redding died aboard
- Buddy Holly's diploma
- The Sun Studio Presto portable sound mixing board
- Janis Joplin's Porsche
- Madonna's bustier
- A quilted David Bowie jumpsuit
- Michael Jackson's sequined glove
- Mick Jagger's velveteen jumpsuit
- Roger Daltry's buckskin suit
- One of Bob Marley's dreadlocks
- Pink Floyd's *The Wall*
- Charles Manson's letter to *Rolling Stone* magazine
- Bruce Springsteen's *Born in the U.S.A.* outfit
- Stevie Nicks's dress from the *Rumours* album cover

RockWalk

Guitar Center
7425 Sunset Boulevard
Hollywood, California
323-874-1060

Founded in Hollywood by Wayne Mitchell in 1961 as The Organ Center, a retailer of electronic organs for home and church usage, this store became a major seller of Vox electric guitars and guitar amplifiers, changing its name to The Vox Center in 1964. Toward the end of the 1960s, Vox's line—whose sales derived largely from its association with The Beatles, who made extensive use of its amplifiers—fell in popularity as Marshall amplifier users Eric Clapton and Jimi Hendrix captured musicians' imaginations. Accordingly, Mitchell once again changed its name, this time to Guitar Center.

The Sunset Boulevard location in Los Angeles hosts Hollywood's RockWalk, a hall of fame honoring notable musical artists ranging from Chuck Berry and Bill Haley and His Comets to Queen and Stevie Ray Vaughan. Artists are invited to place their handprints into cement blocks that are put on display at the Guitar Center. There's even a guitar museum located within the store. Guitar Center is the largest chain of musical instrument retailers in the United States.

Rodgers, Jimmie

Jimmie Rodgers Museum
1725 Jimmie Rodgers Drive
Meridian, Mississippi
601-485-1808

Jimmie Rodgers, the father of country music, was born and raised in the Meridian area. The museum, fashioned after an old train depot, displays the original guitar of "The Singing Brakeman" and other memorabilia of his life and career, as well as railroad equipment from the steam engine era. Notable Rodgers songs include "Waiting for a Train," "In the Jailhouse Now," "Jimmie the Kid," "Miss the Mississippi and You," "Looking for a New Mama," "Jimmie's Mean Mama Blues," and "Train Whistle Blues."

The 113 songs he recorded have hardly ever been out of production. Incredibly, his musical career lasted only six years. Rodgers died from tuberculosis in 1933 in New York's Taft Hotel at age 35. His last recordings were made in Manhattan less than a week before his death. He had been bedridden for several years before this last session and had to rest on a cot between takes. When the Country Music Hall of Fame was established in 1961, Rodgers was one of the first three to be inducted. He was also elected to the Songwriters Hall of Fame and his song "Blue Yodel No. 9" is ranked number 23 on "The Rock and Roll Hall of Fame's 500 Songs that Shaped Rock and Roll."

Soulsville U.S.A./STAX Museum

926 East McLemore Street
Memphis, Tennessee
901-946-2535

Today you can stand right where the great Otis Redding stood when he recorded many of his most popular songs, see the microphone he sang into, and much more here at

the STAX Museum of American Soul Music. Built on the historic site of STAX Records, the Soulsville Museum provides an outstanding collection of STAX memorabilia, a reconstruction of its recording studio, interpretive exhibits describing Memphis's contribution to soul music, memorabilia from other Memphis soul and R&B record companies, and a music training academy.

The Stage of Stars

Shreveport Municipal Auditorium and Stage of Stars Museum
705 Elvis Presley Avenue
Shreveport, Louisiana
800-551-8682

More than 30 of Nashville's Country Music Hall of Famers got their start on the *Louisiana Hayride* in Shreveport, Louisiana. The historic Shreveport Municipal Auditorium was home to the *Louisiana Hayride* radio program every Saturday night in the 1950s and 1960s. It was considered the Junior Grand Ole Opry and the auditorium housed Elvis Presley's first appearance in front of a national radio audience on KWKH.

Built in 1929, the Shreveport Municipal Auditorium was also at one time the nation's largest veteran's memorial. It recently opened as a museum to showcase the numerous stars that have performed there.

When visiting the museum and auditorium, you can stand on the stage where Elvis first performed professionally to a national radio audience. Or you might take a seat in the original chairs and imagine some of the numerous performers that played on its stage in the 1950s and 1960s, such as Hank Williams, Tex Ritter, and Kitty Wells, or speak with the tour guides, some of whom were present at many of the shows in the Municipal's famous past.

Starland Cafe

5125 MacArthur Boulevard NW
Washington, D.C.
202-244-9396

Remember the 1970s hit "Afternoon Delight" by the Starland Vocal Band? Then you'll get the reference to the name of this restaurant, the Starland Cafe. Co-owner Bill Danoff was one-quarter of the group and in addition to the band he's also had great success with this place, which serves moderately priced comfort food and does an exceptional job of providing an outlet for local (and other) musicians to play.

The Strand

Broadway and East 12th Street
New York, New York
212-473-1452

The Strand Book Store is an independent bookstore famous for its giant collection of new, rare, used, and out-of-print books; its advertising slogan "18 miles of books"; and the creative chaos on and around its shelves. And there's some rock 'n' roll history here, too, because back in the early 1970s both Patti Smith and soon-to-be Television leader Tom Verlaine both worked here together.

Theo's Rock and Roll Museum

113 E. Second Street
Clarksdale, Mississippi
901-605-8662

The Rock and Roll Museum in Clarksdale is loaded with rock 'n' roll memorabilia from the '50s and '60s. On the walls and in colorful display cases you'll find beautiful art-work on LP record covers, autographs, photos, 45 and 78 rpm records and acetates, guitars autographed by Chuck Berry and B. B. King, magazines, news articles, movie and concert posters, concert tickets, and lots, lots more.

Waters, Muddy

Delta Blues Museum
1 Blues Alley
Clarksdale, Mississippi
662-627-6820

The Delta Blues Museum contains thousands of artifacts related to the blues, but perhaps none is as stunning as the cabin where Muddy Waters grew up. In the cabin sits the life-size wax statue of former Clarksdale resident Muddy Waters. Muddy was a sharecropper on the Stovall Plantation in the 1920s and early 1930s. Discovered by

musicologist Alan Lomax, he would be a part of the northern migration of African-Americans in the 1930s. Muddy Waters would be credited with electrifying the blues when he plugged his guitar into an amplifier in order to be heard over the noise of the city of Chicago. The suit on the statue was once owned by Muddy.

Williams, Hank

Hank Williams Museum
118 Commerce Street
Montgomery, Alabama
334-262-3600

The official Hank Williams Museum is located in downtown Montgomery, where the country legend lived from 1937-1953. Appropriately, it houses Hank's 1952 Cadillac, in which he made his final journey. Hank Williams's death at age 29 remains a mystery to this day. The precise cause of death, and what happened in the crazy last 48 hours of his life, may never really be known, but we do know that on December 30, 1952, Williams loaded up his '52 Cadillac in the late morning and headed for West Virginia. A couple of days later, the 29-year-old singer was pronounced dead at Oak Hill Hospital in Oak Hill, West Virginia. The car that Williams cruised around in those last fateful days remains one of the most haunting artifacts in music history. Incidentally, Oakwood Cemetery, which is the resting place of Hank and Audrey Williams, is located only five minutes away from the museum. A life-size statue of Hank is also located in Lister Hill Park in downtown Montgomery, just across from the City Auditorium where Hank's funeral service was held.

YesterDave's Auto Museum

10601 Montgomery Boulevard NE
Albuquerque, New Mexico
505-293-0033

Inspired by the legendary Carroll Shelby, creator of the Cobra, the Ford Cobra Mustang, and the Dodge Viper, the museum is home to many celebrity and collector automobiles, from John Lennon's Rolls Royce and Elvis Presley's Mercedes Lime to Carroll Shelby's team race car.

B-Sides: Record Stores, Road Trip Music Suggestions, and Other Rock 'n' Roll Miscellany

In this chapter I wanted to include some reflections and collections of things from my own rock 'n' roll experiences. As fans, we all have our favorite records, shows, etc. We debate, argue, and hash these things out so much that I thought I'd include some of my favorite things. So here goes.

100 Classic Road Trip Songs

If you travel with this book in search of some of the landmarks or are just hitting the road in general, the music you play is important. I could probably list 1,000 songs, but in the interest of space, here are 100 that I think can enhance any car trip, no matter where you are headed. Are any of your top 100 on here?

1. "Tumbling Dice"—The Rolling Stones
2. "Six Days on the Road"—Flying Burrito Brothers
3. "Still Crazy After All These Years"—Paul Simon
4. "Baba O'Reilly"—The Who
5. "Ventura Highway"—America
6. "Bohemian Rhapsody"—Queen
7. "Thunder Road"—Bruce Springsteen
8. "Layla"—Eric Clapton (Derek and the Dominos)
9. "Honky Tonk Women"—The Rolling Stones
10. "L.A. Woman"—The Doors

11. "No Expectations"–The Rolling Stones
12. "Werewolves of London"–Warren Zevon
13. "On the Road Again"–Willie Nelson
14. "Up On Cripple Creek"–The Band
15. "Slow Ride"–Foghat
16. "Born to Run"–Bruce Springsteen
17. "Me and Bobby McGee"–Janis Joplin
18. "Like A Rolling Stone"–Bob Dylan
19. "Take it Easy"–The Eagles
20. "Midnight Train to Georgia"–Gladys Knight
21. "Sweet Home Alabama"–Lynyrd Skynyrd
22. "New York, New York"–Frank Sinatra
23. "American Girl"–Tom Petty
24. "Luca"–Suzanne Vega
25. "The Weight"–The Band
26. "Walk on the Wild Side"–Lou Reed
27. "Sweet Jane"–The Velvet Underground
28. "Isn't It Ironic"–Alanis Morissette
29. "Do It Again"–Steely Dan
30. "The Highwayman"–Stevie Nicks
31. "Come Fly With Me"–Frank Sinatra
32. "Route 66"–Nat King Cole
33. "Ramblin' Man"–The Allman Brothers
34. "Horse With No Name"–America
35. "Box of Rain"–The Grateful Dead
36. "The Promised Land"–Chuck Berry
37. "Over the Hills and Far Away"–Led Zeppelin
38. "I've Been Everywhere"–Johnny Cash
39. "Frederick"–Patti Smith Group
40. "People Who Died"–Jim Carroll
41. "The Road"–Jackson Browne
42. "Changes"–David Bowie
43. "All the Young Dudes"–Mott the Hoople
44. "Stay With Me"–Rod Stewart
45. "Maggie May"–Rod Stewart
46. "Black Maria"–Todd Rundgren
47. "Tusk"–Fleetwood Mac
48. "Oh Boy"–Buddy Holly
49. "The Wonder of You"–Elvis Presley
50. "She"–Gram Parsons
51. "Rock and Roll All Night (Live)"–KISS
52. "Idiot Wind (Live)"–Bob Dylan
53. "Too Cool To Fall in Love"–Jill Sobule
54. "Paradise by the Dashboard Light"–Meatloaf
55. "Blitzkrieg Bop"–Ramones

56. "Mind Games"—John Lennon
57. "Town Called Malice"—The Jam
58. "Beautiful Day"—U2
59. "Waiting in Vain"—Bob Marley
60. "Crossroads (Live)"—Cream
61. "Hello Old Friend"—Eric Clapton
62. "Wouldn't It Be Nice"—The Beach Boys
63. "I Saw the Light"—Todd Rundgren
64. "Personality Crisis"—New York Dolls
65. "Marquee Moon"—Television
66. "Crosstown Traffic"—Jimi Hendrix
67. "Wasted on the Way"—Crosby, Stills and Nash
68. "Coyote"—Joni Mitchell
69. "Distant Lover"—Marvin Gaye
70. "Brandy"—Looking Glass
71. "Dancing Barefoot"—Patti Smith
72. "Blue Suede Shoes"—Elvis Presley
73. "Ripple"—The Grateful Dead
74. "Hurricane"—Bob Dylan
75. "Holdin' Back the Years"—Simply Red
76. "Must'a Got Lost"—The J. Geils Band
77. "My Best Friends Girl"—The Cars
78. "Dream On"—Aerosmith
79. "Wait For Me"—Hall & Oates
80. "Rosalita"—Bruce Springsteen
81. "Ol' 55"—Tom Waits
82. "Here Comes My Girl"—Tom Petty
83. "Get Off My Cloud"—The Rolling Stones
84. "You Get What You Give"—The New Radicals
85. "Thunderstorm"—Matthew Sweet
86. "Love My Way"—The Psychedelic Furs
87. "Someone To Lay Down Beside Me"—Linda Ronstadt
88. "You're Only Lonely"—J.D. Souther
89. "Only The Lonely"—Roy Orbison
90. "Carolina In My Mind"—James Taylor
91. "Rock and Roll Fantasy"—The Kinks
92. "Local Girls"—Graham Parker
93. "Mona Lisas and Madhatters"—Elton John
94. "American Band"—Grand Funk Railroad
95. "Tin Man"—America
96. "You Can't Always Get What you Want"—The Rolling Stones
97. "A Day in the Life"—The Beatles
98. "California Dreaming"—The Mamas and the Papas
99. "Wild World"—Cat Stevens
100. "Like a Hurricane"—Neil Young

100 Rockin' Road Trip Albums

Of course, there has to be an album list, too, right? Here, in no particular order, would be my top 100 albums to have handy when you're on the road.

1. *Exile on Main Street*–The Rolling Stones
2. *London Calling*–The Clash
3. *Revolver*–The Beatles
4. *Sweethearts of the Rodeo*–The Flying Burrito Brothers
5. *16 Biggest Hits*–Johnny Cash
6. *Silk Degrees*–Boz Scaggs
7. *Greatest Hits*–The Spinners
8. *The Spirit Room*–Michelle Branch
9. *Red*–King Crimson
10. *Hard Rain*–Bob Dylan
11. *New York Dolls*–New York Dolls
12. *Something/Anything?*–Todd Rundgren

13. *L.A.M.F.*–Johnny Thunders & the Heartbreakers
14. *Raindogs*–Tom Waits
15. *Marquee Moon*–Television
16. *Flashlight*–Tom Verlaine
17. *Orphans*–Tom Waits
18. *American Beauty*–The Grateful Dead
19. *Cadillac Walk*–The Mink DeVille Collection
20. *This Is Spinal Tap*–Spinal Tap
21. *Live at the Sands with Count Basie*–Frank Sinatra
22. *Hotel California*–Eagles
23. *American Pie*–Don McLean
24. *Houses of the Holy*–Led Zeppelin
25. *Get Yer Ya-Ya's Out*–The Rolling Stones
26. *Dark Side of the Moon*–Pink Floyd
27. *Parallel Lines*–Blondie
28. *The Ramones*–Ramones

29. *Hasten Down the Wind*–Linda Ronstadt
30. *Rumours*–Fleetwood Mac
31. *After The Gold Rush*–Neil Young
32. *Station to Station*–David Bowie
33. *All Mod Cons*–The Jam
34. *The Cars*–The Cars
35. *Greatest Hits*–America
36. *Frampton Comes Alive*–Peter Frampton
37. *KISS Alive*–KISS
38. *Greatest Hits*–Tom Petty and the Heartbreakers
39. *Running on Empty*–Jackson Browne
40. *Four Way Street*–Crosby, Stills, Nash and Young
41. *100% Fun*–Matthew Sweet

42. *Gene Autry's Greatest Hits*–Gene Autry
43. *Collection*–Robert Johnson
44. *Compilation*–Charlie Parker
45. *The Pretenders*–The Pretenders
46. *Greatest Hits*–Grand Funk Railroad
47. *Greatest Hits*–Chuck Berry
48. *Live at the Sands*–Frank Sinatra and Count Basie
49. *Metallic K.O.*–Iggy and the Stooges
50. *Highway 61 Revisited*–Bob Dylan
51. *The Last Waltz*–The Band
52. *Wave*–The Patti Smith Group
53. *Kaya*–Bob Marley
54. *Greatest Hits*–The Partridge Family
55. *The Hissing of Summer Lawns*–Joni Mitchell
56. *I'm Your Man*–Leonard Cohen
57. *Born to Run*–Bruce Springsteen
58. *The Velvet Underground*–The Velvet Underground
59. *Beggar's Banquet*–The Rolling Stones
60. *Brussels Affair*–The Rolling Stones
61. *Bella Donna*–Stevie Nicks
62. *Rocks*–Aerosmith
63. *Live at the Fillmore East*–The Allman Brothers
64. *David Johansen*–David Johansen
65. *Shaved Fish*–John Lennon
66. *Pet Sounds*–The Beach Boys
67. *What's Going On*–Marvin Gaye
68. *Kind of Blue*–Miles Davis
69. *Astral Weeks*–Van Morrison
70. *Innervisions*–Stevie Wonder
71. *Let it Bleed*–The Rolling Stones
72. *Goodbye Yellow Brick Road*–Elton John
73. *20 Golden Greats*–Buddy Holly
74. *Squeezing Out Sparks*–Graham Parker
75. *Post*–Bjork
76. *Modern Lovers Live*–Modern Lovers
77. *The Rutles*–The Rutles
78. *For Your Pleasure*–Roxy Music
79. *Grievous Angel*–Gram Parson
80. *Kid A*–Radiohead
81. *All The Young Dudes*–Mott the Hoople
82. *Desire*–Bob Dylan
83. *Out of the Cradle*–Lindsay Buckingham
84. *Sticky Fingers*–The Rolling Stones
85. *A Mighty Wind*–Various
86. *Along The Red Ledge*–Hall & Oates

87. *Gratitude*—Earth, Wind & Fire
88. *Ziggy Stardust And The Spiders From Mars*—David Bowie
89. *Greatest Hits*—Lynyrd Skynyrd
90. *The Sun Sessions*—Elvis Presley
91. *Flashlight*—Tom Verlaine
92. *Venus and Mars*—Wings
93. *Monterey Pop*—Various
94. *Live at Leeds*—The Who
95. *This Year's Model*—Elvis Costello
96. *Tim*—The Replacements
97. *Aja*—Steely Dan
98. *Anthology*—Muddy Waters
99. *Wish You Were Here*—Pink Floyd
100. *Another Live*—Todd Rundgren

My Top Live 25

I love getting into discussions and debates with friends about what some of the best shows in history were, so I thought I'd share some favorites. Growing up in the New York area in the 1970s, there were a lot of opportunities to see the bands I listened to most. So I tried to see as many as I could. While I'm sure I'm forgetting some, here are 25 shows from my last 30 or so years that still feel as if I saw them all yesterday. I'll tell you too, just sitting down and forcing myself to think about this was a fun drill that brought back countless memories. I highly recommend it as a cathartic exercise. And if you'd ever like to share your top shows, I'd be interested in hearing about them. Shoot me an e-mail.

1. The Rolling Stones, Madison Square Garden, 6/22/75—My first concert ever. What can I say? I remember it like it was yesterday, the thrill has yet to wear off and I thank my parents for actually letting me, my sisters, and my best pal Bryant see this show (which featured Eric Clapton encoring on "Sympathy for the Devil").
My dad got the tickets through his company and my older cousins Chip and Helene took us to the show. I had been a total Stones freak for about a year or two at this point and seeing them in person as they opened their New York run at the Garden was mind-boggling.

2. The Ramones, CBGB's, 1978—I would always catch the Ramones if they were playing nearby but at CBGB's it was different. The famed New York dive felt like their spawning ground, their own personal basement. Plus, when Iggy Pop and Johnny Thunders are watching from the bar, as they happened to be doing on this night, it adds another level entirely to what was already a classic New York show.

3. Bob Dylan, The Forum, 2006—My son and I caught this show recently and though I'd seen Dylan before, this for me was the best. Charlie (13 at the time of the show) likes Dylan a great deal so this was special seeing him watch one of the greats (if not the best) while he's still touring. On the heels of the great *Modern Times* album, Dylan was focused, intense, and mysterious . . . just like always. As he gets

older, as his growl deepens, and as he reworks his classics further, Dylan seems to have reached yet another level of brilliance. Long live Bob.

4. David Johansen, Gemini, 1978—Two feet of snow on a freezing December night up in the suburban country of Westchester County, New York. I had recently discovered the New York Dolls, who had disbanded a few years earlier. Lead singer David Johansen had emerged from the wreckage with a terrific self-titled record full of soulful, desperate Lower East Side rock 'n' roll, including the songs "Funky But Chic," "Cool Metro" and "Frenchette."

I'd read about him for years in magazines like *Circus, Rock Scene,* and *Hit Parader* and I couldn't believe he and his band were actually playing near our town. Or was he? Would they make the one-hour drive from New York in the snow? I called the Gemini (our local rock "nightclub") and they said it was on, so off we went, our friend Patti at the wheel and crunching about five miles an hour through the snow. Once we arrived, we noticed there were maybe 30 people there, in a club that held about 300. But it didn't stop Johansen and company. They performed like there were 3,000 people there and as many times as I saw Johansen later in life, nothing even approached the energy and passion the night of this blizzard.

5. Johnny Thunders, The Mudd Club, 1982—While attending Emerson College in Boston, I had an idea (for a class) to create a documentary about a band called The Lords of the New Church. The band featured musicians from a variety of former punk bands, including Stiv Bators from the Dead Boys and Brain James from The

Damned. For about three days, a camera guy and I drove around with them in their van and documented their compressed little world from hotels to clubs to bars and back again.

One of these nights we ended up in New York City where their old pal Johnny Thunders was playing at the Mudd Club. Given how close the band was with Thunders, we had access to him as well, which made for some interesting footage. Thunders at this point in time was a drug-ravaged wreck, actually brought to the stage in a wheelchair. But once under the lights, he exploded. Backed by The Heartbreakers, he even produced a samurai sword at one point and began smashing it into one of the Mudd Club's concrete pillars near the stage, causing sparks to fly. His guitar playing this night was brilliant. After the show he said to me, "Hey man, how'd that sound?" I said I thought it sounded great and he replied, "Nah, it was just okay. Good but not great." No. It was great.

6. Todd Rundgren, Central Park, 1978–I am a huge Todd Rundgren fan and this was the first time I ever saw him, on a warm summer night when he was in absolute classic form. Todd and New York City always seemed to be a good fit and at this point in his career Todd had everything firing: A great new album (*Hermit of Mink Hollow*), a great band in Utopia, and some wildly successful productions under his belt (including Meatloaf, Grand Funk Railroad, and others). One of the most under-appreciated showmen in rock 'n' roll, Todd's tongue-in-cheek lyrics blended with his soulful singing and the ferocity of his guitar playing made for a classic New York night under the stars.

7. Elton John, Madison Square Garden, 1977–Elton John was one of the premier arena acts in the mid-1970s and though this Louder Than Concorde tour in support of the *Rock of the Westies* album was scaled down from his more lavish productions, I don't think he ever sounded better live. He always had one of the best live bands (including Davey Johnstone, Nigel Olsen, and Ray Cooper) and at this point Elton John hadn't really released a bad record so the set list was bulletproof. (Also, Alice Cooper and Billie Jean King sang backup on the encore, "Saturday Night's Alright (for Fighting).")

8. Patti Smith, Central Park, 1978–At this time in music there were not many dyed-in-the-wool female rock stars. Debbie Harry was certainly getting big, Stevie Nicks had the whole ethereal-arena-witch thing covered, and the Runaways had made a bit of noise on the West Coast. But Patti Smith, the streetwise, defiant poetess, was different. She had the look, the attitude, and, most important, the sound of a bona fide rocker. Her bond with all crowds was special, but summertime in New York (and I think it was raining) was the perfect environment to watch her lead her disciples.

9. The Allman Brothers, Central Park, 1978–It was actually a show by Dickey Betts and his band Great Southern. At this time The Allman Brothers

were not together, but on this night they regrouped during Betts's second set to play a long set of Allman Brothers classics. The crowd went absolutely bananas, nearly tipping a truck over that was parked near the side of the stage. The next year, the regrouped band released *Enlightened Rogues.*

10. Neil Young, Madison Square Garden, 1978–This was part of the *Rust Never Sleeps* tour that yielded not just a live album, but a concert film as well. Young played the first set acoustic and alone and then brought out his band Crazy Horse for set two. This concert showcased both sides of Young, the quiet and the stormy, and for me totally cemented Young's place as one of the last great rebels in music. A high point was the fan machine they dragged out and pointed at Neil during "Like a Hurricane."

11. The Clash, Bond's Clothing Store, 1981–This was chaotic, but fun. The series of Clash shows at the old Bond's Clothing Store in Times Square was marred by *tons* of counterfeit tickets, which caused near riots in the streets. Once inside though, it was fantastic. Bond's was nothing more than a big old warehouse which was a perfect backdrop for The Clash, who played for a solid couple of hours and ended with the encore, "London's Burning." The Stray Cats, who had just released their first album, opened up.

12. David Bowie, Madison Square Garden, 1978– This tour (documented on the double live LP *Stage*) is sandwiched between the stark Thin White Duke tour of 1976 and the much-hyped Let's Dance extravaganza of 1983. The exceptional band (including Adrian Belew and Roger Powell) and the offbeat Brian Eno collaborations made this a cool show. He still played his hits, but mixed in a lot of lesser-known stuff from *Low* and *Heroes.*

13. Lou Reed, The Ritz, 1985–He still had lots of bite in 1985, as this was before Lou drifted into the elder statesman-like role he seemed to adopt with the album entitled *New York.* He ranted and vented in between playing some of his best stuff (and a selection of Velvet Underground tunes) in all their cranky glory. Lou Reed, like Patti Smith, always seemed to belong to New York City and local fans picked up on the subtlest of things. Extra notes, unexpected glances, a head nod–the crowd

always went nuts when it noticed a little something special or different.

14. The Grateful Dead, Englishtown, 1977—I was dragged to this by a Deadhead friend. We had to park and trudge maybe three miles to the raceway, part of the typical communal parade that was the trademark of so many outdoor Dead shows. Openers were New Riders of the Purple Sage and The Marshall Tucker Band, and then the Dead came on around sunset. I never had listened much to the Dead up until now and was sort of dreading this. But you know what? It was a great show. I starting understanding the Dead on this impossibly muggy, rainy summer day in the mud, and while I never came close to being a Deadhead, I enjoyed a lot of their music later on after being turned on to them (and their fans) in the middle of a New Jersey racetrack.

15. Bruce Springsteen, Buffalo War Memorial Auditorium, 1980—I was also dragged to this show, while in college. At that point I was not part of The Boss brigade; I liked a few of his singles but that was about it. To be honest, I found his most ardent fans sort of annoying and in your face, but hey, it was a free ticket. Three-and-a-half hours later, on a subzero winter night in Buffalo, I got it. He played something like 34 songs, as documented by the Springsteen nut next to me. Awesome show.

16. Pink Floyd, Nassau Coliseum, 1980—The Wall . . . what else can you say? They only played this show in two cities, Los Angeles, and New York. The "tour" consisted of seven nights (February 7th to the 13th) at the Los Angeles Sports Arena and five nights (February 24th to the 28th) at the Nassau Coliseum. This was a historic show that's been well documented and I'm glad I got to go. We even managed to grab a couple of the styrofoam bricks when the Wall came crashing down, though I don't know what became of mine.

17. Tom Petty, Universal Amphitheater, 1989—I don't think there's ever been a bad time to see Tom Petty play. He's as solid and dependable a crowd pleaser as I think exists and this show (in which Dion opened) was excep-

tionally entertaining, made better by the fact that I was there with my future wife.

18. Led Zeppelin, Madison Square Garden, 1977–The last real tour the band did was this one so I'm glad I got to go. I mean, who'd want to miss Jimmy Page in a white jumpsuit with bright green embroidered snakes running up the side? Or that big green laser pyramid that pulsed to the beat of "Kashmir"? During Bonham's drum solo on "Moby Dick," many of us hit the men's room. I can still remember, through the thick tiled bathroom walls, the muffled thunder of Bonzo's solo seeping through. Guy next to me: "Dude, Bonzo even sounds good in *here*."

19. Queen, Madison Square Garden, 1977–This was Queen on their News Of The World tour. As over the top and dramatic as you'd expect, and who knew Queen's time as a band would be cut so short? I remember thinking that Freddie Mercury controlled a crowd as well as Mick Jagger. Since then, I'd probably have to add Springsteen and Bono to that group, but I don't think I've ever seen Madison Square Garden held in such tight grip as the one Mercury had on them back in '77. A friend of mine's dad was a New York City cop who had security detail that night protecting the band. What was Mercury like up close according to him? "Freaking nuts."

20. Fleetwood Mac, Verizon Amphitheater, 2004–I saw Fleetwood Mac back in the late 1970s during the frenzy of *Rumours* and then later in the early 1980s when *Mirage* came out, but what made this night memorable (in addition to how well the band played) was that we attended as a family, the four of us, up on the lawn of this pretty outdoor venue on a perfect summer night. I'd look at the group, and then our kids, then aged 11 and 9, and found it hard to believe we could all be there, listening to that band, after almost 30 years. Long live longevity.

21. Earth, Wind & Fire, Madison Square Garden, 1977–This was actually a sort of "date." At least it was in my mind; sorry to say she didn't quite feel the same way. Either way, in their heyday Earth, Wind & Fire put on a spectacular arena show, full of soul, joy, and some ahead-of-their-time special effects. There are not many bands today that could attract that diverse an audience either, at 20,000 strong.

22. Lindsay Buckingham, The Wiltern, 1992–Lindsay Buckingham may be best known as lead guitarist and singer in Fleetwood Mac, but his solo career is, in my opinion, very impressive, both eclectic and extremely innovative. When he toured in support of his album *Out of the Cradle* he had a band that included *seven* other guitarists. The sound was rich and complex, with Buckingham pushing himself into that manic ether where, for a moment, you actually feared for his health.

23. Tom Waits, The Wiltern, 1987–Parts of this, the Frank's Wild Years tour, was filmed for the concept/concert movie *Big Time*. It's the only time I ever saw Tom Waits, who still seems just as mysterious and shadowy as when he oozed onto the scene back in the early 1970s. The show was wonderfully inventive and imaginative, with Waits adopting the persona of a strange vaudevillian. Tom Waits, for me, is in that

rare company of artists who have never strayed from their own vision to try and keep up with current tastes. He does what he wants to do, no more, no less, and this show was a pure example of that.

24. Television, CBGB's, 1978—I could watch Tom Verlaine play guitar all night, especially when his sounds intertwine with Richard Lloyd, the other Television guitarist. The era of Television was, for me, the most thrilling. On this particular summer night it was hot and humid even at two in the morning, the windows were fogged up, and "Marquee Moon" went on for what seemed like about 45 minutes. As I type this entry, I am listening to a live version of "Marquee Moon" . . .

25. The Rolling Stones, Dodger Stadium, 2006—Right back where I started in 1975, only this time my wife and son are with me (the Rolling Stones do nothing for our daughter, who stayed with my twin sister this night). What Mick Jagger did this evening (we saw four shows on this Bigger Bang tour) was unfathomable. Seventy-one U.S. shows and this was to be the last of the tour. He was as animated, passionate, and energetic as ever, transforming Dodger Stadium into no less than a revival hall. Will they tour here again? Who knows. But when I read a review of this show, where the writer said, "I don't even want to think about a world without the Rolling Stones," I knew exactly what she felt. God save the Stones.

30 Great North American Music Stores

It seems, to the pleasure of some of us, that vinyl is making a comeback. If you grew up reading liner notes and studying album cover art, lyric sheets, and other related materials included in the jacket, this is positive news. With CD sales on the way down due to the myriad downloading options, it only makes sense. After all, you can't download a record. Vinyl needs to be held, examined and studied, and the best place to do that is in a record store. For staying the traditional course in a digital age, I wanted to make you aware of some special places that still understand the importance of the music-buying experience. Places where the employees are passionate, knowledgeable rock 'n' roll fans with a frame of reference that goes back more than a year or two. Sure they sell CDs and DVDs too, but they also sell lots of records; beautiful, glorious records. If you're ever in their town, go visit these places. They are among the best that are left. To them, and the others not contained in this book, thank you.

Arizona

Stinkweeds
1250 E. Apache Boulevard
Tempe, Arizona
480-968-9490
Stinkweeds is an independently owned and operated store based in Tempe. Since 1987, they've primarily focused on imports and independent label releases and the selection is fantastic. Tucked away in a strip mall, it's easy to miss so keep your eyes

peeled. (And also watch for the store's list of upcoming events, too. The in-store stage has become locally renowned for featuring stars on the rise.)

California

Amoeba Music
1855 Haight Street
San Francisco, California
415-831-1200

2455 Telegraph Avenue
Berkeley, California
510-549-1125

6400 Sunset Boulevard
Hollywood, California
323-245-6400
Amoeba Music is an independent music chain of three stores located in Berkeley, San

Francisco, and Hollywood, California. The stores are massive and the San Francisco store (opened in 1997) is particularly huge. Built in a 24,000-square-foot bowling alley, the store regularly stocks upwards of 100,000 CDs, vinyl records, and audiocassettes, both new and used. The Southern California location was added in November 2001 and it stocks more 250,000 titles. Amoeba Music also sell movies, DVD, VHS, Laserdiscs, posters, books, and tons of other stuff. You really have to see these places to believe them. A large portion of Amoeba's business is in used merchandise. Patrons of the store can sell their used music and movies to the store for half of the retail value in cash or 2/3 retail value in store credit. Many think this is the greatest record store chain in the world. It's hard to argue the point.

Fingerprint Records
4612 B East 2nd Street
Long Beach, California
562-433-4996

I live not too far from this shop and it's become a regular haunt for my son and I. There's a variety of CDs both new and used, as well as a serious vinyl collection and a good buying policy if you have some LPs or CDs you're looking to sell. Great, knowledgeable staff, and well worth a drive from Los Angeles if you're in the area.

Connecticut

The Mystic Disc
10 Steamboat Wharf
Mystic, Connecticut
860-536-1312

Dan Curland has done an amazing job here pro-viding record buyers with hard-to-find gems for more than 17 years. Their specialty is rare and collectable vinyl from 1964–1974, though the selection certainly isn't limited to that. Next time you're on the road between New York and Boston, stop in and do some record shopping while also checking out the posters, books, and other rock 'n' roll ephemera displayed all over the place. Must be seen to be believed.

Georgia

Circle Sky Records
3633E Chamblee-Tucker Road
Atlanta, Georgia
877-491-2100

Circle Sky Records was designed by serious record collectors as the record store that they would want to shop in. You'll find new and used LPs, 45, 78s, CDs, cassettes, 8-tracks, and vintage magazines (such as *Teen Beat, 16, Hit Parader*) as well as a wide variety of music magazines (like *Goldmine, Ugly Things, Beatlefan*). Also, there are T-shirts, posters, stickers, buttons, patches, and rock incense and accessories (such as a Jimi Hendrix incense burner). Circle Sky also carries record cleaning supplies and record protection items (such as poly sleeves, paper sleeves, record storage boxes) along with music related books, DVDs, VHS tapes, and rock 'n' roll memorabilia items like Yellow Submarine trading cards, rock ashtrays, and coffee mugs. There are in-store appearances, great staff, and, on a trivia note, the store is named after the Monkees' song "Circle Sky" from the movie Head.

Wuxtry Records
197 East Clayton Street
Athens, Georgia
706-369-9428

It was at this legendary new and used record store that store assistant Peter Buck met Michael Stipe and the two decided to try and form a band. Years later, Buck tried again to work here, but his success with R.E.M. got in the way because too many fans asked him to sign records. The store, as well as its sister shop in Atlanta, remain vital resources for music lovers (and they also have an upstairs area with tons of comics and other pop culture ephemera).

Illinois

Rolling Stones Records
7300 West Irving Park Road
Norridge, Illinois
708-456-0861
Rolling Stones Records (not related to the band) is one of the largest music stores in the area and carries lots of vinyl, cassette tapes, radios, headphones, and other music gear. They

also let you hear most of the music before you buy it and you'll also find a ton of in store appearances and band autograph sessions here.

Iowa

Zzz Records
424 East Locust Street
Des Moines, Iowa
515-284-1401

The idea for Zzz Records was conceived in the late 1990s. After Archives Records closed its doors in 1995, Des Moines was without a vinyl-friendly independent store for several years. Convinced that there was still a market for records in Des Moines, Zzz decided to open up a store that featured an eclectic mix of rock and roll, indie, electronica, jazz, country, and more. They quickly outgrew their original space, and on January 2, 2002, moved here to the up-and-coming East Village neighborhood of Des Moines. Today they stock over 17,000 items. Although the majority of them are used LPs and 45s, they also have a growing selection of cassettes and CDs.

Maryland

The Sound Garden
1616 Thames Street
Baltimore, Maryland
410-563-9011

The Sound Garden opened in 1993 and quickly established itself as Baltimore's best independent record store. Located in historic Fells Point, the Sound Garden carries an immense and eclectic selection of music in all genres. What makes them stand out from other record stores is the breadth and depth of their selection. They stock thousands of new and used CDs and DVDs. You'll also find a variety of imports, obscure and rare titles, and releases from smaller independent labels, all at low prices. Add to that a great selection of vinyl, posters, T-shirts, and stickers and you'll see why the store has won many awards, including "Best CD Store" from *Baltimore* magazine and from the *City Paper*.

Minnesota

The Electric Fetus
2000 Fourth Avenue South
Minneapolis, Minnesota
612-870-9300

The Electric Fetus was created in June 1968, by current owner Keith Covart with partners Dan Foley, Ron Korsh, and Roger Emalie. Minnesota Public Radio said of the Electric Fetus that it is "widely regarded as the pre-eminent indie record store in Minnesota." An incredible place, the inventory runs deep in rock, jazz, R&B, and hip hop with great prices. Tons of cutouts, used CDs, an expanded selection of used and new vinyl, DVDs, and all sorts of pop culture ephemera in the gift area make this a "must visit" if you're ever in the area.

New Jersey

Princeton Record Exchange
20 South Tulane Street
Princeton, New Jersey
609-921-0881

Founded in 1980, Princeton Record Exchange is a huge independent record store in historic downtown Princeton, New Jersey, located just about an hour from New York City and Philadelphia. Their store spans 4,300 square feet and houses 160,000 titles, the largest selection of any independent music store in the northeast. While the store offers an extensive selection of mainstream categories like rock, alternative, hip hop, and punk, it also features a selection of over 15,000 classical CDs and jazz CDs. In addition to music, Princeton Record Exchange also carries over 10,000 DVDs. And if you're selling, they also buy private collections, estate collections, reviewer/radio station surplus, and entire inventories of retail stores.

New York

Academy Annex
96 North 6th Street
Brooklyn, New York
718-218-8200

Academy Annex has two other locations (in Manhattan) besides this one in Brooklyn. The store in Greenwich Village focuses on jazz and pop vinyl, the shop on 18th Street focuses on classical vinyl and CDs from all genres, and here in Williamsburg the focus is on rock and jazz. All locations are great for collectors and music lovers in general, and all feature refined selections that reflect creative, eclectic musical tastes.

Bleecker Street Records
239 Bleecker Street
New York, New York
212-255-7899

Located on a great part of Bleecker Street, this store is crammed with vinyl and CDs and for years has been a favorite of music lovers. The prices at this two-level store are decent and the staff is great. A real New York institution.

House of Oldies
35 Carmine Street
New York, New York
212-243-0500

The House of Oldies has been owned and operated since 1968 by Bob Abramson. The store now has over 1,000,000 vinyl records in stock and has been featured on several television specials. They feature rare and out-of-print vinyl records from the '50s, '60s, and '70s (this was my favorite record store when I lived in New York).

North Carolina

Nits Nats Music
105 West Nash Street
Louisburg, North Carolina
919-496-8010

Nits Nats Music has been in business since 1969 providing north central North Carolina with the latest releases as well as all of the classics. Rock, rap, country, blues, beach, jazz, gospel, and more, it's all here. Nits Nats Music also sells thousands of new and used CDs, LPs, accessories, guitar strings, and new and used DVDs and is considered by many music purists to be a place that truly caters to those who know a lot about music.

Oregon

Thunderbird Records and CDs
2407 NE Alberta Street
Portland, Oregon
503-282-6608

Thunderbird Records and CDs is an independent music shop run by music lovers catering to music lovers. As they say here at the store, "If you are passionate about music you will find friends in our store. We will sit and listen to records in the store with you all day. Our favorite customers are the ones that help us get the store messy with records or cds everywhere—even if you don't buy anything!" Thunderbird specializes in all genres of music from independent or mainstream punk, soul, jazz, disco, funk, blues, folk, world, electronica, techno, classic rock—you get the picture.

Pennsylvania

Repo Records
538 South Street
Philadelphia, Pennsylvania
215-627-3775

A great place to stock up on rarities and B-sides, boxed sets, import singles, and other hard-to-find items. It may be a small space but don't be fooled, as there are thousands upon thousands of used records and CDs here, including many an out-of-print treasure. And make sure you check out Repo's downstairs, where 7-inches, used CDs, and other special bins are tucked away.

Trac Records
464 N. Main Street
Doylestown, Pennsylvania
215-348-5633

I used to shop here in the late 1970s (it was then called Key Records) when I'd visit my cousins in the historic hamlet of Doylestown. It's where I discovered my first bootleg album, *Bedspring Symphony*, by the Rolling Stones. They sell more than just vinyl here, and they've been in business for more than 30 years. Trac Records has also been voted by the readers of the Intelligencer Record as the Best Music Store in Bucks and Montgomery Counties.

Tennessee

Poplar Tunes
308 Poplar Avenue
Memphis, Tennessee
901-525-6348

This is where Elvis Presley supposedly bought his first LP and also where his very own record was first sold. Of course, Elvis memorabilia hangs on the walls. Founded by John Novarese and Joe Cuoghi in 1946, Poplar Tunes has been credited with breaking records, boosting careers, and creating hit records through breakthrough promotions, in-store charting and research, and distribution of material to smaller markets throughout the Southeast. Today, the company still supplies products to hundreds of jukebox accounts, making it one of the top suppliers and warehouses of vinyl stock in the country.

Texas

Waterloo Records and Video
600A N. Lamar Boulevard
Austin, Texas
512-474-2500

Perhaps the best music store in the entire Southwest. Since 1982, Waterloo Records has spoiled music lovers with a mind-bending selection and knowledgeable staff. The

inventory spans all styles, with a special propensity for Texas artists. There's a simple, genre-free, A-Z filing system, which customers have raved about for years. Voted "Best Used Record/CD Store" in a recent *Austin Chronicle* readers poll, Waterloo also has won 24 consecutive Austin Music Awards and is a six-time winner of the National Association of Recording Merchandisers (NARM) Retailer of the Year Award. You've got to check this place out if you're even close to Texas.

Vermont

In the Moment Records
143 Main Street
Brattleboro, Vermont
802-257-8171
In the Moment Records is a family run, independently owned music store featuring tons of LPs of nearly every genre with a stock that changes daily. They concentrate on jazz and classic rock, but also carry folk, country, bluegrass, classical, R&B, funk, blues, metal, punk, soundtracks, lounge, hip hop, reggae, comedy, new vinyl, new releases, and much more. A variety of new and used turntables and turntable accessories are also available. You'll also find a large selection of used and hard to find CDs, featuring many out-of-print jazz selections and box sets.

Washington

Bop Street Records
5219 Ballard Avenue NW
Seattle, Washington
206-297-2232
According to J. Greenwood of the band Radiohead, this "store takes the cake in the country." They have over half a million items in stock and owner Dave Voorhees knows his stuff. This place is absolutely crammed with thousands of records, floor to ceiling, as I learned recently when my friend Mike Maitland brought my son and me here. You could probably spend days  hunting and talking with the guys who work here. They stock over 650,000 used vinyl

records from blue note jazz to '70s punk, from doo-wop and soul to the heaviest metal, tons of reggae, blues, classical, all kinds of '50s, '60s, '70s, '80s, and '90s rock. Everything.

Easy Street
20 Mercer Street
Seattle, Washington
206-691-3279
Live at Easy Street is an EP by the band Pearl Jam that includes songs taken from a surprise in-store performance here at Easy Street Records in Seattle on April 29, 2005. Pearl Jam performed in support of the Coalition of Independent Music Stores and in celebration of their 10-year anniversary. So does that say a lot about this place or what? Tons of new and used vinyl is located in the back of the store, rock 'n' roll of all kinds lines the large store on both sides, and hip hop is stocked up near the front along with blues—a good mix. And they also stock a great assortment of pop culture kitsch, from Beatles lunchboxes and KISS thermos sets to T-shirts, books, and more. Great staff, too.

Canada

Beatnick
3770 St-Denis
Montreal, QC
514-842-6944
Retro truly rules here at this specialty record shop in Montreal, where you'll discover more than 15,000 CD and vinyl titles, a tremendous staff, and countless pop culture artifacts. A great place—especially if you're a collector.

Sam the Record Man
349 Yonge Street
Toronto, ON
416-977-4650
Quite simply, this is Canada's largest music/video/DVD store. You'll find a huge selection of videos, DVDs, and all types of music (along with extensive classical and jazz sections, a rarity these days). It's truly a fantastic spot to track down hard-to-find recordings. Plus, you can enjoy their great cafe before or after you shop.

She Said Boom!
372 College St. (East of Bathurst)
Toronto, ON
416-944-3224
Crammed to the gills with used records and books, She Said Boom! is regularly voted Toronto's Best Used Record Store and Best Used Book Store by the local *NOW Magazine*. Located just a few blocks from the University of Toronto (they have a second location as well), the selections here are wildly eclectic and great values abound.

Vertigo Records
193 Rideau Street
Ottawa, ON
613-241-1011
Vertigo Records opened in December 2003, taking over from the site of another record store called Spinables, which had been a long-running music shop in the area. Located in downtown Ottawa, Vertigo caters to the widest range of customers, stocking lots of rock, jazz, soul, funk, hip hop, electronic, punk, metal, indie, reggae, and other genres. They also carry turntables and DJ equipment, offering a wide range of brands and models from companies such as Stanton, Numark, Technics, Shure, Teac, and more.

Zulu Records
1972 West 4th Ave
Vancouver, BC
604-738-3232
Located on Vancouver's trendy West 4th Avenue, Zulu has an incredible selection of new music and a great used record section upstairs. They specialize in alternative music (both local and imports), and there's a huge selection of magazines, too. You can also get great tips from their knowledgeable staff.

Rock 'n' Roll Landmarks by State

Alabama
Alabama Music Hall of Fame - 269
The Rolling Stones - 113

Arizona
Alice Cooper's Town - 273
Bonaduce, Danny - 19
Stinkweeds- 308
"Take It Easy" - 69

Arkansas
The Rolling Stones - 109

California
Abdul, Paula - 13
Altamont Raceway - 117
America - 167
American Graffiti - 160
Amoeba Music - 308
Avalon Ballroom - 119
Ball, Ernie - 226
The Band - 16
Band Shell - 120
Beach Boys - 16, 17, 167
The Beatles - 78, 79
Belushi, John - 204
Ben Frank's - 18
Bingenheimer, Rodney - 19
Bloomfield, Michael - 227
Boarding House - 120
Bono, Sonny - 205
Browne, Jackson - 168
Buckley, Tim - 205
Cal Jam - 123
Capitol Records - 161
Carpenter, Karen - 232
The Carpenters - 21
Central Avenue - 187
Charles, Ray - 162, 235
Cochran, Eddie - 236

Cooke, Sam - 207, 237
Crash, Darby - 207
Creedence Clearwater Revival - 169
Croce's - 273
Crosby, Stills and Nash - 169
Dead Man's Curve - 24
Denver, John - 208
Devonshire Downs - 124
The Doors - 25, 26, 27, 28, 29, 30, 125
Dr. John - 170
Duke's - 274
The Eagles - 126, 171
The Experience - 127
Fender Guitars - 31
Fender, Leo - 240
Fillmore West - 128
Fingerprint Records - 309
Fleetwood Mac - 163
Fox Venice - 129
Frampton, Peter - 129
Fuller, Bobby - 209, 241
Garcia, Jerry - 210
Gaye, Marvin - 210
Gazzarri's - 130
Gibb, Andy - 242
Gold Star Studios - 165
Graham, Bill - 211
The Grateful Dead - 32, 33
Greek Theater - 132
Green Day - 34
Guns N' Roses - 34
Haight Ashbury Free Medical Clinic - 35
Hard Rock Cafe - 36
Hardin, Tim - 211
Hatfield, Bobby - 243
Hendrix, Jimi - 36, 132
Hollywood Bowl - 133
Hollywood Palladium - 134
I-Beam - 134
Idol, Billy - 41

Jackson, Michael – 43, 44
Jefferson Airplane – 44
Joplin, Janis – 45, 214
Journey – 45
King, Carole – 172
KMPX – 135
Laurel Canyon Country Store – 46
Lennon, John – 81
Lewis, Huey – 171
Los Angeles Memorial Coliseum – 153
"Louie Louie" – 166
MacArthur Park – 49
The Masque – 138
Maverick's Flat – 138
McCabe's – 283
McCartney, Linda – 139
McCartney, Paul – 84
McKernan, Ronald C. "Pigpen" – 251
Metallica – 50
Michael, George – 51
Milli Vanilli – 51
Mitchell, Joni – 52
Miyako Hotel – 52
Monterey Pop Festival – 140
Morrison Hotel Gallery – 284
Museum of Making Music – 286
Mydland, Brent – 253
Neil, Vince – 53
Nelson, Rick – 253
Newport Pop Festival – 141
Nilsson, Harry – 254
No Doubt – 54
Notorious B.I.G. – 216
Orbison, Roy – 256
Osbourne, Ozzy – 55
Pandora's Box – 141
The Panhandle – 142
Parker, Charlie – 196
Parsons, Gram – 218
The Partridge Family – 176
Paul, Les – 56
Phillips, John – 257
Pink Floyd – 173
Presley, Elvis – 97, 100, 101
Preston, Billy – 260
The Ramones – 178

Ramone, Dee Dee – 260
Ramone, Johnny – 262
Rendezvous Ballroom – 144
Rhoads, Randy – 263
"Riot" House – 59
RockWalk – 289
Rolling Stone – 59
The Rolling Stones – 113, 114, 175
Ronstadt, Linda – 173
The Roxy – 145
Santa Monica Civic Auditorium – 149
Shannon, Del – 221
Shelley's – 146
Slovak, Hillel – 263
Smith, Elliot – 221
Spears, Britney – 63
Spencer, Jeremy – 64
Spinal Tap – 182
Spirit – 174
The Starwood – 147
Stevens, Rick – 67
Sunset Grill – 68
Sunset Sound – 181
Surf Music – 147
The Sweet – 174
Thriller – 182
Tropicana Motel – 69
Turner, Ike & Tina – 70
U2 – 151
US Festival – 150
Valens, Ritchie – 265
"Valley Girl" – 70
Valley Music Center – 151
Van Halen – 70
The Village Recorder – 183
Wally Heider's Studio – 183
"We Are the World" – 184
Wells, Mary – 267
Whisky a Go-Go – 154
The Who – 73, 74
Wilson, Brian – 75
Wilson, Carl – 267
Wilson, Dennis – 223
Winterland – 156
The Youngbloods – 174
Youth Opportunities Center – 158

Zappa, Frank - 268

Colorado
Dylan, Bob - 87
Led Zeppelin - 136
Presley, Elvis - 98
Red Rocks - 143

Connecticut
The Doors - 28
The Mystic Disc - 309
Pitney, Gene - 259

District of Columbia
The Beatles - 84
Ellington, Duke - 189
The Starland Cafe - 291

Florida
The Beatles - 79
Bee Gees - 17
Clapton, Eric - 162
The Doors - 26
Gram's Place - 277
Thee Image - 150
Limp Bizkit - 48
Lynyrd Skynyrd - 49
Presley, Elvis - 99
Rhoads, Randy - 220
The Rolling Stones - 109, 110
Saturday Night Fever - 179

Georgia
Allman Brothers - 15
Allman, Duane - 204
Atlanta Pop Festival - 119
Ballard, Hank - 227
Ballard-Hudson High School - 16
Brown, James - 20
Circle Sky Records - 309
Geldof, Bob - 164
Georgia Music Hall of Fame - 276
Lopes, Lisa "Left Eye" - 249
McCartney, Paul - 173
Oakley, Berry - 255
R.E.M. - 57, 58

The Sex Pistols - 61
Wuxtry Records - 310

Hawaii
Hendrix, Jimi - 133
Presley, Elvis - 96

Illinois
The Beatles - 77
Browne, Jackson - 179
Chess Records - 187
Disco Demolition Night - 25
The Grateful Dead - 131
Harrison, George - 279
Hendrix, Jimi - 38
Howlin' Wolf - 231
Rolling Stones Records - 310
Waters, Muddy - 266

Indiana
Hoon, Shannon - 245
Jackson Five - 42
Jackson, Michael - 43
Presley, Elvis - 102

Iowa
Big Bopper - 213
Bolin, Tommy - 228
Holly, Buddy - 213
Museum of Iowa Rock and Roll History - 285
Osbourne, Ozzy - 55
Valens, Ritchie - 213
Zzz Records - 310

Kentucky
Pickett, Wilson - 258

Louisiana
Croce, Jim - 208
Delta Music Museum and Hall of Fame - 274
The Doors - 126
The Grateful Dead - 33
Hoon, Shannon - 214
Jazz - 192
Led Zeppelin - 47

Little Richard - 166
Parsons, Gram - 256
Sea-Saint Studios - 180
The Stage of Stars - 291
Tad Gormley Stadium - 148
Thunders, Johnny - 222
Walker, Jerry Jeff - 184
Williams, Hank - 75

Maryland
Browne, Jackson - 179
The Sound Garden - 311

Massachusetts
Aerosmith - 14
Alice's Restaurant - 15
Berklee School of Music - 271
Boston Arena - 121
Boston Tea Party - 121
Hula Moon Café - 282
Joplin, Janis - 136
Marley, Bob - 137
The Rat - 143
The Rolling Stones - 112, 114
Springsteen, Bruce - 146
Synchro Sound - 182

Michigan
Eminem - 31
Franklin, Aretha - 32
KISS - 135
McCartney, Paul - 83
Michigan Theater - 139
Motown Museum - 285
Nugent, Ted - 287
The Supremes - 68
The Who - 73

Minnesota
Dylan, Bob - 85, 86, 87, 91, 93
The Electric Fetus - 311
Prince - 56
The Replacements - 58
Springsteen, Bruce - 65
Tiny Tim - 222

Mississippi
Blues Alley - 186
Blues & Legends Hall of Fame Museum - 272
Handy, W.C. - 200, 201
Johnson, Robert - 193, 248
Lewis, Jerry Lee - 48
Lynyrd Skynyrd - 215
Presley, Elvis - 104, 106
Rodgers, Jimmie - 290
Smith, Bessie - 198
Theo's Rock and Roll Museum - 292
Tutwiler Train Station - 199
Waters, Muddy - 293

Missouri
The American Jazz Museum - 270
Berry, Chuck - 18
Blueberry Hill - 272
Clark, Gene - 235
Elvis is Alive Museum - 275

Nevada
Collins, Albert - 236
Entwistle, John - 209
Presley, Elvis - 99, 104, 105
Shakur, Tupac - 221
Sixx, Nikki - 62

New Hampshire
Aerosmith - 14

New Jersey
Atlantic City Pop Festival - 119
Dylan, Bob - 90
Glory Days - 164
Princeton Record Exchange - 312
Ramone, Joey - 261
"Rock Around the Clock" - 144
Springsteen, Bruce - 65, 66
Stone Pony - 147
The Velvet Underground - 72
Wilson, Jackie - 223

New Mexico
Holly, Buddy - 165
YesterDave's Auto Museum - 294

New York
Academy Annex - 312
Apollo Theater - 118
Armstrong, Louis - 270
B.B. King's - 271
The Beastie Boys - 168
The Beatles - 79, 80
Big Pink - 160
Bleecker Street Records - 312
Bobbysoxers - 186
The Bottom Line - 122
Bowie, David - 19, 122
Brill Building - 161
Carr, Eric - 233
CBGB - 124
Chapin, Harry - 206, 234
The Clash - 169
The Cotton Club - 189
Davis, Miles - 189
The Doors - 170
Dylan, Bob - 85, 86, 87, 88, 89, 91, 92, 93, 94
Danko, Rick - 239
Festival for Peace - 127
Fillmore East - 128
Freed, Alan - 240
A Great Day in Harlem - 190
Great Lawn - 131
Hathaway, Donny - 212
Hendrix, Jimi - 36, 37, 38
Holiday, Billie - 191
House of Oldies - 312
James, Rick - 247
Jam Master Jay - 214, 252
Joel, Billy - 45
Kate's Lazy Meadow Motel - 282
KISS - 46, 135
Leadbelly - 195
Led Zeppelin - 172
Lennon, John - 81, 82, 215
Love, Courtney - 49
Lymon, Frankie - 249
Madison Square Garden - 137
Madonna - 50
Manny's - 282
Max's Kansas City - 138
Mayfield, Curtis - 50

Minton's - 195
MTV - 176
New York Dolls - 53
Nolan, Jerry - 254
Pappalardi, Felix - 217
Paramount Theater - 142
Parker, Charlie - 196, 197, 217
Peppermint Lounge - 142
Presley, Elvis - 107
Ramone, Joey - 57
The Record Plant - 177
"Rock Around the Clock" - 177
Rodgers, Jimmie - 198
The Rolling Stones - 110, 111, 112, 113, 115, 175
Roth, David Lee - 60
Rubin, Rick - 61
Rundgren, Todd - 60
The Scene - 145
School of Rock - 179
Simon and Garfunkel - 61, 174
Stern, Howard - 67
The Strand - 292
Thunders, Johnny - 264
Tin Pan Alley - 199
The Velvet Underground - 71, 72
Watkins Glen - 153
The Who - 155
Wollman Rink - 157
Woodstock - 158

North Carolina
Coltrane, John - 188
Council, Floyd - 238
Nit Nats Music - 313

Ohio
Bowie, David - 123
Costello, Elvis - 24
Freed, Alan - 164
La Cave de Café - 23
Pirate's Cove - 23
Record Rendezvous - 23
Rock and Roll Hall of Fame - 288
Swingo's - 23
The Who - 74

Oregon
"Louie Louie" – 166
Thunderbird Records – 313

Pennsylvania
American Bandstand – 159
"Blue Train" house – 188
Croce, Jim – 238
Haley, Bill – 35
Hall and Oates – 35
Live Aid – 136
Mount Pocono Festival – 141
Melvin, Harold – 252
Presley, Elvis – 97
Repo Records – 313
Sigma Sound Studios – 180
Trac Records – 314

Rhode Island
Dylan, Bob – 92
The Rolling Stones – 115
The Talking Heads – 69

South Carolina
Anderson, Pink – 226
Brown, James – 20

Tennessee
American Sound Studio – 160
Buckley, Jeff – 230
Cash, Johnny – 233
Cline, Patsy – 205
Gibson Guitar Factory – 276
Grand Ole Opry – 130
Green, Al – 34
Handy, W.C. – 201
Lewis, Jerry Lee – 48
Perkins, Carl – 257
Phillips, Sam – 258
Poplar Tunes – 314
Presley, Elvis – 95, 99, 101, 103, 105, 106,
    107, 108, 219
Soulsville U.S.A./STAX Museum – 290

Texas
Ace, Johnny – 203
Antone's – 185

Crosby, David – 24
Dazed and Confused – 163
Holly, Buddy – 39, 40, 41, 244, 280
Hopkins, Sam "Lightnin'" – 246
Jackson, Janet – 42
Johnson, Robert – 194
Joplin, Janis – 45
Nelson, Rick – 216
Orbison, Roy – 287
Osbourne, Ozzy – 55
Presley, Elvis – 100
Selena – 220
Texas Pop Festival – 149
Waterloo Records – 314

Utah
Emerson, Greg – 31

Vermont
In the Moment Records – 315

Virginia
Buchanan, Roy – 229
Carter Family – 22
The Doors – 27
George, Lowell – 211
Presley, Elvis – 100

Washington
Bop Street Records – 315
Cobain, Kurt – 206
East Street Records – 316
Experience Music Project – 275
Hendrix, Jimi – 37, 38, 243
Led Zeppelin – 47
Nirvana – 54
Soundgarden – 62

Wisconsin
Holly, Buddy – 40
Redding, Otis – 219
Vaughan, Stevie Ray – 223
Violent Femmes – 152

Canada
Bata Shoe Museum – 271
Beatnick – 316

Dylan, Bob – 90
Lennon, John – 80
The Rolling Stones – 111
Sam the Record Man – 316
She Said Boom! – 316
Toronto Rock and Roll Revival – 150
Vertigo Records – 317
Zulu Records – 317

Jamaica
Marley, Bob – 250, 283

Acknowledgments

Thanks to my publisher/editor/friend, Jeffrey Goldman; his wife, Kimberly; their son, Nathaniel; and their daughter, Madeleine. Also to Amy Inouye and Brittany Yudkowsky for their excellent work in designing and producing and editing this book.

I also want to acknowledge Hampton Inn Hotels for allowing me to be part of the award-winning Save-A-Landmark program, specifically Hidden Landmarks. To know that a corporation does so much in the way of preservation and historic education is impressive. To be a part of it is a privilege. I encourage you to visit www.hamptonlandmarks.com to experience all that Hampton Inn is doing. Specifically, thank you to (at Hampton Inn and Hilton Hotels Corp.): Judy Christa-Cathey, Kendra Walker, Monica Gaston, and Tori Walsh. It is such a pleasure to work with you. Same goes to my friends at Cohn/Wolfe, Los Angeles: Jeremy Baka, Dawn Verhulst, Ian Jeffries, Kelly McAlearney, Esther Rawlings, and Seth Grugle. (And a special thanks as well to Melissa O'Brien.)

Thank you to my associates at *Chicken Soup for the Soul* magazine, Mignonne Wright, Lansdale Franklin, Shay Pearce, Amy Lorton, and Amy Stewart. I admire and appreciate all that you do (and if you haven't seen the magazine, check it out at newsstands, bookstores and at www.chickensoupmagazine.com).

Thanks also to the folks at Tourcaster: Matthew Dusig, Gregg Lavin, and Vanessa Auburn.

To Devon Wade and Zac Rivera at Maloney Fox, and Angela Morrow and Justin Osmer at Microsoft's Live Search Maps, I really enjoyed working with you!

Thanks to OnPoint designs for tending to www.chrisepting.com. (Thanks Oscar!)

To my old friends, John Mungo and Bryant Lewis for all the years.

On a personal note, to my wife, Jean; son, Charlie; and daughter, Claire—and Mom, Margaret and Billy—thank you as always. You all rock.

And to you holding this book right now, thank you so much for the support. There are many books out there to choose from and I appreciate that, at least for this moment, you have this one in your hands. I hope you enjoy it.

Chris Epting

Photo Credits

Jay R. Rury, p. 15
David McAleer, p. 36, 71, 85, 88, 89, 172 (bottom), 190
CBS, p. 80
Truckee Hotel, p. 84
Duluth National Guard Armory, p. 87
Sun Studio, 108
Bryant Lewis, 111 (bottom right)
Memory Motel, 112
Steve Luftman, p. 126
Jim Brennan, p. 156
Jean Epting, p. 157
E.J. Stephens, p. 176
Patrick D. Shediack, p. 193
Gram's Place, p. 277
Morrison Hotel Gallery, p. 284 (bottom)
A.J. Marik from www.findagrave.com, p. 237, 241, 242
Mike Adrian, p. 303 (top)

All remaining photos were either shot by the author or culled from the author's personal collection. All appropriate lengths were taken to secure proper photo credits and permissions. Any omissions or errors are deeply regretted and will be rectified upon reprint.

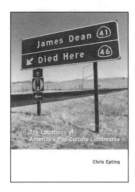

James Dean Died Here
The Locations of America's Pop Culture Landmarks
by Chris Epting

James Dean Died Here takes you on a journey across North America to the exact locations where the most significant events in American popular culture took place. It's a road map for pop culture sites, from Patty Hearst's bank to the garage where Apple Computer was born. Featuring hundreds of photographs, this fully illustrated encyclopedic look at the most famous and infamous pop culture events includes historical information on over 600 landmarks – as well as their exact location. *James Dean Died Here* is an amazing portrait of the bizarre, shocking, weird and wonderful moments that have come to define American popular culture.

Chapters and Sample Entries

Americana: The Weird and the Wonderful
• Bigfoot
• Groundhog Day
• McDonald's (First Location)

History and Tragedy
• The Hindenburg Crash
• Abraham Lincoln's Log Cabin
• Rosa Parks' Bus Ride

Crime, Murder, and Assassination
• Bonnie and Clyde are Killed
• Patty Hearst Bank Robbery
• O.J. Simpson

**Celebrity Deaths and
Infamous Celebrity Events**
• John Belushi
• Hugh Grant
• John Lennon

Let's Go to the Movies
• The Casablanca Airport
• Diner's diner
• The "Field of Dreams"

R&B, Rock 'n' Roll, and All That Jazz
• The American Bandstand Studio
• Jimi Hendrix Burns His Guitar
• Sid & Nancy's Hotel Room

Channel Surfing
• The Brady Bunch House
• The Andy Griffith Lake
• The Seinfeld Diner

Play Ball!
• Wilt Chamberlain Scores 100
• Eddie Gaedel
• Willie Mays' Famous Catch

$16.95 • ISBN 1-891661-31-0 • Trade Paper • 312 pages
6 × 9 • Hundreds of Photos • Travel / Popular Culture

Other Books by Chris Epting

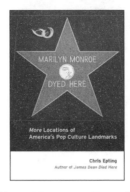

Marilyn Monroe Dyed Here
More Locations of America's Pop Culture Landmarks
by Chris Epting

In 1945, a watershed moment in pop culture history occurred when Norma Jeane Baker walked into a beauty salon at 6513 Hollywood Boulevard and changed her hair from brunette to blonde. With *Marilyn Monroe Dyed Here*, Chris Epting follows-up his critically acclaimed *James Dean Died Here* with another collection of the locations where the most significant events in American popular culture took place. This fully illustrated encyclopedic look at the most famous and infamous pop culture events includes historical information on over 600 landmarks—as well as their exact locations. *Marilyn Monroe Dyed Here* is an amazing portrait of the bizarre, shocking, weird and wonderful moments that have come to define American popular culture.

Chapters and Sample Entries

Americana: The Weird and the Wonderful
- *Saturday Night Live*'s "Cheeseburger!" restaurant
- Elvis Presley gets a haircut

History and Tragedy
- Little Rock, Arkansas high school integration
- The Great White concert fire

Crime, Murder, and Assassination
- Elizabeth Smart kidnapping
- Central Park jogger

Celebrities: The Tragic and the Ugly
- Frank Sinatra landmarks
- Marilyn Monroe's America

Let's Go to the Movies
- Woody Allen's New York
- Alfred Hitchcock's California

Rock 'n' Roll, R&B, and the Blues
- A Bob Dylan walking tour
- Rolling Stones landmarks

Channel Surfing
- *Laverne & Shirley*'s brewery
- *Welcome Back Kotter*'s high school

The Write Stuff
- Steinbeck writes *Grapes of Wrath*
- Ernest Hemingway commits suicide

$16.95 • ISBN 1-891661-39-6 • Trade Paper • 312 pages
6 × 9 • Hundreds of Photos • Travel / Popular Culture

Call 1-800-784-9553 to Order

Other Books by Chris Epting

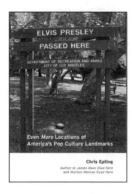

Elvis Presley Passed Here
Even *More* Locations of America's Pop Culture Landmarks
by Chris Epting

Elvis Presley Passed Here is an amazing portrait of the bizarre, shocking, weird, and wonderful moments that have come to define American popular culture. The follow-up to the critically acclaimed *James Dean Died Here* and *Marilyn Monroe Dyed Here,* this third collection of the locations where the most significant events in American popular culture took place offers a fully illustrated encyclopedic look at the most famous – and infamous – pop culture events, providing historical information on more than 600 landmarks as well as their exact locations (including, of course, the Los Angeles park where Elvis Presley and his entourage would organize spirited touch football games against other celebrities).

Chapters and Sample Entries

Americana: The Weird and the Wonderful
• "Uncle Sam's" House
• America's Stonehenge

Born in the USA
• The Birthplace of Coca Cola
• Famous Restaurants and Retailers

History and Tragedy
• Ben Franklin Flies a Kite
• The Titanic's Dock

Crime
• The Cheerleader Murder Plot
• Butch Cassidy's Hole-in-the-Wall

Celebrity Deaths and Infamous Celebrity Events
• Pete Rose Places His Bets
• Rob Lowe's Hotel Romp

Let There Be Music
• Jazz Landmarks
• Velvet Underground Tour

Movies and TV
• Charlie Chaplin's Los Angeles
• *Napoleon Dynamite*'s Town

Art and Literature
• Tennessee Williams Writes *A Streetcar Named Desire*
• Alfred Steiglitz's First Gallery

$16.95 • ISBN 1-59580-001-8 • Trade Paper • 312 pages
6 × 9 • Hundreds of Photos • Travel / Popular Culture

Call 1-800-784-9553 to Order

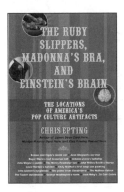

The Ruby Slippers, Madonna's Bra, and Einstein's Brain
The Locations of America's Pop Culture Artifacts
by Chris Epting

Anyone who has ever wondered where Dorothy's ruby slippers, George Washington's teeth, or the world's largest olive are located will be thrilled to take this journey to find hundreds of the most important items from America's popular culture. Found in such major institutions as the Smithsonian and the Baseball Hall of Fame as well as in such offbeat collections as the Sing Sing Prison Museum and the Delta Blues Museum, these pop culture treasures include the most famous—and quirkiest—items from movies, crime, TV, sports, music, history, and America's roadside attractions.

Chapters and Sample Entries

American Curiosities
• Buffalo Bill's Coat • The Dionne Quintuplets' Baby Bottles • The Cardiff Giant • Thomas Edison's Last Breath

Roadside Relics
Giant Artichoke • World's Largest Catsup Bottle • Corn Palace • World's Largest Light Bulb • Giant Killer Bee • The Thing

Historic Artifacts
Stonewall Jackson's Horse • Isaac Newton's Apple Tree • Rosa Parks's Bus • Mahatma Gandhi's Ashes • George Washington's Teeth

Criminal Remains
Birdman of Alcatraz's Cell • Abraham Zapruder's Camera • Lee Harvey Oswald's Rifle • John Wilkes Booth's Thorax

Celebrity Antiquities
James Dean's Car Door • Tom Thumb's Wedding Cake • Clark Gable's Boyhood Sled • Harry Houdini's Straitjacket

Movie and Television Keepsakes
The African Queen • The Lone Ranger's Mask • *Casablanca* Piano • Frank Capra's Typewriter • *The Exorcist* Staircase

Music Mementos
Elvis Presley's Report Card • Muddy Waters's Cabin • Hank Williams's Last Cadillac • Jimi Hendrix's Woodstock Guitar

Sports Memorabilia
Paul "Bear" Bryant's Hat • Alan Shepard's *Apollo 14* Golf Club • Miracle on Ice Skates • Babe Ruth's First Bed

$16.95 • ISBN-13 978-1-59580-008-4 • Trade Paper • 304 pages
6 × 9 • Hundreds of Photos • Travel/Popular Culture

Books Available from Santa Monica Press

Atomic Wedgies, Wet Willies & Other Acts of Roguery
by Greg Tananbaum and Dan Martin
128 pages $11.95

The Bad Driver's Handbook
Hundreds of Simple Maneuvers to Frustrate, Annoy, and Endanger Those Around You
by Zack Arnstein and Larry Arnstein
192 pages $12.95

The Butt Hello
and other ways my cats drive me crazy
by Ted Meyer
96 pages $9.95

Calculated Risk
The Extraordinary Life of Jimmy Doolittle
by Jonna Doolittle Hoppes
360 pages $24.95

Can a Dead Man Strike Out?
Offbeat Baseball Questions and Their Improbable Answers
by Mark S. Halfon
192 pages $11.95

Captured!
Inside the World of Celebrity Trials
by Mona Shafer Edwards
Text by Jody Handley
184 pages $24.95

Creepy Crawls
A Horror Fiend's Travel Guide
by Leon Marcelo
384 pages $16.95

Dogme Uncut
Lars von Trier, Thomas Vinterberg and the Gang That Took on Hollywood
by Jack Stevenson
312 pages $16.95

Elvis Presley Passed Here
Even More Locations of America's Pop Culture Landmarks
by Chris Epting
336 pages $16.95

The Encyclopedia of Sixties Cool
A Celebration of the Grooviest People, Events, and Artifacts of the 1960s
by Chris Strodder
336 pages $24.95

Exotic Travel Destinations for Families
by Jennifer M. Nichols and Bill Nichols
360 pages $16.95

Footsteps in the Fog
Alfred Hitchcock's San Francisco
by Jeff Kraft and Aaron Leventhal
240 pages $24.95

French for Le Snob
Adding Panache to Your Everyday Conversations
by Yvette Reche
400 pages $16.95

Haunted Hikes
Spine-Tingling Tales and Trails from North America's National Parks
by Andrea Lankford
372 pages $16.95

How to Speak Shakespeare
by Cal Pritner and Louis Colaianni
144 pages $16.95

James Dean Died Here
The Locations of America's Pop Culture Landmarks
by Chris Epting
312 pages $16.95

The Keystone Kid
Tales of Early Hollywood
by Coy Watson, Jr.
312 pages $24.95

L.A. Noir
The City as Character
by Alain Silver and James Ursini
176 pages $19.95

Marilyn Monroe Dyed Here
More Locations of America's Pop Culture Landmarks
by Chris Epting
312 pages $16.95

Movie Star Homes
by Judy Artunian and Mike Oldham
312 pages $16.95

Offbeat Museums
The Collections and Curators of America's Most Unusual Museums
by Saul Rubin
240 pages $19.95

A Prayer for Burma
by Kenneth Wong
216 pages $14.95

Quack!
Tales of Medical Fraud from the Museum of Questionable Medical Devices
by Bob McCoy
240 pages $19.95

Redneck Haiku
Double-Wide Edition
by Mary K. Witte
240 pages $11.95

Route 66 Adventure Handbook
Expanded Third Edition
by Drew Knowles
384 pages $16.95

The Ruby Slippers, Madonna's Bra, and Einstein's Brain
The Locations of America's Pop Culture Artifacts
by Chris Epting
312 pages $16.95

School Sense
How to Help Your Child Succeed in Elementary School
by Tiffani Chin, Ph.D.
408 pages $16.95

The Shakespeare Diaries
A Fictional Autobiography
by J.P. Wearing
456 pages $27.95

Silent Echoes
Discovering Early Hollywood Through the Films of Buster Keaton
by John Bengtson
240 pages $24.95

Silent Traces
Discovering Early Hollywood Through the Films of Charlie Chaplin
by John Bengtson
304 pages $24.95

Tiki Road Trip, 2nd Edition
A Guide to Tiki Culture in North America
by James Teitelbaum
336 pages $16.95

Order Form 1-800-784-9553

	Quantity	Amount
Atomic Wedgies, Wet Willies & Other Acts of Roguery ($11.95)	_____	_____
The Bad Driver's Handbook ($12.95)	_____	_____
The Butt Hello . . . and Other Ways My Cats Drive Me Crazy ($9.95)	_____	_____
Calculated Risk ($24.95)	_____	_____
Can a Dead Man Strike Out? ($11.95)	_____	_____
Captured!: Inside the World of Celebrity Trials ($24.95)	_____	_____
Creepy Crawls ($16.95)	_____	_____
Dogme Uncut ($16.95)	_____	_____
Elvis Presley Passed Here ($16.95)	_____	_____
The Encyclopedia of Sixties Cool ($24.95)	_____	_____
Exotic Travel Destinations for Families ($16.95)	_____	_____
Footsteps in the Fog: Alfred Hitchcock's San Francisco ($24.95)	_____	_____
French for Le Snob ($16.95)	_____	_____
Haunted Hikes ($16.95)	_____	_____
How to Speak Shakespeare ($16.95)	_____	_____
James Dean Died Here: America's Pop Culture Landmarks ($16.95)	_____	_____
The Keystone Kid: Tales of Early Hollywood ($24.95)	_____	_____
L.A. Noir: The City as Character ($19.95)	_____	_____
Marilyn Monroe Dyed Here ($16.95)	_____	_____
Movie Star Homes ($16.95)	_____	_____
Offbeat Museums ($19.95)	_____	_____
A Prayer for Burma ($14.95)	_____	_____
Quack!: Tales of Medical Fraud ($19.95)	_____	_____
Redneck Haiku: Double-Wide Edition ($11.95)	_____	_____
Route 66 Adventure Handbook ($16.95)	_____	_____
The Ruby Slippers, Madonna's Bra, and Einstein's Brain ($16.95)	_____	_____
School Sense ($16.95)	_____	_____
The Shakespeare Diaries ($27.95)	_____	_____
Silent Echoes: Early Hollywood Through Buster Keaton ($24.95)	_____	_____
Silent Traces: Early Hollywood Through Charlie Chaplin ($24.95)	_____	_____
Tiki Road Trip, 2nd Edition ($16.95)	_____	_____

Subtotal	_____
CA residents add 8.25% sales tax	_____
Shipping and Handling (see left)	_____
TOTAL	_____

Shipping & Handling:
1 book $4.00
Each additional book is $1.00

Name _____

Address _____

City _____ State _____ Zip _____

☐ Visa ☐ MasterCard   Card No.:_____

Exp. Date _____   Signature _____

☐ Enclosed is my check or money order payable to:

Santa Monica Press LLC
P.O. Box 1076
Santa Monica, CA 90406